Insight into a Career in
Pharmaceutical Sales

Sixth Edition

By Anne Clayton

pharmaceuticalsales.com
655 Deerfield Road
Suite 100-262
Deerfield, IL 60015

pharmaceuticalsales.com, Incorporated.
© 2004 pharmaceuticalsales.com

International Standard Book Number (ISBN)
ISBN , 0-9665121-6-2, Sixth Edition, Published 2004

Previous Editions
ISBN 0-9665121-4-6, Fifth Edition, Published 2003
ISBN 0-9665121-5-4 Fourth Edition, Published 2002
ISBN 0-9665121-2-X Third Edition, Published 2001
ISBN 0-9665121-1-1 Second Edition, Published 1999
ISBN 0-9665121-0-3 First Edition, Published 1998

Library of Congress Cataloging-in Publication Data
Insight into a Career in Pharmaceutical Sales/Marketing Essentials Incorporated
76-2-4K

This pharmaceuticalsales.com publication is available
to businesses, universities, and organizations
at a special discount when ordered in large quantities.
For more information, contact:
pharmaceuticalsales.com
655 Deerfield Road
Suite 100-262
Deerfield, IL 60015
or on the Internet at www.pharmaceuticalsales.com

Published in the United States of America
Printed in the United States of America

To our readers:

Anne Clayton and other contributors have provided
you with an excellent resource for marketing yourself
and building a career in the pharmaceutical industry.
As you pursue this profession, feel free
to contact us through our web site.
http://www.pharmaceuticalsales.com

pharmaceuticalsales.com
655 Deerfield Road
Suite 100-262
Deerfield, IL 60015

Table of Contents

Introduction

Your Mission

Congratulations! You have just chosen pharmaceuticalsales.com for first-hand insight and career guidance into the pharmaceutical industry. You have taken an important step toward a vital and challenging profession, and are about to embark on a step-by-step journey to a professional career. The pharmaceutical industry is one of the most sought after jobs in sales and marketing professions. This industry has consistently shown exceptional growth over many years and promises to continue as one of the greatest industries of the century. The ever-challenging, ever-changing health care market will provide the dedicated individual with professional, business, and personal satisfaction over the course of a life-long career. Again, congratulations, and welcome to your future!

Think of yourself as starting on an exciting mission. You can see the end-point quite clearly. You see yourself enjoying and excelling in a challenging, respected career. You are the consummate sales professional in one of the most prosperous industries in America. You are making a great salary, plus bonus, a company car, and have plenty of benefits! However, you are not exactly sure how to get there from wherever you are now. You have the desire, but need a little push in the right direction.

That is where pharmaceuticalsales.com comes in! Our mission is simple: provide job candidates seeking entry-level sales representative positions in the pharmaceutical industry--like you--with the necessary tools to succeed. That's it! Reading, learning, and applying the lessons in this book provides you with an "insiders" guide to the course of action for greatest success. By practicing the simple down-to-earth steps, you will land the job of your dreams and thereby launch yourself into a highly rewarding and highly compensated life-long professional career.

Insight into a Career in Pharmaceutical Sales (*Insight*, for short) will support you through the important steps. *Insight* provides pertinent industry knowledge, key-networking strategies, essential interviewing preparations, and critical organizational tools that empower you to excel in today's competitive job-hunting environment. In addition, we will do this from the inside perspective by sharing many years of pharmaceutical industry experience and special insights that can only come from being there. The guidance you receive from *Insight* is the combined results of substantial professional involvement in many facets of the sales and marketing of pharmaceutical products, including, and perhaps most importantly, sales management.

Many hours were spent researching, designing, and developing *Insight*. The strategies and tools revealed in this guide were developed from first-hand personal interviews and focus groups. Additionally, we address the career requirements based on many years of experience with professional sales representatives, district sales managers, sales training managers, marketing managers, and regional sales directors, within the pharmaceutical business.

We also have compiled information on specific pharmaceutical companies into a convenient reference (Appendix). Pharmaceuticalsales.com utilizes published sources, such as industry periodicals, annual reports, quarterly 10K filings with the Securities and Exchange Commission, personal interviews, and other such resources to answer your questions and guide you to a rewarding career. The information in *Insight* reflects current and historical research, and can be used as an entree into the industry.

Chapter 1 gives you an overview of this dynamic business. **The Future of the Pharmaceutical Industry** includes current issues and the outlook of this very important industry.

In Chapter 2, **The Sales Representative**, *Insight* gives you an in-depth view of today's pharmaceutical representative on the job. You will see typical compensation packages, job description, career advancement, and positive and negative aspects of the position.

Chapter 3, **Best Foot Forward**, discloses that, although no resume will win you employment, many common mistakes will quickly eliminate you from the process. You will learn the twenty simple rules for resumes and cover letters.

Preparation is the backbone of your job-hunting endeavor. Understanding your target market is perhaps the most important step in securing the perfect job. How to gather and compile this relevant research is outlined in Chapter 4, **Vital Research**.

In Chapter 5, **Networking News**, *Insight* discloses our unique way to show you how to market yourself within the industry. This is key to successful employment. All avenues to reach this goal are explained through each stage of your process.

Now it is time to advance your career in the pharmaceuticalsales.com way. Chapter 6, **The Interview,** shows you the way by providing insight into successful interviewing strategies. It focuses on frequently asked interview questions and suggests ways to tailor your responses in order to maximize your impact with every answer. Most commonly, your first dialogue is via the telephone. Present yourself well and you will enter first, second, and final interviews. The possibilities are discussed with reference to what behavioral characteristics companies are seeking. Also included is a list of guidelines for professional attire that is imperative for outstanding presentations.

Chapter 7, **Your Questions**, provides questions for you to ask in the interview that complement you as a candidate, and generate information that you need to win the job. This chapter also shows you the most intelligent way to turn the tables and take control of the interview.

There are three outcomes from every interview process. Chapter 8, **Decisions, Decisions**, reveals how to handle each situation with the composure that insures positive results.

The Conclusion emphasizes **Your Commitment** to this career choice. It focuses on the continuous implementation of the tools you acquired through *Insight*. The knowledge and skills contained in this guide will work for you to maximize your potential for professional employment in this rewarding and dynamic industry.

The Appendix profiles over fifty companies, offering a comprehensive reference to today's pharmaceutical companies and contract sales organizations (CSO's). This is a convenient resource on the companies. This section also offers advice to help you organize your newly acquired information and document your networking contacts for future interviews. It includes several worksheets which provide a means to record your progress, document the details of your job search, and organize your growing network of contacts in the pharmaceutical companies.

Chapter 1

The New Golden Age: The Future of the Pharmaceutical Industry

It was many years ago that discussions concerning national price controls weighed heavily on the pharmaceutical industry and its investors. More recently, there have been other worries for this golden industry, such as intense competition from generics, patent expirations on major products, rising costs of research, difficulty developing new blockbuster products, pricing constraints from managed care and government markets. Though still very strong, growth in prescription drug sales has slowed slightly. According to the Centers for Medicare and Medicaid Services (CMS), the amount Americans spent on prescription drugs grew 13.3 percent in 2003, down from a peak of 19.6 percent in 1999. On Wall Street, drug company stocks began to grow at a slower rate than the overall stock market. However, according to Business Week (June 2003), stocks are on a rebound. Regardless of these recent challenges, the pharmaceutical industry is among the largest, most stable, and fastest growing businesses in the entire world. In fact, it not only succeeds but it thrives, able to respond quickly to changes in domestic and global markets. There is reason for optimism and enthusiasm in the industry and among investors. According to Standard & Poor's (S & P) Industry Surveys, pharmaceutical company earnings increased by 10 percent in 2003 and are expected to grow as much in 2004. There are promising new products in the pipelines of many companies (see Company Profiles). Total global pharmaceutical sales grew by 7 percent to $428 billion and will continue to grow in the 7-8 percent range through 2007. According to *IMS Health* (the foremost provider of global marketing research in this industry), North America (U.S. and Canada) remains the largest market by far, representing 51 percent of total worldwide sales. The U.S. is not only the largest but also the fastest growing pharmaceutical market in the world, with sales up 14.3 percent in 2002 and another 13.3 percent in 2003 for a total of $182 billion. U.S. drug sales are expected to increase at an annual rate of at least 12 percent through 2005.

Based on Standard & Poor's (S & P) Industry Surveys, *global* sales of pharmaceuticals were up 8.0 percent to over $428 billion in 2003. This includes both prescription (ethical) and over-the-counter (OTC) drugs. *PhRMA* estimates that the percentage of total sales by U.S. companies in global markets is 35 percent and growing. The strongest competitive foreign markets are Europe and Japan, followed by Asia, Africa, Australia and Latin America. This booming global market provides opportunity in long-term sales careers and the possibility of international travel.

Pharmaceutical research, manufacturing and sales is an almost recession proof business, remaining somewhat insulated from economic cycles that affect other commercial endeavors. *Fortune* magazine's yearly survey shows that CEO's award the "most highly respected" rating on a consistent basis to Pharmaceutical Sales Organizations. Investors will continue to make funds available for Research and Development (R&D), and more salespeople will be needed. This means job security, promotions, and competitive compensation packages.

Despite a long and successful record of accomplishment, the pharmaceutical industry, as described above, is not immune to change. Major shifts are taking place that constitute both threats to and opportunities for drug companies. The healthcare system is in flux due to the pressures of cost, managed care, consolidations, vertical integrations among health care companies, government regulations, doctor recommendations, and patients who purchase the products. As the clientele becomes more knowledgeable and powerful, their demands increase and they take charge of their own health care. Rapidly changing demographics create new markets. Many new drugs carry patents that are in effect for a shorter timeframe, and existing patents on 42 major drugs are expiring in the next five years. Salespeople must adapt well to change and remain well educated about the company and the products they represent in order to succeed in their careers.

Several positive changes in the pharmaceutical industry include corporate mergers, vertical integration, alliances, and outsourcing within the industry. Mergers have given rise to larger, more secure companies with greater economies of scale. Alliances have grown the capabilities for research and development ensuring the flow of new drugs. Outsourcing has given rise to contract sales organizations (CSO) in providing an effective way to employ a large sales force. CSOs will be discussed in later chapters of this book.

The U.S, is expected to remain the largest and fastest growing among the world's ten major drug markets over the foreseeable future. The future is bright and demands qualified salespeople. The market for pharmaceuticals will generate a 6 to 7 percent annual growth in worldwide sales over the next five years and beyond. In fact, prescription drug spending will double in the next five years, according to *Merck-Medco Managed Care LLC's* 2001 drug trend report. The forces that will increase the demand are listed below. Each of these will be discussed in the remainder of this chapter:

- Aging global population and increasing life expectancy
- Increasing incidence of chronic diseases
- Successful industry track record on Wall Street
- Investments in R&D and a constant flow of new drugs
- Innovation and advances in technology
- New markets for pharmaceuticals
- Growing healthcare expenditures and demand for cost-effective health care
- Medicare drug coverage legislation
- Identifying and treating overlooked patient populations
- A high demand for better lifestyle and improved quality of life
- Shorter FDA approval times and relaxed marketing restrictions
- Expanding promotional spending and consumer oriented marketing
- Educated health-conscious consumers
- Industry giants, growth companies, and blockbuster drugs

THE AGING GLOBAL POPULATION AND INCREASING LIFE EXPECTANCIES

The two most powerful demographic trends are the aging population and increased life expectancies. These two factors are generating growth demands for pharmaceuticals as both dramatically increase the number of elderly persons. The over-65 population in the U.S. is expected to expand by about 31 percent from 2001 through 2015, according to the U.S. Census Bureau. Every day more than 6,000 Americans celebrate their 65th birthdays. This phenomenon is a reflection of the baby boomer generation. Aging will provide a tremendous marketing opportunity for prescription drugs. A global study by The World Health Organization shows that this older population will increase from the current level of 380 million to over 800 million by 2025.

At the turn of the 19th century, the average life expectancy was only 47 years. A child born today can expect to live to be almost 80. These longer life spans are due to advances in medical care, improved standards of living, and the development of innovative medications and vaccines to treat deadly diseases such as polio, diphtheria, heart disease, and the various forms of cancer.

As more people live longer, they will naturally experience an increase in health problems due simply to aging. Additionally, the long-term effects of unhealthy habits such as smoking, over-eating, poor diet, and lack of exercise result in increased incidence of diseases. Thus, the over-65 population becomes candidates for various treatments including increased ethical and OTC drugs. On the average, the elderly consume three times more prescription medications than persons under the age of 65.

Major problem conditions in the elderly are heart disease, stroke, arthritis, cancers, depression, impotence, osteoporosis, Parkinson's, and Alzheimer's disease. Pharmaceuticals targeting these diseases will be in greater demand. The industry will dedicate the majority of its massive $30.5 billion annual R&D spending over the coming years toward the development of new treatments for these health problems.

INCREASING INCIDENCE OF CHRONIC DISEASES

In addition to diseases that will increase as a result of aging, the World Health Organization reports that many chronic diseases will increase in the years ahead due largely to unhealthy habits and conditions such as smoking, obesity, poor diet, lack of exercise and stress management. Our high speed, stressful lifestyle is feeding this frenzy. These unhealthy habits are well-known risk factors for many common diseases such as ulcers, depression, obesity, and impotence. The four largest therapy classes in the world can be linked to unhealthy lifestyles-- they are, in the order of global sales: Antiulcerants, Cholesterol Reducers, Antidepressants, and Antihypertensives. These drug categories treat conditions that have been described as "diseases of civilization" because they are a largely a phenomenon of Western culture.

The outbreak of severe acute respiratory syndrome (SARS) has been alarming to medical experts around the world. SARS is a contagious viral disease that became more widely spread as a result of international travel. As such, it represents a new challenge based on the increasing frequency and ease of international air travel brought about by the relatively new global economy. Governments and pharmaceutical companies are working independently and together to develop vaccines and treatment to combat SARS.

SUCCESSFUL INDUSTRY TRACK RECORD ON WALL STREET

The pharmaceutical industry is considerably insulated from changes in the economic climate. Simply put, people will always be sick and will always require medications regardless of the economy. Drug pricing inelasticity indicates that patients will buy a needed prescription despite the price. If an alternate medication is available, but not as effective, the more costly product will still be purchased. For many patients, insurance affects the price of the medication by requiring a small co-pay or expenditure, which usually means that price is not an issue.

Historically, this business has provided excellent growth for investors. The stock market recorded unparalleled growth in the 1980's and 1990's. Operating profit margins (earnings as a percentage of sales) have come down in recent years due to reduced pricing flexibility, but the industry average still exceeds 30 percent--more than twice that of the typical corporation in the S & P Industrial Index. The drug industry pretax and net income returns are substantially higher than in other industries. The net earnings as a percentage of sales averaged 16.8 percent for the five-year period through 2002, compared with 5.6 percent for general industry. Return on equity (ROE), or net earnings, as a percentage of average stockholders' equity, is approximately 25 percent--ranking pharmaceuticals among the highest of all industries. The ROE reflects the impressive profit margins.

According to the Wall Street Journal, drug company stocks slumped in 2003 in favor of technology and industrial stocks which are benefiting from an overall economic rebound. As a result, pharmaceutical stocks are trading at a price-to-earnings ratio of about half the value of the overall market. From a value perspective, this makes them a more attractive buy according to market analysts, and are rebounding well. No doubt pharmaceuticals will continue to be an excellent investment.

This industry has come under fire in past years from claims that its profits are greater than necessary to provide a return on investment in research and development. The fact is, in financial terms, drug manufacturing is a high-risk business. Economists at Tufts University estimate that it takes ten to fifteen years to develop a new drug from the laboratory to FDA approval. Growing complexity and length of the drug development process has increased R&D costs. For example, larger and longer clinical studies are required by the FDA. Researching, developing and introducing a new drug now costs nearly three and a half times more than it did only 15 years ago, with the average cost now over $800 million. Included in the cost are expenses of research projects that failed to produce a viable or marketable compound. For every 5,000 compounds discovered, only one ever reaches the market. Of those that do make it to market, only three of ten drugs will sell enough to recoup their R&D costs. However, when a newly marketed drug is widely successful, the sales on that product can be in the billions of dollars. This is the primary reason for the industry's high profit margins. Continued growth depends on private investors having the confidence that they will receive a competitive return on their investment that is commensurate with the risk. A June 1994, a study by the Congressional Budget Office (CBO) found that measures of industry profitability do not take into account the inherent riskiness of pharmaceutical R&D.

INCREASED INVESTMENTS IN R&D AND A CONSTANT FLOW OF NEW DRUGS

Today's top corporations are research and development driven. New products are the lifeblood of the industry. Research-based pharmaceutical companies invested $32 billion in R&D in 2002, a 21 percent increase over 2000 and four times the 1990 level. These expenditures include $26.4 billion spent within the United States by both U.S.-owned and foreign-owned firms, plus an additional $5.7 billion spent abroad by U.S.-owned firms (*figure 1*).

FIGURE 1: **PRESCRIPTION PHARMACEUTICAL R&D EXPENDITURES AT RESEARCH-BASED PHARMACEUTICAL COMPANIES, IN BILLIONS OF DOLLARS**

Source: ***Pharmaceutical Research & Manufactures Association***

FIGURE 1: Prescription Pharmaceutical R&D Expenditures
At research-based pharmaceutical companies, in billions of dollars

Source: Pharmaceutical Research & Manufacturers Association

Over the past 20 years, the percentage of sales allocated to R&D has increased from 11.4 percent in 1970 to 18.2 percent in 2002. Meanwhile, the average R&D-to-sales ratio for other U.S. industries is less than 4 percent. Based on corporate tax data compiled by Standard & Poor's *Compustat*, pharmaceutical manufacturers invest a higher percentage of sales in R&D than any other industry, including high-tech electronics, aerospace, automobile, and office equipment such as computers, printers, and peripheral devices. The nature of the drug industry requires the most intensive R&D structures in the U.S. economy. R&D spending is rising sharply, both in dollar terms and as a percentage of total sales; it has doubled every five years since 1970.

The United States industry is the world leader, and invents about 70 percent of the world's new medical therapies. Of the 100 most widely prescribed drugs, 94 were discovered with private funds without any government support. However, publicly funded health research, administered by the National Institutes of Health (NIH) has also increased substantially in recent years. The NIH invested $24 billion in pharmaceutical research in 2002, up from $18 billion in 2000. Government and academic scientists lead the way in basic research about diseases. Then drug industry scientists translate these academic advances into medications to prevent, cure, and treat the diseases. According to PhRMA, the partnership that exists in the U.S. between private industry and the government is one reason why this country has surpassed Europe as the leader in pharmaceutical R&D.

The most significant result of the industry's continued investment in R&D is the constant flow of new drugs to treat disease, extend life and increase the quality of life. The Pharmaceutical Industry Profile 2003 published by PhRMA reports there are over 370 biotechnology products are in the pipeline addressing cancer and some 200 other diseases. In addition to the biotechnology advances, there are close to 800 traditional pharmaceutical compounds in development: 402 to fight cancer, 123 for heart disease and stroke, 83 for HIV/AIDS, and 176 for neurological diseases such as Alzheimer's and Parkinson's. Close to 320 anticancer drugs are in the pipeline, 187 drugs and vaccines for children, over 130 AIDS treatments, 100 for heart disease and strokes, 85 for mental health, and 30 for arthritis. This proliferation should keep both the industry and the public healthy for many years to come.

Besides drug development, there are other major results of pharmaceutical R&D. First is its contribution to the advancement of scientific knowledge, technology and new manufacturing processes. Second is its contribution to the American economy. Since 1990, the pharmaceutical industry has grown twice as fast as the overall economy. According to a report by the American Enterprise Institute, the key factor is the heavy investment in R&D, and the fact that effective medicines increase the productivity and growth of every sector in the economy, producing social returns much greater than private returns produced by the companies themselves. The industry has been a significant source of new, highly skilled jobs, and is one of the nation's largest employers with approximately 223,000 employees nationwide, including an estimated 50,000 scientists and 90,000 pharmaceutical sales representatives!

INNOVATION AND ADVANCES IN TECHNOLOGY

There is also a constant demand from the consumer for quality health care. Americans have come to expect the best and latest in health care technology.

In the past, valuable discoveries were often made by accident. The twenty-first century, however, brings sweeping changes in biomedical and pharmaceutical industries. The U.S. Human Genome Project unlocked the mystery of DNA. By completing the map of the human genome, researchers will be able to design medicines for specific patient populations. This will result in a future that provides medications tailored to an individual's genetic makeup. Physicians will be able to treat and prevent the root causes of cancer, heart and arthritic conditions, and

Alzheimer disease. New products will combat illnesses that were once considered the inevitable consequences of old age: frailty, vision failure, sexual dysfunction, and loss of mental acuity.

Most of the top corporations are aligning with genomic companies or have established genomic research facilities of their own. Pharmaceutical companies using scientific data from genome research will gain a significant competitive advantage. This advantage, according to industry analysts, will not prove profitable in the near or medium term, but could potentially take the form of a rich research and development pipeline leading to highly effective and lucrative medicines in the next decade.

The biotechnology industry is having an impact on medicine right now. It is on the forefront of innovation and high technology resulting in new discoveries every day. These "biotech" companies, specializing in genetically altered drugs, gene research, and molecular biology will provide new therapies and also improved therapies over existing problems.

New corporate marriages between biotechnology companies and pharmaceutical concerns are common. This practice provides small, innovative biotech companies with the financial backing for research, plus management and marketing efforts to successfully launch new products into the marketplace.

NEW MARKETS FOR PHARMACEUTICALS

Recent events in major markets around the world are opening tremendous growth opportunities for today's global pharmaceutical corporations. The "Third World" is becoming more developed economically. Rising standards of living in Latin America, Asia, Africa, and Eastern Europe are also good news for U.S. companies. As emerging nations raise the economic standing of the population, one of their top priorities is to improve healthcare. An increased demand for medications to provide better healthcare in many countries equates to a longer life expectancy for their residents.

The forecast calls for an explosion of growth in developing countries over the next five years, and in specific pharmaceuticals to aid the global aging population. The world pharmaceutical market is projected to grow at the rate of seven to eight percent annually through 2007. The North American, European, Japanese, and Latin American markets will continue to dominate, accounting for 92 percent of all global sales during that time (*figure 2*). Globally, the Middle East, Australia, Southeast Asia, and China are expected to grow most quickly. In Europe, Poland has the fastest growth rate, followed by Sweden, the Czech Republic, and Ireland.

FIGURE 2: 2002 Global Rx Sales in $US billions
*Source: IMS World Review 2003   *% change from 2001*

Japan
13%
*(+8%)

Latin America
4% *(-10%)

Europe
24%
*(+8%)

North America
51% *(+12%)

Africa, Asia and
Australia
8% *(+12%)

The top five companies in 2003 global sales, based on *IMS Health* data, are Pfizer, GlaxoSmithKline, Merck, AstraZeneca and Novartis. China, with over one billion people, is a major potential market. According to S & P's *Industry Surveys*, major U.S. companies doing business in both Russia and China include Johnson & Johnson, Merck, Bristol-Myers Squibb, Eli Lilly, and Schering-Plough. The pharmaceutical industry provides excellent opportunities for career advancement in sales and marketing to various global markets. Adding to the potential for global pharmaceutical sales and marketing careers is the fact that many of the major U.S. companies are divisions or subsidiaries of large parent companies based primarily in Europe or Japan.

There is an inherent risk in global markets. Economies can be unstable, shaped by politics and world events. Recent problems in Russia, Eastern Europe, Afghanistan, England, the United States, and other countries may cause more U.S. drug companies to lose money in their total global portfolios. However, health is a growing global concern. Moreover, the threat of bioterrorism presents challenges and opportunities for the industry.

GROWING HEALTHCARE EXPENDITURES AND DEMAND FOR COST-EFFECTIVE HEALTH CARE

Prescription drug therapy is cost-effective. This means that a treatment or medication meets a specified goal at an acceptable cost compared to surgery, hospitalization, physician visits, and nursing care. Pharmaceuticals often eliminate the need for these more expensive interventions. However, this is a fact that is not widely recognized or acknowledged which can have negative fallout for the industry. According to an article in Forbes (Mar. 31, 2003), the pharmaceutical industry is fighting a public relations battle. "It's easy to target [drugmakers] as

the big, greedy, soulless international industry and forget about the value we produce," says Novartis Chief Executive Daniel Vasella. From the same article, Columbia University economist Frank Lichtenberg found that every additional dollar spent on newer drugs reduces other medical costs by three dollars or more! For example, putting an AIDS patient in the hospital costs $1,500 a day. A protease-inhibitor cocktail at $12,000 a year is a comparative bargain. In another disease category, prescription drug therapy for ulcers costs $1,000 per year, but replaces the need for ulcer surgery costing $25,000. Nearly $400 billion would be saved by taking advantage of more cost effective medicinal treatments and cures for the seven major uncured diseases (Cardiovascular, Cancer, Alzheimer's, Diabetes, Arthritis, Depression, Stroke, Osteoporosis). Nearly 300 medicines are in development for these diseases.

The expense of caring for patients with migraine headaches is being lowered primarily by one drug. The expenditures for this drug increased dramatically, but the costs of treating migraines declined 41 percent because of treatment with the medicine. These costs include health care, lost time at work, lost wages, etc. Using this particular therapy for treating migraines, one study showed that this drug saved employers $435 per month per employee due to a reduction in lost productivity on the job.

However, healthcare delivery can be inefficient, and this has given rise to "managed care." Eliminating inefficiencies in the system is the goal of managed care organizations (MCOs), such as health maintenance organizations (HMOs) and preferred provider organizations (PPOs). These MCOs manage and administer the overall healthcare benefit for employers at relatively lower cost than traditional "fee for service" insurance plans. The goal of management care is to lower cost, which often results in decreasing the access to specialists, or limiting patients' choice of healthcare provider to a specific list of doctors, hospitals, etc. Another area where choice may me limited is in the pharmaceutical benefit. Essentially offshoots of managed care, pharmaceutical benefit manager companies (PBMs) function as intermediaries between pharmaceutical manufacturers and large drug purchasers. In 2003, about 90 percent of HMOs and 80 percent of PPOs use PBMs to manage their drug benefits. PBMs insist on the use of lower cost generics whenever possible and have established formularies, or lists of preferred drugs approved for reimbursement. This list may exclude newer or more expensive medications. Although prescriptions account for only 15 percent of the MCOs medical costs, they are the fastest growing expense for managed care.

PBMs also provide services such as claims processing, mail order pharmacy, utilization management, and physician monitoring and education. PBM's can represent millions of members, or "covered lives" and wield broad decision-making power over which drugs their members can buy. These members give PBM's a powerful influence against pharmaceutical manufacturers. They are able to negotiate discounts or rebates from a manufacturer in return for increasing usage of the manufacturer's product. These rebates can be passed along by way of lower premiums to the employer and lower co-payments for the patient. Managed care has become the dominant domestic market for pharmaceuticals. Based on data from the Kaiser Family Foundation, about 95 percent of U.S. workers with insurance were covered under managed care plans in 2002 versus five percent under fee for service. This is an incredible growth rate for managed care over the past fifteen years. In fact, in 1988 only 27 percent of U.S. workers were enrolled in MCOs in 1988. In terms of total prescriptions covered, based on data provided by *IMS Health*, persons covered by managed care plans accounted for over 75 percent of all prescriptions dispensed in the U.S. in 2002. This compares with 30 percent in 1992 and 60 percent in 1997 (see *figure* 3). An estimated 115 million Americans are enrolled in drug benefits managed by PBM's, or close to 75 percent of all employed persons.

The growth of managed care has a positive impact on the pharmaceutical industry by covering prescription drugs for its members. First, managed care has favored drug therapies because of their cost-effectiveness compared to surgery and hospitalization. Secondly, Drug coverage by a third party, such as managed care, or other insurance companies, removes or minimizes price as a factor for the individual who seeks medical care and ultimately fills a prescription at the pharmacy. In fact, the dominance of third party payment is one of the primary forces behind the increasing number of prescriptions being written and dispensed.

A growing tool for managing drug costs by managed care is the "tiered co-pay" pricing system. Under this system, generic drugs have the lowest co-payments, preferred drugs listed on the HMO's formulary require a higher co-payment, and brand drugs not on the formulary require the highest out-of-pocket payment. According to Scott-Levin, a market research firm, about 40% of all HMO covered lives are enrolled in three or four-tier plans.

**FIGURE 3:   MANAGED CARE TRENDS -- PERCENTAGE OF TOTAL PRESCRIPTIONS
                    BY PAYER TYPE**

Source: ***IMS HEALTH***

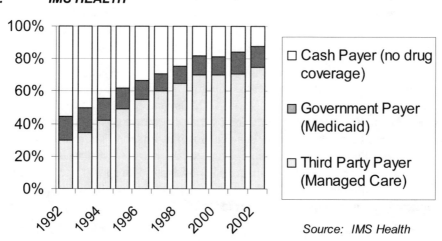

Source: IMS Health

Automated mail order processing using sophisticated computer technology to handle large volumes of prescriptions is one of the PBM's strongest tools. Through economies of scale, a PBM can sell drugs by mail at lower prices than retail pharmacies can. There is also a financial incentives for the patient to use mail order pharmacies. For example, a 90-day supply of a chronic medication can often be purchased by mail order for a single copay instead of only a 30-day supply purchased at a retail outlet for the same copay.

FIGURE 4:   U.S. NATIONAL HEALTH CARE EXPENDITURES, 2001
Source: *Centers for Medicare and Medicaid Services*

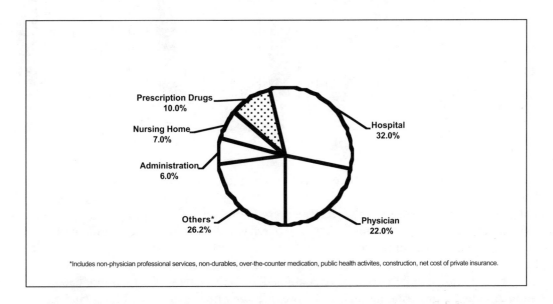

*Includes non-physician professional services, non-durables, over-the-counter medication, public health activites, construction, net cost of private insurance.

Total health care spending in the U.S. increased 8.7 percent in 2002 reaching $1.4 trillion, according to a review conducted by the federal government. This is the greatest rate of increase than any of the previous ten years. With the focus on containing healthcare costs, there has been a popular notion that hospitals, physicians, and pharmaceutical companies have benefited from increased pricing. It is also a popular notion that the culprit in the high cost of healthcare is the high cost of medicines, and that Americans are spending more on prescription drugs than on other health care items or services. This is a false assumption. In fact, prescription drug spending is a small fraction of the total costs. It is estimated that expenditures for prescription pharmaceuticals made up only 9 percent of the healthcare bill in the United States in 2002 (*figure 4*). This is an increase from 7.9 in 1999. This rise is due to increased prescription utilization, and remains a small percentage of the total healthcare cost. However, the percentage of healthcare cost attributed to pharmaceuticals is projected to increase over the next several years reaching 11.4 percent in 2005 and 13.9 percent in 2010. That is due to a predicted jump in pharmaceutical spending of 16-17 percent annually over the next two years and then slowing to 10 percent annually through 2010. The lower rate of increase is predicted due to health plans and private insurance payers becoming more restrictive, and health insurance premiums increasing, plus an overall economic downturn. Even with the projected lower rate of increase, total healthcare expenditures for prescriptions drugs will double from 1999 to 2005 and nearly double again by 2010 (*figure 5*).

FIGURE 6:   **U. S. EXPENDITURES FOR PRESCRIPTION DRUGS: 1980 - 2010 (BILLIONS)**
Source: Health Care Financing Administration.

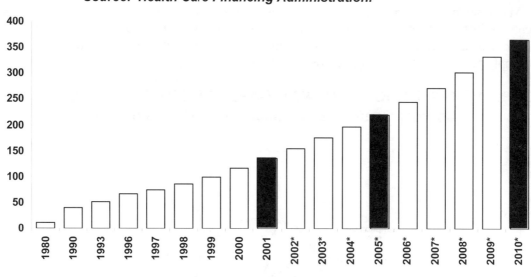

* Projected

   The money spent on drugs, questions of pricing, and insurance coverage of prescriptions will continue to draw the critical attention of politicians and the media. Most discussions on the role of pharmaceuticals in the health care system focus, not on their long-term value, but on their short-term cost. One reason for this is that drug purchases are one of the few health care expenses paid directly out of pocket, especially for the elderly who do not have drug coverage under Medicare. Despite all the measures implemented by government and private third-party payers, prices for prescription drugs have continued to increase by a wider margin than general inflation. In the 7 year period through 2002, prescription prices increased at an annual rate of 4.3 percent compared with 2.4 percent for the Consumer Price Index (CPI). Following several years of relative pricing stability, prescription prices moved notably higher in 2002 in both the branded and generic sectors of the market. Based on data from the Bureau of Labor Statistics, drug prices rose 5.2 percent in 2002 versus a rise of 4.7 percent for the average of all healthcare products and services, and an increase of only 1.6 percent in the CPI. In addition to price increases, overall increasing demand also influences spending for pharmaceuticals--more people are filling prescriptions now than in the past. To illustrate, U.S. total health-care spending rose 7.3 percent in 2003. In the same year, U.S. prescription drug spending increased 13.3 percent. Again, it is both the demand for prescription drugs and higher drug prices that are fueling growth. According to IMS, only 3.8 percentage points out of the 13.3 percent increase resulted from increased prices. Of the remaining 9.5 percent increase, 6.8 points resulted from a higher volume of existing prescriptions dispensed, and 2.7 points from the added use of new medicines (***figure 6***). Historically the use of pharmaceutical products has been lamented, rather than applauded regardless of the improvements they bring to healthcare.

FIGURE 6:   PRESCRIPTION PHARMACEUTICAL SALES GROWTH RATE, INCREASING DUE TO VOLUME NOT PRICE, U.S. MARKET.

Source: IMS America

Growing evidence supports the assertion that increased use of innovative medications can help people avoid more expensive and invasive treatments. In other words, pharmaceuticals are slowly being recognized as the most cost-effective method of treating many conditions. Scientific evaluation and education acknowledges that medications protect the quality of care and control the costs. Therefore, not only would more spending on drugs make and keep more people well, it would shrink the overall cost of care. No one is more interested in the overall cost of care than MCOs. Many MCOs have initiated "care management" or "disease management" programs for patients with chronic diseases, many of which rely heavily on prescription medications and increased drug utilization. The purpose of these programs is to control costs associated with treating chronic illness and improving the quality of care. So it follows that with intensified focus on disease management by managed care and with increasing numbers enrolling in managed care, we will see more drug utilization. As managed care grows, so will the demand for cost-effective ways to treat diseases--and that means greater demand for pharmaceuticals. The development of innovative pharmaceuticals is the most promising and cost-effective method to keep Americans out of hospitals, out of operating rooms and out of nursing homes. In short, pharmaceuticals help keep people healthy and productive.

MEDICARE DRUG COVERAGE

Another factor that will significantly increase demand for pharmaceuticals is the implementation of drug coverage for all senior citizens under the Medicare program. Medicare is the federal program that pays healthcare expenses for 40 million of the elderly population in the U.S. While Medicare currently pays for most medical and hospital services, it does not cover outpatient prescription medications. Thus, the elderly must pay cash, purchase supplemental insurance to cover prescriptions, or rely on existing retirement benefits, which often include ongoing prescription benefits.

However, this scenario changed for the better in November 2003 as Congress finally passed legislation to add a long overdue drug benefit to Medicare. The legislation will provide much-needed pharmaceuticals to millions of people, especially the elderly. It also allows insurance companies and managed care organizations in the private sector to compete for Medicare beneficiaries. This was preferred over having Medicare administer the entire benefit in order to help keep prices competitive. The major disagreements among policy makers, between Democrats and Republicans, was on how the plan should be structured. The argument runs along the lines of conservative (less government) and liberal (more government) approaches. Republicans favor a plan run by private companies such as existing MCOs and the role of government is simply to pay for it. Democrats desire the expansion of Medicare, a comprehensive federal bureaucracy that would directly provide drug benefits. The Democratic plan would have cost $500 billion over ten years and put the government in a powerful position as the largest purchaser of prescription drugs. While pharmaceutical companies would benefit from the large increase in product demand, they fear that the plan would carry with it the 30-40 percent price discounting that exists in other government-run drug coverage programs such as state Medicaid, Tricare, Champus, and the Veterans Administration. Fortunately, the Medicare Bill that passed and was signed into law by President Bush, was a bipartisan legislation that includes the competitive nature of private companies to hold down prices instead of government mandated price controls or discounts.

Even with market competition in force, the new Medicare drug benefit is estimated to cost $400 billion over ten years. The greater access to necessary pharmaceuticals by Medicare beneficiaries will mean increased sales by the pharmaceutical industry. However, the drug benefit does not take effect until 2006. In the meantime, seniors will be able to purchase a discount card that provides 10 to 25 percent off prescription drugs. There is also available right away a $600 subsidy for those with low-incomes defined as individuals below $12,124 and couples below $16,363.

Beginning in 2006, Medicare will pay for 75 percent of prescription drug costs for most people who choose to enroll, after a $250 annual deductible, up to $2,250. Medicare will pay 75 percent of drug costs between the deductible and $2250. Beneficiaries will then pay for drug costs between $2250 and $5100. Medicare then pays 95 percent of drug cost above $5100. Once a beneficiary spends $3,600 of their own money on drugs ($5,100 in total prescription drug spending) Medicare will pay 95 percent of the rest of their drug costs. The Prescription Drug Benefit includes a more comprehensive coverage for people with low income and limited assets. Most significantly, people with incomes below 100 percent of the federal poverty level will pay no premiums, no deductibles, and minimal copays of $1 for generics and $3 for brand name prescriptions. The legislation provides $88 billion in subsidies for employers (both public and private) to retain existing retiree drug coverage.

Prior to the passage of the Medicare Bill, to alleviate pressure on Medicare enrollees due to price concerns, seven major drug companies banded together and launched a discount card for prescription purchases by low-income senior citizens, called the "Together Rx Card." In what Secretary of Health and Human Services, Tommy Thompson, called a "tremendous new initiative," the card entitles Medicare beneficiaries to price discounts of 20 to 40 percent on more than 170 popular prescription drugs. Approximately 11 million seniors may be eligible for Together Rx. The only requirements are that you are a Medicare enrollee, have annual income less than $28,000/singles or $38,000/couples, and have no other prescription drug coverage.

This card has been well received by seniors, with over one million enrollees who have received more than $228 million in savings. The companies offering discounts via the Together Rx card are Abbott, AstraZenica, Aventis, Bristol-Myers Squibb, GlaxoSmithKline, Janssen, Ortho-McNeil and Novartis.

IDENTIFYING AND TREATING PREVIOUSLY OVERLOOKED PATIENT POPULATIONS

We are in an age of ever expanding knowledge, technological advances, and new scientific and medical discoveries. Our knowledge of the human body, the processes of disease, and our genetic makeup will be translated into new capabilities to study, diagnose, and treat a variety of illnesses. Even in a time of recession, we are also in an age of an expanding access to the healthcare system.

The methods and extent to which common diseases can be detected is improving. More sophisticated, sensitive, and less expensive diagnostic technologies are leading to widespread use of screening programs, which lead to better analysis. Thus, diagnosis and treatment for common diseases such as elevated cholesterol, osteoporosis, and prostate cancer can be addressed at the onset.

DEMAND FOR "LIFESTYLE" OR "QUALITY OF LIFE" PHARMACEUTICALS

More than ever, people want pharmaceuticals to enhance their lives, not simply treat illnesses. Generally, the baby boomer generation is not staying healthy by exercising, eating well and getting enough sleep, but rather by aggressively pursuing medical care when--and even before--health problems arise. Their expectations are that modern healthcare should fix their medical problems. This led to the "new drug culture"--the concept of drug products that will improve a person's functional capacity and overall well being. Baby boomers are attracted to "better-for-you" products, which has created greater demand for new pharmaceuticals.

Another growing therapy class is the treatment of erectile dysfunction for men, for which there are now three competing products on the market. Attention is turning to medications for women's sexual function as well. Weight management is also a rapidly growing therapeutic category, as is cosmetic surgery and procedures such as Botox injections for removing wrinkles. These therapies give rise to questions about what should or should not be considered a medical problem or a disease, and more importantly raise the questions of who should pay for their treatment. That definition may be expanding to include problems that can be treated with "quality of life" and "lifestyle" medications. Examples of such problems include the appearance of wrinkles and loss of hair.

FDA APPROVAL TIMES AND MARKETING RESTRICTIONS

As the principal federal agency responsible for enforcing U.S. drug laws, the Food and Drug Administration (FDA) regulates the introduction of new drugs. Pharmaceutical companies must submit extensive data to the FDA demonstrating both the safety and the effectiveness of new drugs before receiving approval for sale in the U.S. In addition, the FDA requires that drugs be produced according to specified "good manufacturing practices" (GMP) guidelines. Manufacturing plants are subject to FDA approval and must be inspected periodically. Once a product is approved, the manufacturer must also receive FDA authorization for its marketing practices. In other words, the FDA must approve what the pharmaceutical companies can say about their products, as well as how they go about publicizing them. The claims that Pharmaceutical Sales Representatives make to physicians must meet FDA standards.

Pharmaceutical companies until recently were benefiting from a friendlier regulatory environment for new drugs. To help bring down the high cost of drug development, the FDA began streamlining the review process in 1992. The average review time for a newly introduced drug is now 12-18 months, down from 35 months in 1996. Current drug approvals had almost doubled from an average of only 70 each year from 1990 to 1994. The number of new drugs approvals declined in 2000 through 2002, while the time it took to approve them increased. The good news is that for 2003, according to a report by Lehman Brothers, there was a modest rise in new drug approvals to 30 novel drugs, up from 25 in 2002. The analysts estimated that, in terms of product value, the sales potential of drugs likely to be approved in 2003 is $21 billion; the corresponding figure for 2002 was $18 billion.

The FDA had been operating without a commissioner from early 2000 until the appointment of Mark McClellan in late 2002. This is more good news. According to the 2003 S&P Industry Review, Dr. McClellan is committed to streamlining and speeding up the new drug approval process, and his directives since assuming office have for the most part been favorable to the drug industry

Another role of the FDA, in addition to approving new products, is to monitor marketing guidelines which regulate how pharmaceutical companies promote their products. Marketing guidelines have become less restrictive in recent years. For example, restrictions on direct-to-consumer (DTC) advertising, particularly via the television, have been lifted. This contributed to an increase in DTC advertising by pharmaceutical companies, leading more patients to make specific requests for brand-name products to their physicians. Another restriction that has been eased is the limitation on discussions by Sales Representatives concerning "off-label" or unapproved uses of their products. This means that companies can expand the types of patients or diseases that their existing products can be prescribed to treat.

EXPANDING PROMOTIONAL SPENDING AND CONSUMER ORIENTED MARKETING

Pharmaceutical companies have stepped up marketing efforts on all fronts to take advantage of favorable conditions in the market. Money spent by pharmaceutical companies for research and development was $30.5 billion in 2001; promotional spending was $8.6 billion in the same year (*IMS Health*). Sampling costs were valued at $10.5 billion, according to *Med Ad News*. These three costs alone--R&D, promotional spending and sampling--consume nearly half of pharmaceutical sales revenue. See *figure 7* for the break down in promotional spending for 2001.

Typically, sales and marketing of prescription drugs fall into two main categories--professional promotions and direct to consumer advertising (DTC). Professional promotion includes: sales presentations in doctors' offices, hospitals and pharmacies; medical journal advertising; drug samples; meetings and events including continuing medical education (CME); direct mail; Internet-based programs; and promotional items (pens, pads, office trinkets). The various strategies in the promotional mix are changing as DTC and Internet-based promotions expand. However, the overall strategy continues to be spearheaded by large sales forces of professional Pharmaceutical Representatives.

FIGURE 7:   **PROMOTIONAL SPENDING FOR YEAR 2001**
Sources: *IMS, Scott Levin*

Doctor Office Promotion (includes sales force)	$4.8 billion
Hospital Promotion (includes sales force)	$760 million
Journal Advertising	$380 million
Direct to Consumer Advertising	$2.7 billion
Retail Value of Sampling	$10.5 billion
Total Promotional Spending Mix	**$19.1 billion**

Direct-to-consumer advertising targets specific groups of customers in print and broadcast media such as television, radio, billboards, magazines, and newspapers. The practice was almost non-existent in the industry until the mid-nineties and has nearly doubled every year since 1994. This growth has been helped by several trends.

1. The FDA has relaxed regulations on DTC advertising.
2. Patients today want to be more involved in their own healthcare so they are more receptive to advertising.
3. The public's medical knowledge is expanding.
4. The public's desire and ability to access the Internet is expanding.
5. Physicians are more willing to comply with patients' requests for drugs seen in DTC ads.

Increased DTC advertising has led to greater consumer recognition of the benefits of pharmaceutical therapies, and created brand recognition and loyalty. This strategy is not always popular among physicians, but such advertising makes more patients aware of ailments and encourages them to see their doctors to learn more. One poll of 1,200 people showed 74 percent believe these ads help them be more involved in their own health care; 67 percent say the ads teach them about risks and benefits of drugs. Of patients who talked to their doctors about a drug that they saw advertised, 50 percent asked for a prescription by name and 70 percent of them received a prescription for the brand they wanted. According to Scott-Levin, a pharmaceutical industry market research firm, there is a direct correlation between the spending on DTC and product sales; those products that are heavily advertised are the ones most often requested by patients.

FIGURE 9:   **SPENDING ON DIRECT TO CONSUMER ADVERTISING, IN BILLIONS**
Source: ***IMS, Scott Levin***

Source: IMS; Scott Levin

DTC is expected to continue at a steady pace in the years ahead. Though television is the dominant medium, companies are increasing their annual budgets for more varied types of DTC advertising. After six years of expansion, total expenditures on DTC advertising declined seven percent in 2002, to $2.3 billion. ***Figure 9*** shows yearly trends in spending for DTC. ***Figure10*** presents the top ten prescription drugs leading the industry in DTC spending.

FIGURE 10:   TOP 10 COMPANIES BY DIRECT-TO-CONSUMER SPENDING, IN MILLIONS
Source: Verispan   ***January- November, 2002**

Drug Company	DTC Expenditure*
GlaxoSmithKline	$459
Pfizer	350
Merck	294
Johnson & Johnson	233
AstraZeneca	188
Aventis	166
Pharmacia	165
Schering-Plough	143
Bristol-Myers Squibb	106
TAP	69

Although the pharmaceutical industry was slow to embrace the Internet as a marketing tool, today virtually every company has a product information web site and some have e-business divisions. According to Cyber Dialogue, a New York-based Internet market research firm, companies spent close to $100 million on Internet marketing, or about 9.65 percent of the total DTC budget. A growing number of pharmaceutical companies are using the Internet to make sales presentations directly to physicians. Some doctors respond to the convenience of logging on to a web site from their office and then speaking with a Pharmaceutical Representative. Early research shows that physicians may be willing to spend more time with the representative when the sales call is conducted on line. Companies with the top 15 products spent $14.6 million promoting online in 2000 and increased to over $18 million in 2002. AstraZeneca is the top spender, with online campaigns using the latest in streaming media. Other top spenders include Aventis and Schering-Plough.

Pharmaceutical Sales Representatives are the industry's most critical tools for promoting its innovative product offering. During the early 1990's, the industry began to cut back on its sales force size. The assumption was that once managed care dominated the healthcare system the physician would no longer be the decision-maker and there would be no need for large forces in the physician offices. However, experience in recent years has shown that even under managed care physicians remained the ultimate decision-makers in choosing prescription medications. Successful companies have returned to traditional "detailing" and sampling strategies, greatly expanding their representative staff in the process. The return on investment is obvious for the physician office-based sales force. Market share increases when you add additional sales representatives. Sales forces, including contract sales representatives, grew by 15 percent from 1997 to 1998. That trend continues today. In 2000, sales force growth continues at the rate of 16% among the top 40 companies, according to Scott-Levin. In 1995, there were approximately 40,000 sales representatives in the U.S. By 2000, there were more than 80,000, as reported by *IMS Health*. **Figure 11** presents the largest U.S. companies by sales force size.

FIGURE 11:   TOP TWENTY LARGEST U.S. SALES FORCES
SOURCE: Med Ad News; Verispan

Company Name	Number of Sales Reps
Pfizer, Inc. (includes Pharmacia)	12,000
GlaxoSmithKline Plc.	8,000
Merck & Co.	6,500
AstraZeneca, Plc.	6,000
Novartis	6,000
Johnson & Johnson	5,400
Eli Lilly & Co.	5,300
Aventis SA	5,200
Wyeth/American Home Products	4,900
Bristol Myers Squibb Co.	4,400
Abbott Laboratories	4,000
Schering-Plough Corp.	3,500
Bayer	2,400
Sanofi-Synthelabo	2,300
Forest	2,300
Roche (Hoffmann-La Roche)	1,750
Boehringer Ingelheim	1,700
Allergan	1,325
Takeda	1,200
Total Top 20	**84,175**

The year 2002 brought a major shift in the pharmaceutical industry's promotional tactics. Led by PhRMA member companies, the industry revised its voluntary guidelines concerning the marketing of drugs to physicians. While this new code still allows treating physicians to reasonably-priced meals, guests who are not part of the medical practice (spouses, for example) would not be allowed to participate. The purpose of the revisions is to keep the sales representatives focused on educating and informing physicians and less focused on business related entertainment. The venue for educating physicians is now mandated to be "conducive to providing scientific or educational information," according to a report by the Associated Press. Promotional items that are no longer acceptable include, among others, logo-imprinted golf balls, floral arrangements and tickets to sporting events, the theater and concerts. There is no mechanism for enforcing the revised code, but companies who participated in the process, as well as other companies, are expected to voluntarily adhere to the guidelines.

Why the change in promotional tactics? Scrutiny by the media and politicians of pharmaceutical promotional practices has been intense. A survey conducted by the Kaiser Family Foundation found that perks from sales representatives such as meals, event tickets and travel were received by 61 percent of the more than 2,600 U.S. physicians polled, and that a substantial portion of the promotional budget of pharmaceutical companies was directed at these activities. The assumption is made that these "perks," rather than physician education activities, are unduly impacting physician prescribing. "We think there are some very valid concerns and as an industry we are looking at ways to address concerns while still continuing the very important work of educating and communicating to physicians information about new products," said Jeff Trewitt, a spokesman for PhRMA. Many sales representatives welcome this change in tactics in order to alleviate the concern over physician gifts, level the playing field among large and small companies and focus on face-to-face physician interaction in daily selling situations.

AN EDUCATED, HEALTH-CONSCIOUS CONSUMER

The consumer movement has expanded the public's medical knowledge. The information age has made it possible to find in-depth medical information fairly easily with the help of proliferating healthcare magazines, detailed and priority reporting in the news media, medical programs on radio and television, and widespread use of the Internet. The extensive news coverage of the medical problems of celebrities and political figures in recent years is a good illustration of the public's attention to medical information.

Many pharmaceutical companies have taken it upon themselves to expand promotional efforts into this vast area of medical information. They have developed consumer education initiatives, customer service hotlines, referral networks, and screening programs to detect diseases for which their products can be subsequently prescribed. Most companies now have Internet sites that include special areas for consumers offering detailed information, interactive capabilities, and coupons for rebates. In fact, according to Harris Interactive, of patients with chronic medical conditions, 27 percent visit Web sites sponsored by pharmaceutical companies.

INDUSTRY GIANTS, GROWTH COMPANIES AND BLOCKBUSTER DRUGS

The pharmaceutical industry saw unprecedented consolidation through the 1990's, and it continued unabated in 2000-2002. In 1990, the world's top 10 players accounted for just 28 percent of the global market. Ten years later, that proportion is greater than 45 percent and still gaining. In 2002, the top ten companies represented 50 percent of the U.S. pharmaceutical industry. The U.S. market giants are listed according to 2002 sales in *figure 12*.

The largest merger was Pfizer's acquiring Pharmacia only a year or so after Pfizer completing a merger with Warner-Lambert (Parke-Davis), and within two years of Pharmacia & Upjohn completing a merger with Monsanto (Searle).

Mounting pressures from third-party reimbursement, looming patent expirations for major products, the need for rich product pipelines, and growing globalization of the industry are forcing leading companies to combine. The new drug giants are formidable forces on the global market. They also become more efficient by cutting operating costs, eliminating redundant marketing, manufacturing, and R&D efforts and can offer "one stop shopping" to managed care customers and other large buyers. They put the necessary resources toward important development and marketing of new billion-dollar drugs, known as blockbusters, to fuel ongoing growth. These medications are the lifeblood of the pharmaceutical industry giants. Current blockbuster products are listed by year 2002 sales in *figure 13*.

Many relatively smaller companies are showing incredible growth. The top companies by percent annual growth in 2002 are listed in *figure 14*.

FIGURE 12: **TOP 10 INDUSTRY GIANTS BY GLOBAL PHARMA SALES IN 2002**
Source: **IMS Health, Retail and Provider Perspective, 2002**

Organization	2002 Sales in billions	% Change from 2001	% Market Share	Sales Force Size
Pfizer inc. Pharmacia	40.31	42.5	17.9	12,000
GlaxoSmithKline	28.2	8	11	8,000
Merck	21.63	1	10	6,500
AstraZeneca	17.84	9	7.5	6,000
Aventis	17.25	11	3.5	5,400
Johnson & Johnson	17.2	15.5	6.7	5,500
Novartis	15.36	4	4.1	6,000
Bristol-Myers Squibb	14.7	-2	6	4,400
Wyeth	11.7	7	3.8	4,900
Lilly	11	-4	3.3	5,300

FIGURE 13: **TOP TEN U.S. BLOCKBUSTER PRODUCTS IN 2002**
Source: **IMS Health**

Product	Company	Therapeutic Category	Diagnosis	2002 Sales in Billions
Lipitor	Pfizer	Cholesterol-reducing statins	Cholesterol	$8.0
Zocor	Merck	Cholesterol-reducing statins	Cholesterol	5.6
Prilosec	AstraZeneca	Proton pump inhibitors	Ulcers	4.6
Procrit	Johnson & Johnson	Erythropoietins	Anemia	4.3
Norvasc	Pfizer	Cardiovascular	Hypertension	3.8
Zyprexa	Eli Lilly	Antipsychotics	Schizophrenia	3.7
Paxil	GlaxoSmithKline	SSRI	Depression	3.2
Prevacid	Tap	Proton pump inhibitors	Ulcers	3.1
Celebrex	Pharmacia	COX-2 inhibitors	Arthritis, pain	3.0
Zoloft	Pfizer	SSRI	Depression	2.7
Total Sales of Top Ten Blockbusters				**$42.0**

THE NEW GOLDEN AGE: THE FUTURE OF THE PHARMACEUTICAL INDUSTRY

FIGURE 14:   **Top Growth Companies by Percent Increase in Global Pharmaceutical Sales Increase Between 2001 and 2002**

Source: ***Pharmaceutical Executive***

Company	2002 Sales in Billions	Percent Growth from 2001	Sales Force Size
Amgen	4.99	40	400
King	1.17	35	1,235
Forest	1.56	33	2,300
Schwarz	1.03	25	
Genentech	2.16	24	700
Altana	1.68	22	300
Allergan	1.38	21	1,325
Eisai	3.39	21	400
Fujisawa	2.49	19	300
Teva	2.51	17	

Chapter 2

The Sales Representative

In this chapter of *Insight*, you will learn about the actual job of the Pharmaceutical Representative. You will see that both a challenging and rewarding career, and an excellent work life is yours for the taking. After discussion and description of a typical workday, this chapter focuses on some of the normal challenges faced by the Representative. Upon completion of this chapter, you will have a basic understanding of the entry-level position, and be able to answer the following questions:

- What is a Pharmaceutical Representative?
- What qualities are companies looking for in job candidates?
- What does the Representative need to know?
- How are they trained?
- What does a typical day look like?
- What does it take to be successful?
- What are some positive and negative aspects of the job?
- How are Representatives compensated, and what are the financial incentives?
- What are the career advancement opportunities?

In later chapters, you will learn how to dig deeper into the job and uncover potential opportunities in your area. For now, take some time to review this chapter. It will give you the solid base of knowledge you will need to begin the networking process, described in Chapters 4 and 5.

WHAT IS A PHARMACEUTICAL REPRESENTATIVE?

For a perspective on this exciting position, begin with a look at some of the various titles used across the industry to designate the Pharmaceutical Sales Representative. Behind these titles are individuals who provide the first line of contact for the many large, medium and smaller sized pharmaceutical manufacturers and marketers across the industry. Each individual possesses a high degree of technical expertise, selling skills and professionalism.

Pharmaceutical Sales Representative	*Professional Medical Representative*
Territory Manager	*Medical Specialty Representative Hospital*
Hospital Representative	*Specialty Representative Senior*
Professional Sales Representative	*Professional Representative Account*
Sales Associate, Sales Consultant	*Manager, Account Executive*

For the Pharmaceutical Sales Representative, the primary target audiences are physicians and pharmacists. Obviously, you will be selling to highly trained and technically oriented professionals. Such an audience demands that you also have a high level of expertise. You must know your customers' business, your products, your competitors' products, and the diseases and health conditions for which your products are prescribed.

Does this mean you have to be educated in a medical or health-related field in order to relate to your customer? Absolutely not! The goal of the Pharmaceutical Representative is no different than that of any sales professional promoting virtually and product or service. Pharmaceutical salespeople are professionals selling the goods and services of an organization. The key to success lies in thorough preparation to guide you in making effective sales calls and following up on your commitments. Success requires determination, attention to customer service, and hard work. It does not need a specialized degree in any one area. It is no different than selling in any other industry. That is why people from all sorts of backgrounds, educational levels, previous sales experiences, and even non-sales backgrounds are successful in the pharmaceutical industry. Successful sales abilities in other product or service areas will transfer well to the pharmaceutical industry. Success is success!

The 30th president of the United States, Calvin Coolidge, captured this concept in the following, one of my favorite quotations and perfect for both the endeavor you are on now and ultimately in your career:

> *"Nothing in the world can take the place of persistence. Talent will not; nothing is more common than unsuccessful [persons] with talent. Genius will not; unrewarded genius is almost a proverb. Education will not; the world is full of educated derelicts. Persistence and determination are alone supreme."*

Now let's drill down a bit in terms of what, and who, a Pharmaceutical Rep is and does. To begin, as a Pharmaceutical Sales Rep, SALES is your middle name! Your responsibility is to increase market share and total volume of prescriptions written for your pharmaceutical products by the prescribers in your territory. Thus, what you are is a Sales Professional. Simple enough! That said, as a sales professional, your job entails everything that goes along with the sales territory: customer profiling, data analysis, tough gatekeepers, entertaining, relationship building, generating reports, product training, selling skills training, sampling regulations, planning, itineraries, scheduling and routing, communication, meetings, appointments, reports, team counterparts, conference calls, managers, evaluations, meetings, travel, reports, and finally, more reports. And, as also goes with a standard sales territory, most of what you do you do alone.

A Pharmaceutical Sales Representative must keep all the balls in the air at once, and achieve a high level of performance and professionalism. You must do what's expected in terms of meeting quotas, and your communication, administrative work and follow through must be impeccable.

Your sale is made when the doctor writes the name of your medication on a prescription and gives it to the patient. The sale is final when the prescription is dispensed by the pharmacy. You need both actions to take place and there are many factors impacting on each one. Many of those factors depend not only on you but on other individuals. And, some factors are not within your control. So the first step is to identify what you as a Sales Rep can control because obviously that is where you should and will spend your time and effort. The quick answer to this question is that the Sales Rep can change physicians' prescribing habits. The term *prescriber* refers not only to the physician but also the Physician Assistants and Nurse Practitioners who also prescribe many medications (varies based on individual state's laws). That said, I will use the term Physician from here on to indicate all prescribers. Physician "habits" merely refers to what medications the physician uses. By and large, this becomes a habit over time, in what actually is prescribed and this can be your challenge to overcome. Your goal is to have him thinking about your products and writing them. These habits can be difficult to change but can be done over the course of the sales cycle.

It takes selling at different levels to change physician prescribing habits. Since not much happens unless you get access to the physician, that is a good place to start. There are ways other than face to face selling that change physician habits, such as speaker programs, continuing education, written notes and information left behind or dropped off for the doctor, entertainment events; selling to partners, nurses and office staff on your side, and so on. But for now let's look at access. Access is the number one challenge you will face because it is through access to the physician that you will maximize the opportunities you have to sell to that customer. Your prospective employer will be interested in what you think about gaining precious minutes of time with your customer. The best approach to this is to be relationship and service oriented—always think in terms of the value you are bringing to the doctor, and the relationship you have with the gatekeepers and entire staff. If there is relationship, service and value, you will get and maintain time with them. If not, you will find yourself shut out. High rapport and high customer service are essential. Read on for more on access and other key skills and responsibilities. To summarize what the Pharmaceutical Rep is, he or she is the consummate sales professional, attentive to every detail of the sales call including pre-planning and careful follow up; he is customer focused, creative, flexible, positive, and technically oriented and an expert in the disease states, products and competitor products. She is also a goal-setter, aggressive, and determined to get the results she desires.

WHAT QUALITIES ARE COMPANIES LOOKING FOR IN JOB CANDIDATES?

The essential qualities desired by a pharmaceutical company are generally the same as those of other sales organizations. Of course, you must demonstrate to prospective employers that you have the competencies that they are looking for in a new employee. You have to convince the first interviewer that you have the qualities that fits the profile his or her company has in mind. You can create the opportunity to do so by following the strategies outlined in this manual.

I would like to take a moment to make a personal comment on this subject, as well as make an appeal to you as a prospective candidate for a Pharmaceutical Sales Position. Please take these words very seriously and in the positive manner in which they are intended. There are many hundreds and even thousands of well-meaning individuals who have the basic qualifications and abilities to get interviews with pharmaceutical companies. However, as a District Manager for many years myself and in discussions with other Managers, there is a frustration that sometimes surfaces during the process of interviewing and selecting the best candidate. This frustration stems from a lack, not an abundance, of candidates that rise to the top and set themselves apart from the average. Even after running classified ads, eliminating hundreds of resumes, receiving referrals from company sources, agencies, job fairs, headhunters, networking sources, etc., there can often be no candidate that goes the extra mile to stand apart. By this I mean the candidate who knows the company, knows the job, is prepared for the interview, and follows up afterwards—what I would consider the standard steps throughout the interview process. So my appeal to you is this: Make the effort to demonstrate your excellence! Position yourself to win by dedicating high effort and energy into this process. It's not easy, but it is simple. Follow the steps, be confident, give it high energy, be devoted to the details, and you will be the one who stands out among the many. Now, I know there are many who feel they are doing this and are still not succeeding. To them I say you must keep trying. Learn something from every contact, phone call, interview and turn-down. It can take many months or even a year or more for qualified candidates to get the job. OK, enough of Anne getting on her soapbox! Now let's continue!

You will discover that these attributes described in this section can be demonstrated clearly in the way you approach and progress through the networking and interviewing process. Central to the strategy is the concept that the job search itself is an ideal opportunity to clearly demonstrate you own potential in a powerful way. You must sell yourself as the right candidate in order to get the job. This is the first opportunity that the interviewer has to assess your talents in sales. You are talking about your skills and at the same time demonstrating them. The employer is the buyer. It is similar to the selling situations you will face as an employee of your new company. Thus, be at your best in all your contacts with prospective employers from the very start.

Most companies have a definitive profile, and interviewers will tailor their questions to identify whether you fit this profile. Each company will have identified certain traits, skill sets, and abilities that they will attempt to evaluate in each candidate through the interview process. These areas are often called "job competencies." Some competencies are considered "core" which means they are inherent in an individual and can not be trained or developed. In other words, the candidate either has them or not. Core competencies are in the areas of positive attitude, motivation, drive for results (goal oriented), and work ethic. Other competencies can be obtained or developed in an individual by training and practice. These are in the areas of selling skills and knowledge. Please note—for those of you without prior sales experience, you CAN learn to sell. Good sales people are the result of training, self-learning and practice. In addition, there are many jobs that, though not titled or typically thought of as sales, are actually utilizing and developing the competencies required to be in sales. Teaching, working on teams, gaining approval for budgets or projects, making presentations, purchasing functions and many other roles provide this experience. In addition, a successful track record, progression in responsibility and salary level, setting and accomplishment of specific goals, use of persuasion and presentation to convince others to take action, etc., all show your ability to sell. Therefore, you need to plan for your interview-- be prepared to illustrate, with examples, each of the qualities you possess. Familiarize yourself with the following attributes. As you prepare for your interview with the questions in Chapter 5, develop your answers to demonstrate these competencies. Whether you have had previous experience in sales or not, you will need to describe or use as examples various activities, responsibilities and accomplishments in your work or school history that will demonstrate these competencies. These will bring you success in pharmaceutical sales.

- Results Oriented or Goal Oriented: Your activities are directed towards an identifiable, stated or written goal.
- Motivation: Show what makes you get up in the morning, and what excites you about the job and company you are pursuing.
- High Energy: The ability to stay focused and enthused in all aspects of the job over time. May include the ability to stay persistent, produce high quantity and quality of work, and put in long hours when necessary (and long hours will be necessary from time to time).
- Flexibility: Able to perform well under changing conditions and demands.
- Communication: Simply put, communications are everything you do and say, and how you do it. As a sales representative, you are in the business of constantly communicating to your customers and your company. This includes listening, speaking, presentation skills, business writing skills, and tele phone skills. Presenting yourself well from the start will go far in demonstrating that you have this talent.
- Determination: You have the intention to get what you want both personally and in business. You succeed in the face of adversity. You do not become discouraged, are not afraid to take risks, and you learn from your own mistakes.
- Drive: You have the zeal to achieve goals, and a sense of urgency to complete large and small tasks. You are not complacent or easily satisfied.
- Confidence: You are calm and attentive; you are not arrogant, but very sure of yourself in front of people. You have straight, relaxed posture, good eye contact, and voice projection. The best way to be confident is to be prepared!
- Reliability and Integrity: This is trustworthiness. It is being responsible for your promises and commitments to the customer. Follow-up is extremely important in pharmaceutical sales. For example, you may be asked a question for which you do not know the answer. How long will it take you to find out and communicate it to the customer? Pharmaceutical selling is an ongoing, consultative process. Your follow-up is what establishes your relationship as the customer comes to trust that you will always keep your commitments. If your customers trust you, they will also trust your com pany and your product. It is not only going the extra mile, but also going every mile.
- Listening Skills: It is a fact that salespersons talk too much instead of listening. Good listening is essential to strong relationships; it involves understanding and clarifying with questions what the customer is saying. With good listening skills, a customer feels heard and will be more receptive. These skills allow you to uncover customer needs so you can direct your product presentation to meet those needs.
- Creativity and Innovation: Create strategies, develop solutions to problems, and take advantage of opportunities. In pharmaceutical sales, for example, creative representatives think of unique, attention-getting ways of opening a sales presentation.
- Teamwork: As sales in the pharmaceutical industry changes to meet the challenges of the health care system, such as managed care, selling in a team approach is becoming more important. A sales team could include a sales representative, hospital specialty representative, managed care account manager, and district manager to achieve a common goal of increasing sales in a given managed care organization or physician group practice.
- Achievement: This can be shown by a history of success in other sales and career areas, in school, and community or extra-curricular activities.

These attributes provide an excellent framework to help you prepare for interviewing. Individual companies or district managers may look for additional traits or possess certain "hot buttons." Hot buttons are specific attributes that a manager feels are especially critical, and they weigh most heavily in his or her selection of candidates. You can find out about these ahead of time through your contacts with a sales representative in that company (described in Chapter 5). During your networking, a good strategy is to ask for the desired requirements for the job as early as possible in the process. By uncovering these early on, you will be able to effectively match your skills and abilities to fit the needs of the company. You will perform this skill for product presentations once you are hired. During your preparation for the interview, determine specific examples from your past experience that you can present to illustrate each attribute you possess. This practice is critical to successfully interviewing.

WHAT DOES THE REPRESENTATIVE NEED TO KNOW?

Simply put, the Pharmaceutical Representative needs to be an expert in the medical specialty area in which his or her products will be used. That may seem daunting at first. How can you know as much as a physician or pharmacist who has all those years of training? There are several reasons you can accomplish this.

First, you will be dealing with a relatively small area of medicine compared to all of medicine. The physician or pharmacist has an extensive background involving hundreds of medications, many different disease states, and multitudes of treatment options. Your knowledge, on the other hand, will be highly specialized, focusing exclusively on a few medications you represent, only one or two diseases, and a limited number of treatment options. You will become an expert in your given areas.

Secondly, as a newly hired representative, you will embark upon an elaborate company training program. The pharmaceutical industry, as a rule, provides training and development that is unparalleled in any other industry. Most companies are proud of the extensive and demanding nature of their training programs. It is helpful in your research of each company to investigate its training program. You will learn when and how to approach this topic in later chapters.

Training is conducted in two broad areas. 1) Knowledge, which is the information you need about your products and your customers and 2) Skills, which are the learned behaviors and habits that you need in order to perform your job.

Examples of knowledge building can be found in the following:
* anatomy and physiology
* diseases for which your products are used, such as asthma, diabetes, cancer, and depression
* diagnosis and appropriate treatments
* your pharmaceutical products and competing products are referred to as product knowledge
* customer types and suggested selling approaches for each type
* the health care system managed care, retail pharmacy, etc.

Specific product knowledge on a medication that you promote is highly emphasized. For example, you will be required to know the following details about your products and their competition:

* mechanism of action (how it works in the body)
* indications of the medication (what it is used for)
* contraindications (when it may not be used)
* dosage regimens
* side effects
* warnings and precautions (under what circumstance is caution advised)
* current scientific medical studies
* costs of therapies

Examples of skill building are:

- call planning and preparation
- business planning and customer targeting, referred to as territory management
- listening and selling skills (ie, opening, closing)
- group presentation skills
- negotiation skills
- call reporting
- computer skills
- analytical skills, sales data interpretation
- strategic and creative processes
- teamwork, leadership, and managing your career
- setting up and managing a home office

Thirdly, many training sessions are company-specific. These include policies and procedures for working day to day within the corporate environment. Examples are reporting procedures for sales call activity, travel and entertainment expenses, and use of your company car.

Why do companies place so much emphasis and investment in training? The goal of each company is to represent itself in the best possible light. When you represent a company, you are the company to that customer. A physician must feel very confident in prescribing a pharmaceutical product. He is placing the health of his patient and his own reputation on the line with each treatment decision. Therefore, it is imperative that you project the utmost professionalism, confidence, and knowledge to that decision-maker.

It would be a liability for a pharmaceutical company if a representative were ill prepared and therefore misinformed its customer physicians. All statements made by a representative are considered "promotional claims" and must comply with FDA guidelines. Pharmaceutical companies must monitor this closely to ensure that their sales force is performing to this standard.

HOW IS THE REPRESENTATIVE TRAINED?

Training programs for all of the top pharmaceutical companies are similar. These programs usually begin with extensive at-home reading assignments over a period of two weeks or more. During the home study period, you will need to absorb a large amount of information from product training manuals including anatomy and physiology, disease states, diagnosis, testing, and treatments including your medications and the competition.

Home-study is followed by two to six weeks of classroom sessions under qualified instructors including role playing sales calls and taking written examinations. Role-play situations are used to practice what you are learning. A trainer will play the role of a customer so the trainee can become familiar with questions and objections he or she will encounter during sales presentations. After this initial period, your training will move into the field. A trainer, manager, or experienced representative will work with you in your territory. You will also observe other representatives working in other territories. Your district manager or a trainer will work with you frequently at first, then perhaps every four to six weeks. Their role is to provide observation, insight, motivation, and coaching to your performance. You will need to be able to accept positive criticism well and have a desire to learn and grow. Many companies will use the training program as an ongoing evaluation of the candidate. You will discover challenges that are unlike those of any college program you have ever experienced. Be prepared to take it very seriously.

Training in the pharmaceutical industry never ends. You need to know about the new drugs that have been approved by the FDA, and the side effects of existing ones. This is an ongoing process. Medical science will continue to provide new advances and scientific breakthroughs for new products, new clinical research studies, recalled drugs, and uncovering new diseases. As in any sales industry, you will continually face the threat of new competitors and the advent of new market opportunities. Nowhere is this more the case than in today's ever-changing healthcare environment. This profession rewards the individual who builds his or her knowledge and skill levels.

WHAT DOES A TYPICAL DAY LOOK LIKE?

As with many other sales professions, Pharmaceutical Representatives work from their homes. There is no one to look over your shoulder every day. Your self-determination is the key to your success. You should emphasize your independent drive and self-motivation as you interview.

First of all, most entry-level Pharmaceutical Sales Representatives are working in a Primary Care (PC) physician office setting. Primary Care physicians make up the majority of offices out there. They are generalists as opposed to specialists. Types of Primary Care physicians include Internal Medicine, Family Practice, and General Practitioners. They can be MD's (Medical Doctor) and DO's (Osteopathic Doctor). Pediatricians are also considered Primary Care, as are some Obstetrician/Gynecologists. A typical day consists of presenting your products to Primary Care Physicians, their Nurses and office staff. Your Manager and your company usually determine the specific number of calls you make, which physicians you will call on, and which of your products you will promote to a given physician. Most companies requ'ire a minimum number of calls, usually in the range or 8-10 physicians per day. In addition to physician calls, you may also call on retail pharmacies and hospital clinic pharmacies. Your "call plan" is a list of targeted physicians in your geography. Armed with your call plan, sales data, sales support materials, product samples and literature, you will prepare for the day's call. This is usually done the night before as you organize yourself for the following day. Only then are you ready to venture out to make your calls on the customers.

Your company's "plan of action" (POA), or similar term, helps you set your overall goals, objectives, strategies and individual tactics. The POA includes what products and promotional messages you will emphasize. The plan of action is based on the priorities of the company as determined by the sales management and marketing teams. To illustrate, imagine that your employer, XYZ Pharmaceuticals, Inc., has decided to promote their antibiotic for the next twelve weeks. Thus, for that period, the activities of the organization will be geared towards this goal. Representatives' presentations will shift to increase market share in this product category. Specific tools such as visual aids (product information), give-away items, speaking programs, sales contests and bonus payout incentives are all geared towards the same goals. After this twelve-week period, selling focus may shift to promote a different product, perhaps a new line of oral contraceptives or anti-inflammatory. Promotional plans often are based on financial or sales periods, such as quarters or trimesters.

As your day begins, you will make sure everything is planned and ready for the day. This includes all the visual aids, product literature, give-away items, samples, computer/PDA, sales reports and data, and even having your cell phone charged and ready to go. Either the night before or in the morning, the Rep will conduct a thorough pre-call plan. This is a vital part of your day and prepares you to make the most impact possible with a given customer. To adequately pre-call plan, you will review your post-call notes from the previous call to that doctor. In addition, you will review sales data to see if that doctor has increased or decreased in the number of prescriptions, or share or prescriptions written for your product and competitive products. Armed with such data, you can determine your objective for the call and how you are going to accomplish your objective. A good Sales Representative will plan the entire call from the initial questions to the material to be presented, left behind, and the specific closes to be used. Each call is tailored to the individual physician in order to have the most impact. Begin your pre-call planning by asking yourself this question: "what do I want the physician to do differently as a result of my call?" From there, the initial questions, product messages, materials and closes should all support the objective. After the call, recording what transpired and planning the next steps right away will ensure you have smooth follow through and transition into the next call.

Close communication is also part of a typical day. Normally, you will start your day by checking voicemail and email to see if there are any communications from your manager and/or counterparts that require immediate action or response. "Counterpart" Reps are those Reps from your own company with whom you "overlap" or share territory, but promote different products (you may or may not have counterparts based on how your sales forcer is structured). Coordination of effort is important among counterparts, as is the concept of team selling—taking a team approach to an individual physician or physician office. You may meet on a weekly basis, perhaps even daily or at the least touch base by phone or voicemail. Your day in the field will begin around 8:00 a.m. or as soon as physician offices and pharmacies are open and available to make calls. During your day, you will enter physicians' offices to make your presentations. This is the major focus of your day, of course. You will be challenged to overcome the obstacles between you and this all-important customer. Obstacles include the constraints on the doctor's time, working with (or through) the office staff, and perhaps being bumped by one of your competitors! Your knowledge of the doctor's preferences and schedule, your rapport with the office staff, and other tricks-of-the-trade will help you meet this challenge.

Once you are in front of the physician, you may have a few seconds or several minutes to perform the skills and communicate the knowledge necessary to gain the doctor's confidence and commitment to prescribe your product. During this time, your preparation is the key to your success. You are a resource of information, providing unique services to the physician and ultimately the patient. Thus, you must understand the physicians' needs and attitudes in order to position your product to satisfy those requirements. Your final goal is to gain the physician's commitment to prescribe your product.

Part of the typical day is, on occasion, a breakfast or lunch meeting with the physician office. This may mean feeding the entire staff, or just the doctor. It may require additional time and planning to physically pick up the lunch, or you may have it catered, which saves time. Regardless, it is a great opportunity to get expanded time with both the doctor and the entire office. Many Reps, depending on the company, will have one to even 4-5 lunches per week. The frequency of lunches depends on how many you can schedule and how much money as been budgeted for this purpose. You may also share the lunch meeting with one of your counterparts. During this sit-down meeting, you both will have the time to fully present your products.

Though not always, it can be part of the typical day to be planning and conducting a speaker program (an expert speaker giving a lecture), a promotional or educational event. First of all, as discussed in Chapter 1, there are limits to what Pharmaceutical Representatives can do regarding entertainment. Due to PhRMA Guidelines adopted in July 2002, most companies are no longer providing entertainment other than meals, such as dinner out at a restaurant. Thus, you will NOT be involved in sporting events, concerts, shows, golfing, etc., which were commonly done in conjunction with an educational programs to make them more attractive and increase attendance. However, educational programs are a staple of your promotional strategy. In a typical day, you may be including oral and written invitations to your customers during sales calls. You may be attending speaker programs in the evenings or on weekends. These are a good opportunity to have your customers hear your product message, and learn from outside experts in the field, rather than from company representatives.

You may also be involved in exhibits or displays at larger symposia, which may be local such as at a hotel or may be out of town and require you to travel. Regardless of the location, working an exhibit is part of the job, offering you a venue in which the physician comes for continuing education and in the process will stop by your booth for information and discussion on your products. You may also have a display at a local hospital where you have made arrangements to set up a table in the hallway or physician lounge in order to meet and call on doctors as they go through their hospital rounds. Again, these are opportunities outside of the typical physician office call for you to affect physician prescribing behavior.

There are aspects of every industry that make it unique, such as product lines, customer audiences, decision-makers, the purchasing environment, sales-cycles, call frequency, and others. The goal of selling pharmaceuticals is the same as for any product. However, this industry has some characteristics that are inherently different from other businesses. For example, the Pharmaceutical Representative does not sell directly to the end user of the product, or the patient. In other words, the "decision maker" does not actually buy or take the medication. In fact, the decision-maker (physician), the consumer (patient), and the payer (insurer) are all different individuals or organizations. The Pharmaceutical Representative presents his or her products to the prescribing physician, dispensing pharmacist, or other purchaser such as a hospital or managed care organization (MCO).

The decision-maker is generally the prescriber. The pharmacist can also decide, in some situations, to dispense a product other than the one prescribed by the physician. This can happen in two ways. The first is generic substitution, whereby the pharmacist dispenses a generic form of the same medication that is prescribed. Secondly, the pharmacist may call the doctor and request permission to dispense a completely different medication, but one that has the same overall effect on the patient. This is a process called therapeutic substitution. Thus, both the pharmacist and the physician influence which medication the patient ultimately gets.

Further complicating the scenario is another decision-maker referred to as the "payer," or the "third party." Think of the patient as the first party, the health care provider (doctor, pharmacist, etc.) as the second party, and the person paying the bill as third party. Third parties are the insurance company, the employer, and the health plan or managed care organization (MCO), or the government in the case of Medicare, Tricare, Champus, and Medicaid. Examples of MCOs are health maintenance organizations (HMO), preferred provider organizations (PPO), and pharmaceutical benefit management companies (PBM). Managed care organizations do have impact in approving which medication the patient ultimately is given by limiting what specific drugs they will pay for or "reimburse." Enforcing a "formulary," which is a list of approved drugs that are "covered" or paid for by the MCO, does this. The formulary is sent out to all doctors and pharmacists to guide them as to which drugs should be prescribed and dispensed for patients enrolled in that MCO. Thus, third party payers are important customer audiences for pharmaceutical companies, particularly MCOs.

Because the prescribing physician and the dispensing pharmacist are the primary audience of the entry-level sales representative, I will, in this book, limit the focus of discussion to office-based physicians and retail-based pharmacists. Other customers, such as MCOs, are the responsibility of experienced account managers and national account executives that have been promoted from sales representative and district manager positions.

Another characteristic of pharmaceutical sales is the unique selling process. First, the process of selling to a physician would not be characterized as a hard sell. There is no push to get the customer to "sign the bottom line" by using aggressive sales techniques and power negotiations. Rather, pharmaceutical selling is characterized as consultative. You are a consultant to the doctor, providing educational and informational data to support his or her decision to use your products. This is not to say that you do not gain a commitment from the doctor. You must close the sale firmly (does not mean aggressively) if you are to change a doctor's behavior. You must ask the physician for a commitment to prescribe your products, and continually reinforce that commitment. However, you must earn the right to ask by winning the trust of the physician, This is accomplished by consistently providing accurate product information, published literature, clinical studies, answers to any questions that come up, patient examples, medication samples, patient education materials, and whatever additional information the physician or pharmacist requires.

The physician is in search of the most medically appropriate product that will achieve optimal results for the varied needs they have. The biggest need, of course, is to provide benefits for the patient. A physician is basing his or her decision on years of extensive education and experience. They also possess unique characteristics, strong attitudes, or hot buttons, which drive their prescribing habits. For example, a given doctor may be more likely to use one medicine over another because it is new or perceived to be more scientifically advanced. This type of physician is an early adopter of new products. Another physician will do the opposite, preferring older and more proven therapies. This type of physician is a late adopter.

Other requirements affect the physician's decision to prescribe a particular medication. These are the professional and personal necessities of the individual physician. Many needs also arise from the physician's consideration regarding third party influences. Such third parties include the group practice in which the doctor is a member, a hospital system where the doctor is on staff, managed care organizations that provide a flow of patients to the doctor, governmental and other health plans, employers, and insurance companies. Your challenge is to uncover all the various needs and attitudes of a given doctor. You can then position the features and benefits of your products to best meet those needs and gain the commitment to prescribe. Physicians are creatures of habit like anyone else. They typically have a small group of medications they have become comfortable with and prescribe repeatedly. Changing their prescribing habits is your challenge.

It may take several sales calls on an individual physician before you successfully close the sale and the doctor prescribes your product. The selling cycle may be longer or shorter for some doctors, depending on the needs and attitudes previously described. A contrast is the retail sales environment, where a sale must be made on a single encounter with the customer. That is not always the case with a physician—it means that you may not ask for the business, or close the sale, on the very first call. Always ask the client for a commitment to try your product.

Another challenge awaiting you on a typical day is differentiating yourself from your competitors, as well as their products. As you now know, selling pharmaceuticals requires a technical and consultative approach. However, this fact does not obviate the benefits of relationship selling. People buy from people, as the saying goes, and physicians are no different. Developing good rapport with your customers is essential to gaining their time and attention. Physicians' offices have 75 to 100 individual sales representatives from different companies and industries calling on them. Sometimes the office staff will have five Pharmaceutical Representatives that call on them in a single day. They are busy and have limited time so it is your job to obtain the doctor's time and attention. Your excellent rapport, product knowledge, communication skills, and professional demeanor can set you apart from representatives of competing pharmaceutical companies.

Physicians differ in their overall attitude towards Pharmaceutical Representatives. These decisions span from complete refusal to speak with pharmaceutical salespeople to an open door policy. This range of mannerisms is one aspect of the job that offers a challenge to the representative. For example, you need to be innovative to create opportunities to get in front of the "hard-to-see" doctor.

Product samples and patient information may be a part of your total offering. If so, this provides the physician with an excellent service for his practice. Most physicians applaud the practice of free samples. These are used to start therapy or sometimes treat a particular patient with that medication. Often the doctor can evaluate the response to the drugs without having the patient incur the full cost of the prescription at the pharmacy. Sometimes physicians will provide a patient with two different medications (such as treatments for allergies), and have the patient try each one at home. The patient will decide which one works best. Physicians will also use samples to assist a patient who cannot afford the cost of the prescription. Product samples are an excellent service that can be offered to the physician who in turn can provide a better service to the patient. I should mention a word here about sampling because sampling is taking a larger piece of the Rep's administrative time through the week. Sampling is a highly regulated area of your job. The federal government regulates how companies handle samples in order to minimize sample misuse and diversion (selling samples). Individual companies must comply, which results in very strict procedures and reporting for how the Sales Reps utilize their samples. Suffice it to say that the result is more time spent counting and recording sample inventories and disbursements. This could be a computerized or paper process.

A large part of the typical day is spent in planning, organizing, and reporting. You will manage your time by planning your calls for the day and routing yourself in the most efficient way, based on appointment times and customer locations. You will assemble all the necessary materials—sales information, visual aids, clinical studies, and product samples. It is important to stock and organize the supplies you need in your company vehicle. This will ensure that you have what you need and your day runs smoothly. Recording and reporting each call is also critical to your success. The method you employ will vary slightly by company. The advantages of recording call activity are that you can retrieve the information later, use it to evaluate your efforts and what you accomplished, remember what the customer commitment was, and importantly, what commitments you made and what you need to do next. Most companies now use laptop computers to enable you to instantly record your calls "in the field." Computers also offer you instant access to customer records and are an excellent tool for sales tracking.

WHAT DOES IT TAKE TO BE SUCCESSFUL?

Many personal characteristics and traits are essential to your success. These requirements were described in this chapter and will be revisited in later chapters—they are the qualities you will want to demonstrate during your sales interview process. The following keys to success are practical applications of your individual talents. This discussion will give examples of successful goals and strategies.

First, excellent product knowledge forms the basis of your sales presentations. Secondly, successful sales representatives consistently *maximize their selling opportunities*. Simply, this means they make the most calls, at the right times, to the right physicians, with the right messages. Thus, they see the highest number of valuable physicians within their territory, and deliver the best marketing message. By doing so, successful reps create the best chance of success in every call. Not to say that every call must or will be a success—there are many obstacles and challenges to most every call; but good sales people know the secret is in the numbers—the more calls you make, the better your odds of closing the deal. Perhaps you will not be friends with every physician you call on, be your best on every call. However, you need only have a relatively few high-writing doctors on your side to be successful. A good Representative lives by the old 80-20 rule. That is, 80 percent of the prescriptions are written by 20 percent of the doctors.

What is good, professional rapport? It means learning the physician's needs, schedule, patient types, current prescribing habits, and hot buttons. Is he clinically or technically focused? Does he prefer a product because it is convenient, inexpensive, or new? Does he pay attention to all those managed care formularies or does he focus on what is best for the patient? Rapport also means trust. It is imperative that what you say is accurate and that you are dependable. It takes time to develop a sales relationship before an actual sale or commitment to prescribe can take place. There are no short cuts, and if you are to learn the intricacies of the industry, you will still need to give yourself two to three years in a given territory to really get up to speed and productivity. This concentrated time at the outset of your career will be invaluable as your progress, whether you remain in sales, pursue management, marketing, or even the office of the Chief Executive.

As you begin in your new territory, you will be assigned a selected audience of physicians, pharmacists, and hospitals. You will be on a schedule that puts you in front of the same customer every four, six, or eight weeks, depending on your company's direction. This schedule is your call cycle and determines your call frequency. The sale can sometimes require several contacts, which you will accomplish as you repeat your call cycle over time. Success is dependent on a consistent selling message, frequency of contacts, and professional relationships.

WHAT ARE SOME POSITIVE AND NEGATIVE ASPECTS OF THE JOB?

As with any career choice, there are positive and negative aspects of a career in pharmaceutical sales. In summarizing the most common job aspects we use the information that we acquired from numerous interviews and focus groups with pharmaceutical representatives.

The job requires autonomy in your daily activities. Some people enjoy this aspect and the freedom to be creative in their sales efforts. Others complain that such autonomy often leaves them feeling isolated from co-workers and without direction. Individuals who are not disciplined and self-motivated will find themselves struggling with distractions. Determination and a drive for success are essential attributes for this reason.

Job burnout can be a problem with Pharmaceutical Representatives just as it is with other demanding professions. One of your biggest challenges is to keep yourself motivated daily. The best way to do so is to set short-term, realistic goals. Look for new challenges and be creative. Have fun with it! Your district manager has experienced the same job stresses that you have, and is responsible for helping you stay motivated. He or she will be a good resource, but it will be mostly up to you.

There is a twelve percent turnover rate in the industry, which indicates that this job is not for everyone. My research suggests that some Pharmaceutical Representatives become complacent in their positions over time and no longer experience the job satisfaction that was present in the beginning of their careers. The day-to-day work can become tedious, and it requires your own creativity and motivation to make it exciting. Having supportive management and a team spirit among your peers is also helpful. Calling on six to nine physicians per day, spending time in waiting rooms, idling in traffic, and going into pharmacies and hospitals is a hard day's work. Sometimes the heat of summer or freezing winter snowstorms challenge your resolve. Will physicians complain if you do not make the sales call? Hardly! Will your manager know if you ended your day early every now and then? Probably not. Your determination and persistence will be the key to the success of your career.

I have spoken with many representatives with ten to thirty years on the job. On the positive side, many experienced veterans reported that job satisfaction increased over the years. The continual learning associated with new products and technologies offers unlimited challenge. The rapport and long-term relationships they have developed with their physicians and pharmacists are personally valuable and important. These long-term customers also appreciate the experienced representative and recognize good salespeople are a tremendous resource. Career sales representatives find satisfaction in the recognition they receive. Multiple sales awards, generous raises, and commission payments come with hard work and experience. The number one reason given for long-term success is practicing a strong work ethic.

To summarize, individuals in this field are as unique as in any profession. You will discover whether this career is a good fit for you only through investigation and research—a process you have already started! Before you decide for or against this career choice, gain the broadest perspective, you can from individuals within the profession.

HOW ARE REPRESENTATIVES COMPENSATED AND WHAT ARE THE INCENTIVES?

Compensation packages in the pharmaceutical industry vary from company to company. Typically, you will receive a combination of base salary plus a bonus or commission on sales achievement. Our research shows that the annual base salary for an entry-level representative may range from $40,000 to $50,000. Bonuses and commissions are generally paid out by quarter, trimester, or year based on sales performance. Industry norms show a wide variance in bonus structure, with annual earnings ranging from $5,000 to $25,000 and higher. Obviously, you should look at both base salary and bonus potential.

With many companies, you may be offered additional compensation. Virtually all pharmaceutical companies provide a company car. This should be considered part of the entire package, and is said to be worth more than $10,000 per year in base pay. Some offer stock options, though these may be reserved for Manager level and above. Cash profit sharing is less common but may be part of the mix for some companies.

To illustrate, consider a Pharmaceutical Representative who works for a company that pays a low base combined with a high bonus structure. Let us say this individual earns a base salary of $40,000, which is at the low end of the range, and is eligible to earn between $20,000 and $30,000 on bonuses and/or commissions. The total package is worth $50,000 to $60,000 per year. In another company, that same representative may earn a larger base salary, say $40,000, but only be eligible for a commission and bonus of $10,000 to $20,000. His total package is the same as in the first example. Again, this varies from company to company. The first-year Pharmaceutical Representative can usually expect a total package of $50,000 to $60,000. In addition, there is compensation for business and entertainment expenses, a company car or car allowance, excellent medical and dental plans, retirement and savings plans, and perhaps stock options. You can expect your base salary to increase yearly if you stay with the same corporation. Many companies have different pay levels associated with certain criteria of performance and length of service within the organization.

HOW IS SALES PERFORMANCE MEASURED?

It is important for any representative to know how sales performance is measured. This is another topic for you to explore during your research into the industry and contacts with prospective employers. It is not advisable to inquire about the amount of compensation early in the interviewing process. However, you should inquire about the basics. For example, what methods of evaluation are used to measure job performance? What percentage of total compensation comes from base salary versus bonus and commission? This information will provide insight into the management style of the company. For example, if a company places emphasis on representatives' autonomy and creativity, they will reward this behavior by placing a larger percentage of total compensation into bonus or commission. Bonus and commission payments are at risk—they are yours to earn, or yours to lose!

Sales tracking and measurement in pharmaceutical sales is historically problematic. In recent years, it has become more of a science. In brief, there are vendors, or specialized companies, who make it their business to accumulate distribution and prescription data from the various points along the supply chain. Then they process it into usable data runs and sales reports, and make it available to pharmaceutical companies for purchase. Thus, your company can provide you with specific sales by market share, numbers of prescriptions written, and tablets sold by territory, zip code, and even by specific doctor. As mentioned earlier in this chapter, physician level prescription data is an indispensable tool in planning and evaluating your own efforts on any individual physician. Imagine knowing exactly what and how many prescriptions your customer has written over the past two months, for example, of not only your product but the competitor's product as well. It is powerful information, but NOT to be shared with the physician, of course, or even let on that you have the information. It is strictly confidential company data. Some doctors are aware the industry has this information

An older method of measuring territory sales (called DDD) was to simply count the amount of product delivered to pharmacies in your territory. To illustrate, let's follow a unit (or bottle) of prescription medication through the chain of distribution. First, it is shipped from the manufacturer to a wholesaler, then from the wholesaler to retail pharmacies. Each unit is tracked by its movement through various market outlets: chain and independent community pharmacies, mail order pharmacies, food store pharmacies, mass merchandise stores with pharmacies, hospitals, nursing homes, and HMOs. When that bottle is sold from an outlet in your territory (as determined by zip code), you receive credit for the sale of that unit. There are some inconsistencies, such as when your doctor writes for your product but the patient has her prescription filled in another Rep's territory. This method of tracking units sold by zip code is no longer used by most companies.

It is now possible to track sales by individual prescription which is a much more accurate way to measure sales performance. Once a doctor writes a prescription and the patient has it filled, the representative responsible for calling on that particular physician is credited with the sale. In this system, it does not matter in which pharmacy or zip code the prescription is filled. It also gives you specific data on the prescribing habits of each one of your customers—an obvious benefit when it comes to evaluating and planning sales strategies for that doctor. This detailed level of data is very expensive for pharmaceutical companies to purchase. However, it is worth it because of its value in evaluating and targeting customers. Your time is also expensive for pharmaceutical companies, and you are more productive when you target doctors that respond well to your selling efforts or have high potential for prescribing your products.

WHAT ARE THE CAREER ADVANCEMENT OPPORTUNITIES?

Advancement opportunities are available and achievable within the pharmaceutical industry. Directions in which to advance are many and challenging. Opportunities may be categorized into three different areas of career specialization, as follows:

• Career Field Sales

• Field Sales Management
• Corporate Office Functions

Advancements in these three categories are accessible to representatives from the entry-level sales position. Each area offers unique experiences, builds additional competencies, and opens more doors for increased responsibility and compensation.

First, field sales opportunities are positions available within different divisions or segments of the sales force. They offer increased responsibility, experience with new customer types, different products, and new career challenges and growth. As the health care system changes, organizations rather than individual practitioners may make decisions about treatment. Such organizations are physician groups, hospital systems, MCOs, and governmental agencies. This shift has created opportunities in the pharmaceutical industry as companies expand and adapt sales forces to service these newer segments of the marketplace. Examples include the following:
• Senior Sales Representative: A life-long career in sales can be rewarding and provide an excellent work-life. This promotion does not significantly change what you are doing, but acknowledges your experience and advancing skills. It is offered to reward those with long-term success as a pharmaceutical sales representative.
• Hospital Sales Representative: This promotion offers new customer types, professional settings, and selling situations. The environment is in teaching hospitals or universities, including schools of medicine and colleges of pharmacy.
• National Accounts Representative: This position requires business shrewdness and knowledge of product distribution. The main accounts include wholesalers and retail pharmacy chains.
• Managed Care Representative: This is an advanced field position, targeting HMOs, PBMs, employers, and physician groups. It requires advanced knowledge of the payer environment and overall health system.
• Government Affairs Representative: Legislation and policy changes will influence the pharmaceutical

industry. Pharmaceutical companies are involved at all levels of government. Customers include state Medicaid programs, regulatory and licensing boards, professional societies, and associations, state public health departments, and formulary committees. This position may involve lobbying and legislative activity.

The second category of career options is sales management. This position is usually referred to as District Manager (DM). The DM's responsibilities include hiring, coaching, and managing an entire district of seven to ten or more representatives. The DM reports to the Regional Director (RD), who has responsibility for five to ten DM's and their subordinates. At the top of the sales force is the Director of Sales, who may be a vice-president (VP), and reports to another VP, usually of sales and marketing, or directly to the CEO. This structure varies from company to company.

The third category includes opportunities in the corporate headquarters. Promotions exist for the ambitious sales representative in many different departments. Some of these positions are listed.

- Sales Trainer: Designs, develops and delivers all types of training.
- Marketing Manager, Product Manager: Develops sales strategies, forecasts, and promotional pro grams for the sales force to implement.
- Communications Manager: Develops sales and corporate communications material and programs in support of marketing and sales strategies.
- Professional Education Manager: Developing educational programs for physicians and pharmacists.
- Sales Administration or Sales Operations Manager: Logistical areas of the sales force, such as computer systems, call planning and reporting, supplies, and bonus compensation plans.

Each of these advancements will require a successful background as a Pharmaceutical Representative for a minimum of two to three years. Progression to Director-level appointments requires experience in the corporate headquarters or "home office." Regardless of your long-term aspirations, your short-term goal is to achieve an entry-level sales position. Once you are working in the industry, develop your knowledge and skills to the best of your ability. Use all the resources available to you through the training department, your manager, experienced representatives, and corporate headquarters contacts. Identify your strengths and weaknesses. Evaluate where you can make the best contribution to the company, how you can maximize your strengths, and what interests you the most. Communicate to your manager that you are interested in development and advancement. Evaluate your situation and develop your goals for the future.

Chapter 3

Best Foot Forward: Resumes, Cover Letters

RESUMES AND COVER LETTERS

Resumes should be meticulously crafted. Their main purpose is to prevent you from being quickly and immediately eliminated as a potential interview candidate. This is an important fact about resumes. They constitute that all-important "first impression" that can either land you an interview, or land you in the wastebasket. Twenty seconds is all the time the average manager takes to look over a resume and decide whether the applicant should be granted the opportunity to impress the management in a face to face interview. You do not want your resume landing in the proverbial "on-file" Neverland from which few ever emerge.

Picture this scenario: XYZ Pharmaceuticals needs to fill new positions created as a result of sales force expansion. The Human Resources Department (HR) places an advertisement in the "job classifieds" section of the weekend newspaper and on posts the job vacancies the company website. In addition, the local District Manager alerts her Sales Representatives to "keep an eye open" for potential candidates. Many companies offer their Representatives an incentive ("referral bonus") for surfacing qualified candidates from the field. In addition, Managers will request a professional recruiter (headhunter) to make contacts and identify qualified candidates for interviews. Combining these multiple recruiting strategies produces hundreds of resumes. It is typical for just a single classified advertisement in a large metropolitan newspaper to generate more than five hundred resumes.

So, what happens next to all the stacks of paper? Picture them being screened according to basic minimum criteria by an individual, perhaps an HR (Human Resources) specialist, or even a secretary. Some companies may use an electronic scanning process that looks for "keywords." After some are eliminated, the remaining are reviewed again using higher standards, as the stack grows smaller. Eventually, there are only twenty-five to fifty remaining. The resume stack has been sufficiently narrowed for the next step—the phone screening and face to face interviewing process.

Wait a minute! What did those remaining twenty-five to fifty applicants do that was so special? The answer may surprise you—it is what they did not do that made the difference. They did not make simple mistakes that resulted in rejection for others. Certain mistakes make you unappealing to the prospective employer. In other words, employers are initially screening out, not in, their applicants from the stack of resumes.

Employers are looking for reasons to winnow out particular applicants based strictly on their resumes. This is an easier and less time consuming process than determining which applicants should be interviewed and can be done by an administrative person, such as a secretary or assistant. As the stack grows smaller, the Manager can now focus on specific criteria such as the career history, education, and recommendations from current Sales Representatives.

So how do you get over the first hurdle? What were the basic criteria and higher standards being used in the XYZ Pharmaceuticals example? Pharmaceuticalsales.com will give you the answers to both of these questions in this chapter. Dedication to the pharmaceuticalsales.com approach in marketing yourself can and will put you in front of the interviewer, including these basic guidelines for writing your resume and cover letter, with examples of both.

First of all, some larger organizations and search firms use a computer technology to scan resumes, store them, screen them, and search them for "keywords" to match them to opportunities. Please note, my recommendation is that you do not spend too much time or concern on this aspect of recruitment efforts. Computer screening is rarely used by pharmaceutical companies, and attempting to tailor your resume for it will have little benefit to you. Resumes are scanned into the candidate database, ATS (Applicant Tracking System). Most will never be read by an actual human being unless a manager decides to search the database for possible candidates. In reality, DM's in Pharmaceutical Sales do not operate this database! Instead, DM's get their resumes the old-fashioned way—from Sales Representatives, recruiters, and from running classified ads. Keep in mind that when it comes to resumes, they should be well-written according to the following guidelines, and be part of the overall networking strategy that I recommend (described in Chapter 5). However, online application forms are sometimes required, and are used for screening purposes. As you fill out this type of application, or any application for that matter, treat it like a resume by putting yourself in the best light. Just be aware that automated resume management programs exist out there, and may be used whenever resumes are in electronic form--posted on the Internet, sent by email, or scanned hardcopy to create the electronic file. You can prepare your resume for electronic sending and scanning by not using formatting features such as bolding, italics, underlining and shading. Using Microsoft Word will make it acceptable for attaching to emails. Rich text format (RFT) is also a good option. Use of a standard font and size (Times New Roman 12 pt for example) is important. Regarding "keywords," you will already have many of these in your resume if you include your degree, job history, objective, achievements, etc. For more information on resume preparation, if desired, you can find help and examples on career Internet sites such as monster.com, careerbuilder.com, and hotjobs.net.

What can you do with your resume to give it the best advantage of surviving the initial cuts? Implementing the resume tips that follow will be an excellent strategy. Considering that the average time spent reading a resume is not more than a few seconds, it must be concise and easy to read. The Manager will be looking first at the header for name and location, then objective, then current position and then education. After that, if he likes what he sees so far, he will look at previous positions and other information. Common problems that will eliminate your resume are perceived lack of experience, lack of four-year degree, geography in terms of where you live versus location of the territory, gaps in employment, perceived job instability or frequent job changes, poor format or too wordy/lengthy, poor grammar and misspellings, and typos.

TWENTY SIMPLE RULES FOR RESUMES AND COVER LETTERS

After conducting focus groups and interviews with managers who have made numerous hiring decisions, and after ten years of personal experience as a District Manager, Anne Clayton and pharmaceuticalsales.com has derived the following guidelines. These twenty rules should keep you from being disqualified by your target company and being dropped from consideration before the interview.

Do not focus on mass mailings or blindly sending resumes to pharmaceutical companies. In the rapidly changing business environment of today, this approach is too passive. Unsolicited resumes rarely, if ever, get a response. One exception is in the use of the Internet. More employers are turning to job/resume Internet sites and also using their own sites to capture resumes. In addition to mailing and posting resumes, spend your time and effort on building a network of contacts (see Chapter 5). Once you make direct contact with a potential employer and they agree to see you, then use your resume. Send it directly to the hiring manager and all your networking contacts, not to the corporate Human Resources Department.

1. Outward appearances count heavily. Regardless of how good your handwriting is, always and without exception, type everything. This includes the mailing address and your return address on the envelopes. Type directly on the envelope if possible. If not, type the information onto a white label, then affix it to the envelope. Many managers state they will not even open a handwritten envelope, and will discard immediately a hand written cover letter or resume. Use a large, full-size envelope. For an extra touch, the envelope should be big enough so you do not have

to fold your resume. This will keep the neat and professional look to your resume and cover letter that you worked so hard to create. It will also make it easier to scan which is what employers will do to make it easier to store and send by email. For the same reason, do not staple your resume to your cover letter.

2. Do not be tempted to use colored paper to differentiate your resume from the horde. No manager with whom we spoke ever gave favor or "extra points" for this. Instead, use 100% white cotton paper for your stock and envelope. No other color is more professional than white, period! Have your resume printed using a high quality laser printer. Print each resume separately and avoid using photocopies. This gives the final copy a neat, sharp contrast. Pharmaceuticalsales.com suggests that you have your resume and sample cover letters stored on a diskette. If you have your own computer, you can do this yourself. If not, a local copy center can type, format, print your entire resume, and store it on a diskette. In other words, the copy center can laser-print it from your own diskette, if you have it, or they will type and format it onto a diskette for you. Then it is a snap to print additional copies including any changes to your resume quickly and easily.

3. How should you send your resume? First, avoid the temptation to fax your resume. Even if you mail the original hard copy after faxing it, your faxed copy ends up being seen first, and probably most often. The best approach is to mail or email your resume. First, emailing your resume as an attachment is quite acceptable, and may be preferred by many managers because or its ease in storage, transporting, forwarding to others. Recruiters prefer email and it is a very acceptable means to use. Include your cover letter in the same email as a separate attachment. Next, mailing is an excellent means to distribute your resume. When timing is crucial, use an overnight mail service. You place value on your work by not faxing it and by sending it via overnight mail. It will get more notice and the person receiving it will respect it. Even if timing is not an issue, pharmaceuticalsales.com recommends that you use USPS Priority Mail or overnight mail. The cost of U.S. Postal Service Priority Mail is around four dollars for delivery in two to three days. Express Mail from the U.S. Postal Service delivers overnight for an extra charge. In addition, the U.S. Postal Service can deliver mail to a post office (P.O.) box. Other overnight services do not have that capability. Finally, because it is mailed in a sturdy 8.5 X 11-inch cardboard envelope, it will be protected from damage and you can avoid folding it.

4. Personalize it! When you are sending a resume in response to a classified advertisement from the newspaper, you will find that the "want ads" often do not list the District Manager's, or Human Resource Representative's name. In this case, you have to rely on the pharmaceuticalsales.com strategies described in Chapters 4 and 5. Use these tactics to discover the appropriate names. Ideally, through your networking efforts, you will find contacts in the company who can inform you of opportunities before new openings are even advertised. If the person screening resumes sees their own name or a District Manager's name on your cover letter, they are more likely to pay attention to your resume. Many times, however, classified advertisements are blinded and do not even mention the company name. You should still respond with your resume and cover letter to these ads. You want every opportunity to interview and gain offers. If you have been following the pharmaceuticalsales.com method of networking from before the advertisement was placed, you may already know which companies are hiring. You may be able to find out which company placed the advertisement anyway!

5. Past performance is the best indicator of future success! Accomplishments are critical because they support your claim that you will be successful in pharmaceutical sales. Whether your previous accomplishments are in sales or any other field, they must be stated concisely in measurable or quantitative terms as much as possible. Show the numbers (sales, profits, quotas, calls made) and other measurable achievements such as recognition (awards, promotions, projects completed). Use short statements that begin with an action word such as "achieved," "earned," "increased," etc. Such statements build confidence that you are able to do the job, and are easier to understand than long accolades in paragraph form. Use of bullet points is fine.

6. Choose an appropriate resume format. The format or style of your resume helps

organize the content and makes it attractive and easy to read. There are two basic formats, chronological and functional. You could use either one or a combination. The chronological format is the most common and widely accepted format for candidates with job experience. List your job history by dates of employment, beginning with your present position and moving in reverse chronological order. Briefly describe the major responsibilities and your most important achievements. Include specific results! Begin each phrase with action verbs. In a functional format, group your work accomplishments, responsibilities and duties according to functional skill such as "Sales" or "Organizational Skills." Choose specific skill headings or use a general heading such as "Key Skills." Sometimes, a combination of the two formats is useful. You would begin you're your career objective, followed by a "Featured Skills" section from the functional format, then add your job history as in the chronological format. See the examples of each at the end of this chapter.

Which format is better for pharmaceutical sales? Personally, in my experience of ten years as a District Manager and sifting through hundreds of resumes, I prefer to see the chronological format. Most managers would hold this same opinion. It is the most widely used and acceptable, easiest to read and assimilate because is emphasizes employment history. By highlighting position titles, company, skills, responsibilities and achievements, it easily demonstrates stability and track record of accomplishments. It is particularly effective when seeking a position is the same or similar field, such as moving from one sales position to another. On the other hand, a functional format may be more effective when changing careers, including diverse work history, emphasizing skills outside of your career path, and minimizing gaps in time.

7. Include the common resume components, regardless of the format. Here is a brief description of the components. Again, see the resumes at the end of this chapter for specific examples of these components. **Heading**: include name, address, phone numbers and email address. **Objective**: concise statement of the job you want. **Summary**: a narrative snapshot of your qualifications, experience, skills, traits and sometimes even your accomplishments. It's a good place to insert "keywords" for electronic scanning. The summary should support your objective, i.e., why you are able to do what your objective states. **Experience/accomplishments**: Also called the "job history," here you provide your current and previous positions, with key results and achievements that give further support to the objective and summary. This section will differ in format depending on whether you choose chronological or functional. In a chronological resume, list your employers with city and state, the positions held and the dates of each position. **Education:** List your education after your job. There is one exception to this rule: If you have been in the workforce under one year, then list your education first followed by your brief job history. List your educational background beginning with the highest degree first (Master's, Bachelor's, Associates) followed by major concentration, name and location of school. Year of graduation is considered optional. The following components can be considered optional. I like to see them on the resume if they add significant information. Leaving them off is fine, of course, if you don't have anything to add to them. **Professional Development**: Under this heading, if applicable to you, include any special training or credentials earned outside of your degree program. This could include courses in sales, public speaking, computers, technical areas, etc. **Associations**: You can list professional organizations both current and former if they support your work objective. Avoid religious or political affiliations, as these are generally not pertinent to your career goal and may be used either consciously or otherwise to discriminate against a candidate.

A final section on the resume can be used to provide personal information. This component is optional and, I feel, should be limited or not included at all. Sometimes labeled Personal or Other Relevant Data, you can use it to generate additional enthusiasm in you as a person. It can include certifications or licenses (such as CPR or first-aid certification), foreign languages, military service, volunteer or community work, sports accomplishments, and so on. Items should, again, support your Objective and/or make the manager curious enough to want to sit down with you for an interview and talk about it.

8. Keep it brief. Resumes should be one side of one page in length, two-pages at the most if you have a longer work history. Personally, I prefer a single side of one page. Regardless of how much information you may desire to communicate, you can always get it down to one page if you focus on the truly critical information. Do yourself and the reader a favor by keeping it to one page! Try different formats to get the look you want. See the sample resumes at the end of this chapter for examples of good formats. Keep one-inch margins. Do not crowd the page with long sentences. Leave blank space between short items of information. Use a simple, easy-to-read font selection. Include your name, address, telephone number, and email at the very top of your resume. This will allow the hiring person to contact you even if your cover letter is discarded or otherwise separated from the resume.

9. Provide a clear objective. Only five percent of job applicants do this. Managers want people who want the job. If you take the time and effort to match them up, your career objective states that you want that specific job. Communicate one specific career objective, listed first after your name and address. This will tell the hiring person exactly what you want right now. It is the "hook" that gets the reader to continue reading the resume. State your objective clearly and simply. Do not be wordy, vague, or say anything about your long-term career goals. Avoid overused expressions about a "challenging opportunity" or a "progressive organization." Such verbiage communicates nothing and can be boring, just taking up space. State your immediate job objective only. You can include more detail in your cover letter, if desired.

10. If you have completed one, and you should, include the "Pharmaceutical Sales Preceptorship" or "Pharmaceutical Sales Field Research" as a separate heading on your resume. Include a brief statement describing key job components that you observed. See example resumes at the end of this chapter and read more on the Preceptorship in Chapter 5.

11. Do not list your salary history, current salary, or desired salary.

12. Do not list personal information such as age, date of birth, marital status, children, religious affiliations, political affiliations

13. Leave out explanations or "reasons for leaving" previous positions.

14. List the time spent in each job, indicating the first and last calendar year in which you were employed. Do not leave any gaps in time.

15. Do not list personal or professional references on the resume. Type your references on a separate sheet of paper. List three personal references and three professional references and bring it with you to present at the interview.

16. Triple check for errors on your resume and cover letter. Make certain that you have used proper grammar, punctuation, and spelling. Typographical errors send the message that you are not serious about the job or you simply lack the skills to produce a proper letter and resume.

17. Make extra copies of your resume and put them in your interviewing file. Bring them with you to all your interviews. Offer your resume to the hiring person as you begin the meeting. He or she should have one already, but do not assume that they have it in front of them. Additionally, this proactive measure communicates that you are attentive and that you anticipate the needs of the interviewer and the customer. A nice touch is to bring your resume in a file folder with your name labeled on the file tab.

18. Cover letters: The cover letter is essentially your way of thanking the employer for reviewing your resume and setting the stage for the interview. You are basically announcing who you are, the position you are applying for, how you learned about it, and why you would be successful in it. Always send a cover letter with your resume, and address it to an individual by name if at all possible. Keep the body of your cover letter under 100 words in length. Your cover letter should be direct and to the point. State clearly that you have researched the position being offered, that you want the opportunity being offered, and you have essential skills that will make you successful. Include a "call to action" explaining that you will take the next step in contacting the Manager. Your own contact information is on your resume, so there is no need to repeat it on the cover letter. You have a lot of information to pack into 100 words or less. Get the readers attention by making it specific

to them and their organization, including how you heard about the opportunity—responding to an ad, for example. Give contacts by name, such as, "Steve Brady suggested I contact you." Use a formal business format for your cover letter and sign it neatly and legibly. Your cover letter should match your resume in format, font, and paper stock. A paper clip affixing it to the resume is appropriate. Refer to the sample letter at the end of this chapter.

19. Regarding GPA, include it if it you have graduated in the past year or two, but only if it is favorable. Once you are in the work force for a couple years and have a documented professional track record, the GPA becomes less important. If it is high, such as over 3.0, it will never hurt to include it. Some managers may place value on it more than others. My view is that academic achievement is one piece of the puzzle, one data point, but is not a reliable indicator of success in the position of pharmaceutical sales.

20. Finally, have a current resume prepared at all times throughout your career. Keeping an updated resume will come in handy as you apply for promotions within your company, or move to another company. Do not force yourself to write one at the last minute when an opportunity presents itself.

For additional help with writing your resume, there are many sources available in publications, the Internet, and from professional resume writers. I have worked with consultants in this field, and have found one in particular that I believe does an excellent job specifically for the pharmaceutical industry and does so at a fair price. Scott Burke of TCA has 25 years experience writing resumes for people trying to break into competitive careers like pharmaceutical sales. For further information, go to http://www.coreynahman.com/TCA.html.

Please continue for examples of resumes using various formats.

[Sample Resume: Sales Experience, Chronological Format]

Helen M. Collins
1994 W. Merrimac Ave., Unit G, Denver, CO 80015
Home: 555-847-9457, Mobile: 555-847-6311
hmcoll2@hotmail.com

Objective
Entry-level position in Pharmaceutical Sales

Career Summary
- A versatile, energetic professional with 5 years successful outside sales and marketing experience with a proven sales record
- Strengths include qualifying and closing deals with a strong ability to build and maintain long-term customer relationships through integrity and follow through.
- Goal oriented, strong work ethic and excellent communication

Professional Experience
January 2002 to Present   Brant Publishing and Advertising/Yellow Book USA, Aurora CO
Account Executive, Outside Sales
Promoted advertising and communications products in 4 state area
- Initiated, developed and maintained accounts. Expanded customer loyalty through excellent customer service relationships and efficient resolution of disputes.
- Increased sales revenue from $15K to $75K (500%) including 15 new accounts in first year on the job
- Increased revenue from $75K to $202 (270%) including 21 new accounts to date in second year
- Ranked #4 nationally out of 81 Sales Representatives

March 2000 to January 2002   Newtones Instruments, Kansas City, KS
Account Manager
Marketed structural systems to the telecommunications industry
- Successfully attained sales growth of 20% with 38% increase in profit margin in year 2000
- Penetrated and established successful relationships with key accounts TTI, SSC, NetWorks
- Achieved "Winners Club of Excellence" award in second year, 2000-2001

June 1998-March 2000   Office Projects, Inc, Overland Park, KS
Territory Manager
Responsible for all aspects of Territory Management, from account acquisition to customer service in office equipment and supplies.
- Ranked top Territory Manager for three consecutive months (January through March 2000)
- Consistently surpassed quarterly sales and gross profit, exceeding budget by 33% in second year

Education: BA, Marketing Communications, Kansas University, 1998

Computer Skills: Proficient in spreadsheet, word processing and database applications

Personal: Successfully trained for and completed three marathons. Enjoy travel and golf.

[Sample Resume: Student or New College Graduate, Functional Format]

Janet Lynn Jones
jljones@aol.com

Home Address:	School Address:
1234 Summer Boulevard	23 Flyers Avenue, Suite #1026
Winter, PA 19123	Walnut, OH 45874
(215) 555-3456	(419)-555-5947

Career Objective: Entry level position in Pharmaceutical Sales

Education:

May 2004	UNIVERSITY OF DAYTON, DAYTON, OHIO

Bachelor of Science in Business Administration, May 2004

June, 2004	XYZ PHARMACEUTICALS

Pharmaceutical Preceptorship
Observed Pharmaceutical Sales Representatives for three days. Gained valuable insight into the sales position, including territory management, product detailing, targeting

Major Accomplishments:

Courses include Marketing, Chemistry, Statistics, and Computer Applications 3.8 GPA in Major, 3.6 GPA Cumulative
Listed: Who's Who in American Universities
Dean's List: All semesters, while working full-time earning 90% of tuition and expenses
Alumni Scholarship Awarded in 2003
Student Council President 2003-2004

College Work Experience:

2002-present   EAST DAYTON COMPUTER, DAYTON, OHIO
Salesperson, Retail computer store. Advised clients on hardware and software purchases. Performed cashier and quality control functions. Promoted to Assistant Manager.

1999-2002   EARL'S DRUGSTORE, WINTER, OHIO
Pharmacy Technician. Cashier in large retail pharmacy. Checked stock in, took inventory, assisted with phone calls to patients and physicians.

1998-2001   UNIVERSITY OF DAYTON, DAYTON, OHIO
Laboratory Assistant, Computer Lab. Assisted students during laboratory hours. Cleaned and repaired computer equipment.

Skills:

Microsoft Office Applications, Lotus, Multimedia and web applications
Fluent in Spanish

Affiliations and Special Interests:

Starlight Children's Foundation, Chairperson
Special Olympics, Event Coordinator

[Sample resume – combination functional and chronological]

Brian K. Shelton
3728 N Harvard
Chicago, IL 60613

Home: (773) 555-3270
Cell: (773) 555-9242
email: **blarimer@yahoo.com**

CAREER OBJECTIVE
Seeking a pharmaceutical sales position

FEATURED SKILLS
- Unique combination of knowledge and success in sales, marketing, negotiating, management and customer service
- Succeeded in a competitive telecommunications market where budgets were being cut and competitors were undercutting prices drastically
- Established mutually beneficial relationships with decision makers ranging from Directors up to Executives of global enterprises across multiple industries
- Successful track record of continuously and quickly learning new skills and technologies to maximize the value to my clients and my company
- Computer literate with extensive knowledge of Microsoft Office, Siebel CRM packages, and general sales tracking and forecasting software

PROFESSIONAL EXPERIENCE
Major Account Manager, AT&T Business, Chicago, IL   (July 2002 – Present)
Responsibilities include proposing and closing new business, selling the customers up AT&T's value chain of products, and managing the care, billing, and maintenance.
- Achieved 108% of year-to-date quota as of the end of April
- Breakfast of Champions participant in October 2002, December 2002, January 2003
- Successfully completed AT&T Rolling Thunder Training Program

Data Network Account Executive, AT&T Business, Chicago, IL (Feb – July 2002)
Responsibilities included prospecting and calling on non-AT&T businesses, proposing value-added services, negotiating contract terms, and closing new business.
- Brought four new clients into AT&T Chicago office
- Created customer leave-behind document that was adopted by my entire sales team
- Successfully completed AT&T Voice Essentials training

EDUCATION
University of Notre Dame   (August 1997- May 2001)   Notre Dame, IN
Mendoza College of Business, BA Business Administration
Minor: Management – Consulting
Deans List Senior Year, Major GPA: 3.75

EXTRACURRICULAR ACTIVITIES
Member of Chicago Lacrosse Club in Midwest Club Lacrosse League
Participate in American Lung Association Young Professionals Board

[Example Cover Letter – personalized to Manager and Company]

[Example Cover Letter – personalized to Manager and Company]

June 4, 2004

Ms. Eleanor Lowe
District Manager
34 Corporate Drive North
Plaza Park, CT 03201

Dear Ms. Lowe:

I am applying to the position of Pharmaceutical Sales with CM Pharmaceuticals.   I believe that my background and experience match the responsibilities and requirements you are seeking.

I have a B.S. degree in Business Administration and 3 years of sales experience. I am a results oriented person with strong relational skills. The following points are highlights of my professional career that have prepared me for the position:

• *A versatile professional with direct sales experience and proven sales record.*
• *Strengths include client need assessment, and consultative selling techniques.*
• *Strong ability to establish and maintain long term client relationships.*

Thank you for taking the time to review my resume, attached. I would like to meet with you to discuss the opportunity further. I will contact you in the next week to follow up.

Sincerely,

Mark Craig

[SAMPLE COVER LETTER: REFERRED BY NETWORKING CONTACT]

August 24, 2004

Michael Buckley
1234 Summer
Boulevard Winter,
PA 23005

Ruth Boardman
District Sales Manager Company
XYZ Pharmaceutical
240 West Argonne Drive
King of Prussia, PA 19414

Dear Ms. Boardman:

Ernie Brown recently told me of an open sales territory in the Philadelphia district due to a promotion. He suggested I contact you.

I am excited about a career with XYZ Pharmaceuticals. From your current product portfolio and pipeline of new products, such as Aspirin XL, I know I will excel in such a challenging work environment. From my own research and from conversations with William, I know I can make significant contribution to your sales team.

I would like the opportunity to interview with you. I will contact you by telephone early next week to discuss it. My resume is enclosed for your review. Thank you for your time and consideration.

Sincerely,

Michael Buckley

[SAMPLE COVER LETTER: NEW COLLEGE GRADUATE RESPONDING TO CLASSIFIED AD.]

August 24, 2004

Mark Kirchoff
1234 Summer Boulevard
Winter, PA 23005

William Betts
District Sales Manager
XYZ Pharmaceutical Company
240 West Argonne Drive
King of Prussia, PA 19414

Dear Mr. Betts:

I am interested in the position of Pharmaceutical Representative (Philadelphia Inquirer, May 13). My resume is attached for your review.

I have focused my education towards a career in the pharmaceutical industry. During the last semester break, I spent three days with Pharmaceutical Representatives to learn more about the sales position.

From your current product portfolio and exciting new drugs in the pipeline, such as Aspirin XL, I know I will excel in such a challenging environment. I am confident that I would make a successful addition to your sales team.

I want the opportunity to prove myself in your interviewing process and as a successful sales representative for XYZ Pharmaceutical Company. I look forward to your reply.

Sincerely,

Martha Kirchoff

Chapter 4

Vital Research

Anne Clayton encourages you to <u>*market*</u> yourself to others who work in the industry. This process is known as "networking," which simply means getting to know people and letting them get to know you. All it entails is presenting your professional skills and abilities effectively, to a specific audience, for a business purpose.

What do networking and research have to do with each other? Networking is the "people" preparation that goes hand in hand with the "paper" preparation. There is a cardinal rule at the core of the system one that you have heard many times, especially if you have been a Girl or Boy Scout. That rule is BE PREPARED. You will find all the tools you need for success in this chapter and the next two. Chapter 5 launches you into people preparation, but let us start here with the paper preparation. Upon completion of this chapter, you will:

- Understand helpful techniques for research and finding sources of information.

- Develop a system to keep any vital information readily accessible, including the use of pharmaceuticalsales.com profiles provided in the appendix.

- Be able to set yourself apart from the candidate field by demonstrating to a potential employer that you are well-prepared for the interview, as you would prepare for sales calls in your territory.

WHY DO YOU NEED TO PREPARE YOURSELF?

The first major pay-off for being adequately prepared is that you are relaxed and confident. Your performance in networking and interviewing situations improves considerably when you are poised and thinking clearly on your feet. The candidate who is unprepared will never be at ease in the situation and will be afraid of what might come next in the interview. This distraction can cause you to stumble over easy questions and will result in poor listening skills and ineffective communication.

Secondly, good district managers are looking for adequate preparation. They know that the individual who prepares well for an interview is demonstrating a key aspect found in the successful sales professional. The manager will correctly assume that, because you are well prepared for your interview, you are the kind of person who will be motivated to prepare well for a sales presentation. The reverse is also true. In other words, why should a manager hire a person who does not take the time and effort to excel in an interview? Will something happen to motivate that person when he or she is hired? No! The manager wants to see you demonstrate now; those things you say you will do for the company later. Thus, the under-prepared candidate has already missed the opportunity to show that he or she is capable of self-directed research and education, a habit that directly relates to success in pharmaceutical sales. Show your motivation.

Next, a manager will be more likely to hire the candidate who knows what is expected in their career rather than someone who is blindly seeking any type of employment. By having an understanding of the pharmaceutical industry and the specific company with whom you are interviewing you differentiate yourself. You can show excitement for specific products, new product launches, therapeutic discoveries, or a recent increase in sales, for example. You can emphasize aspects of your background and personal attributes that relate to the company or product. You can say with confidence that you want to work for this company because you have done the research and know the business and professional commitments of the organization. You will shine when asked the inevitable question, "Why do you want to work for XYZ Pharmaceuticals, Inc.?"

WHAT DOES IT MEAN TO BE ADEQUATELY PREPARED?

Being prepared means that you know what to expect, are ready, and will not only participate in but also control your interview. You should be prepared with your answers to typical questions. Also be ready to ask smart ones of your own. You should be able to demonstrate a basic understanding of a sales representative's job in the pharmaceutical industry, and of the specific company with which you are interviewing. These aspects are presented in following chapters of *Insight*. The central point of this chapter though, is to teach you how to conduct industry research, which is an integral part of the preparation you will need for successful networking and interviewing.

Where do you get the information? Industry information is accessible from these general areas:

- consumer media sources
- company published information
- business publications
- industry publications
- internet sites
- consumer media sources

The most readily available source is the everyday consumer media. The news media frequently and fervently reports on health issues, and consumers are listening. Public awareness is high due to health issues, which attracts attention and raises viewer ratings. These easily accessible sources of information include the following:

- local newspapers
- national newspapers, such as *The Wall Street Journal* and *USA Today*
- news magazines, such as *Time* and *Newsweek*
- business periodicals, such as *Forbes, Fortune,* and *Crain's*
- television news magazine broadcasts, such as *Dateline NBC* and *20/20*

You can start building your own awareness by reading these reports as part of your normal routine. Read thoroughly the daily newspaper for health and medical related stories. Look for any headlines on healthcare, managed care, insurance companies, medical breakthroughs, new prescription drugs, and pharmaceutical manufacturers. Read each article with a questioning eye. What are the issues? What is the main message? Who wrote this and what is the author's perspective? You will not need to buy many subscriptions if you make a habit of stopping by the public library to browse and read. You can also obtain copies of pertinent articles for later reference.

Consumer media sources are also good for information on specific medications. Look for advertisements of prescription drugs in magazines and television commercials. In the ad, the manufacturer is communicating the features and benefits of their product. This will give you insight into how they are positioning the product in the marketplace. Who is the manufacturer? What features and benefits are being offered to the patient? These features and benefits are often the same promotional messages being used by the pharmaceutical representative. Some print advertisements include an abbreviated version of the package insert, which is also called "drug labeling." This is in the fine print section, and it lists indications (under what circumstances the drug is to be used), side effects, dosages, patient instructions, and a brief explanation of how the drug works. Television and radio ads also give information about important side effects.

TIP: *For complete drug labeling information, look in the public library for* The Physician's Desk Reference (PDR). *This book is published annually by Medical Economics, and contains the complete drug labeling for every currently marketed prescription pharmaceutical product and many of the over-the-counter drugs.*

TIP: *Excellent baseline information is available through multiple media sources. Educating yourself on healthcare and the pharmaceutical industry is an excellent way to develop life-long learning habits. However, for more specific and in-depth information, locate a medical library where you can have access to the medical journals and references. The best resources are medical school libraries, large "teaching" hospitals, and other university settings.*

TIP: *Software programs such as Medical Drug Reference provide full descriptions of drugs, and can be used to check the interaction of different medications. Imagine the professional relationship that can be forged by a Rep who can respond to a doctor's question about specific patient issues within a very short period of time.*

Besides accessing general healthcare and pharmaceutical industry information, what can you do to get the business and marketing information you want before interviewing? Where can you find the details about a specific company's financial performance, sales force size, product line, and products currently in research or awaiting Food and Drug Administration (FDA) approval?

There are two main sources for detailed company-specific information:

- company published sources

- sales representatives working for that company

Chapter 5, "Networking," will discuss interacting with Sales Representatives. Let's look now at company-published sources of information. Examples of these are annual reports, 10K filings, current marketing initiatives, and marketing material. Annual reports are available in most cases by calling, writing, faxing, or e-mailing the corporate headquarters, and some companies have web sites with an option that allows you to order annual reports on-line or even download them immediately. Ask for annual reports from the last two or three years. You should receive them in a few days.

After you receive the annual report, study it carefully. Write down any questions you may have about the organization. Read the annual reports chronologically. Is the company on track with its own agenda? Are forecasters' goals being met? Are new products making it to the marketplace as promised in previous years' reports? What is the corporate direction?

Next, directories such as Standard & Poor's and Dunn & Bradstreet are good sources of recent information. All public companies must file a "10K, 10Q Reports" every quarter with the Securities and Exchange Commission (SEC). These are abbreviated annual reports, they are available to you at local libraries that offer a business index, and as always, the companies' website may provide access.

TIP: *A trick of the trade for keeping up with companies over the long term is to purchase a single share of stock. You will receive annual reports automatically every year, and will find it more interesting to track drug company stocks. What a surprise it would be for a manager to hear during the interview that you are a stockholder. You will surely be remembered for it. In essence, you are creating your own mutual fund based on your research and you are as well informed as many so called pharmaceutical industry analyst .*

Your research should also include a review of the business newspapers and periodicals. These include *The Wall Street Journal, Crain's Business, Business Weekly, Forbes,* and *Fortune.* You can use the business index to search for all published articles on a specific company by name. You can then request back issues from the reference desk and read the articles. The most common type of storage is on microfilm, which makes it easy for you to browse nearly all of the publications. Call around to different libraries until you find one with a business index and access to previously published articles.

Your company-specific research should also include a thorough review of the company's Internet web site. These sites are an excellent source for company overviews, product summaries, drug labeling, stock trends, employment opportunities, and even employee benefits. Internet addresses are increasingly available on most company-published materials and advertisements. Of course, searches using the company name or product name will also result in finding the site you want. Anne Clayton has listed many company web site addresses in the "Company Profiles" section of *Insight* and provided additional on-line resources at the end of this chapter.

Your research may also include trade journals of the pharmaceutical industry. These publications often discuss prevailing and emerging business trends, profile organizations, review products, and highlight key individuals. Some examples are *Pharmaceutical Executive, Medical Advertising,* and *F-DC Reports.* Thousands of libraries subscribe to electronic information-retrieval services, such as Nexis, that will speed your research. A listing of the most helpful references is available in the "pharmaceuticalsales.com Suggested Resources" at the end of this chapter.

HOW DO YOU KEEP AND READILY ACCESS VITAL RESEARCH INFORMATION?

You may be collecting articles and doing research over the course of a job search that could last weeks, months, or longer. It may be quite a while before you need to access that information for networking and interviewing. How will you keep track of everything you want to remember or save for future reference?

You need to have a storage method for important research and networking information that is easy to use. We suggest that you create a file on each company for which you have collected information or with whom you have made contact. Save general industry information that does not pertain to any single company in a separate file. As you find articles on companies of interest, print them out from the Internet clip them from newspapers or magazine's, or photocopy them. Take notes during your research and add these to the appropriate file. You can also add product advertisements, computer printouts of web site information, and package inserts that you can collect from pharmacies. All of this will come in handy in preparing for, and in conducting, your interview.

Additionally, you need to document your networking contacts and track your telephone calls, meetings, and correspondence. Save your notes on all calls and interactions with sales representatives and managers, your meetings, and your interviews. Maintain your current resume as well as the original one that you sent to the company. Also, keep copies of your resumes, cover letters, thank you notes, and follow-up letters in another readily accessible file.

COMPANY PROFILES

Anne Clayton has provided a head start for you by creating company profiles of the top fifty pharmaceutical organizations. You can find these Company Profiles in the Appendix. The Profiles include company summaries, history annual healthcare revenue, salesforce size, addresses, current product portfolios and products near the final stages of approval. All the information you require to get you started, save you hours of time and countless trips to the library.

In addition, the appendix, there are several worksheets for recording your notes and research as you prepare for interviews. These worksheets can be removed from the book and kept in your file you create on each company. Make photocopies for additional blank worksheets.

YOUR NEXT MOVE -- NETWORKING

Networking is one of the most important sources of vital company information, and should be an integral part of your research. Your resources are the many current representatives of pharmaceutical companies. Interacting with these people is the way to find out what is important to their respective organizations right now. Furthermore, it allows you to discover what is happening in your region of the country and in specific districts and sales territories. You can uncover success stories, identify essential challenges facing the company, and learn how you can contribute to the organization. Discovering this information first hand from sales representatives will round out your "paper" research. This is a critical part of your interview preparation. The pharmaceuticalsales.com method is described in depth in Chapter 5.

The advantage of performing all this research is realized only if you successfully demonstrate your expertise in the interview. There are several approaches and you may want to use all of them. Now that you have done the preparatory work, how can you best leverage your efforts?

- How do you demonstrate to a potential employer that you are prepared?
- Can you be differentiated from other candidates?
- What is the benefit of hiring you?

As mentioned above, an important benefit to you is the confidence that comes from knowing you are ready. Your confidence will show in your voice, eye contact, and posture. Stand and sit straight, look the interviewer in the eyes, and project your voice loudly by breathing deeply from the diaphragm.

A second benefit, of course, is your ability to discuss specific company information. Make a point of presenting it. Take advantage of the natural flow of the dialogue to interject what you know. Show that you have done your research. You will appear energetic and attentive to detail. It will show you went the extra mile to learn something about the company. Here is an example:

> Interviewer: "The company will launch a new wide spectrum antibiotic this fall."
> Candidate: "Yes, I read about the unique once-a-day dosage of your new entry. It appears to offer some unique benefits to patients and physicians treating pneumonia."

Also, be sure to include names of company individuals you have met with or talked with on the telephone. Here is an example:

> Candidate: "When I met with Helen Ellies, I learned that the sales force is currently undergoing product training for your new ulcer medication. I understand there are several other new products under development as well."

As you are presenting your professional strengths, a brief description of your research and networking method makes a great example of your self-motivation, determination, and other attributes. Bring along your company file and lay it on the table as you talk. If the interviewer shows interest in this, which he surely will, go into more detail and show off what you have.

TIP: *Begin your interview by making the point that you are prepared. State in your opening remarks, "I have researched the XYZ Pharmaceutical Company and the sales representative position. I am an excellent fit for your company." This opening statement will often get a curious response such as, "OK, tell me what you know about the company." The ball is in your court and you are doing just what you prepared to do. Your effort is paying off. You have taken control of the interview.*

Next, you can demonstrate your preparation by providing specific company information. You can also do this by asking intelligent questions. Use specific company information as a lead-in to your questions to the interviewer. Add a prepatory statement that first gives information about the company. For example:

> Candidate: [give information] "I understand that XYZ Pharmaceuticals is focusing on diabetes and high blood pressure medications. [ask question] On what diseases states or therapeutic categories does the company want to focus in the future?"

TIP: *Clip and save prescription drug advertisements from consumer magazines and medical journals. Publications such as the Journal of the American Medical Association or the New England Journal of Medicine, are good sources for this (remember the target reader is the physician, not a consumer). Preferably, find an advertisement for a medication manufactured by the company with which you are interviewing. Bring it to the interview and make a sales presentation to the interviewer on the advertised product. Use the advertisement pages as your sales "visual aid" and make a commanding product presentation as if you were talking with a doctor. Be sure to ask for the commitment from "the customer" to prescribe your "product."*

A FINAL WORD ON RESEARCH

Surprisingly, less than 25 percent of interviewing candidates will perform the industry and company-specific research. I have interviewed many candidates who didn't bother to learn the company's product names or the name of the CEO. This is very sad when the candidate is otherwise showing good potential. In contrast, when a candidate is well-versed in the industry, the job, and the company itself, I know as a Manager that this individual is determined to succeed. It gives me confidence in my decision to hire that individual. The entire working relationship gets off to a great start! NOTE: Only *one percent* of candidates will perform the additional networking steps of company specific research, including networking with company sales reps. These people are the ones who will achieve their desired results.

- Research will take you into networking with individuals.
- This is where you will gain vital knowledge about the company from actual employees.
- Professional pharmaceutical sales representatives and other contacts know the routines of the business.
- Through these individuals, you will discover up-to-date information about the organizations.
- You will learn their sales region/district/territory of the country.
- Identify key challenges facing the company whether nationally/regionally.
- You will discover ways you can contribute to the organization.

This will help you secure yourself a position among the proven 1% that guarantees your success. Challenge yourself to execute the research and begin today!

SUGGESTED RESOURCES

This list contains suggestions for resources from each of the following categories:
- Business Periodicals
- Pharmaceutical Industry Periodicals
- Medical Journals
- Internet Resources

Business Resources

Dunn and Bradstreet's *Million-Dollar Directory:* Lists 160,000 companies that are both publicly and privately held; updated annually.

Standard & Poor's *Register of Corporations:* Lists 45,000 companies with insight to thousands of company executives.

Corporate Technology Directory (Corporate Technology Information Services): Focuses on the products of 35,000 companies including pharmaceuticals.

Personnel Executives Contact book: Lists key personnel and other contacts of 30,000 publicly and privately held companies and government agencies.

Directory of Corporate Affiliations (National Register): Lists information on a company's corporate divisions and subsidiaries.

Industry Resources

Pharmaceuticalsales.com Profiles: *Insight,* Appendix A, which lists vital information on 50 pharmaceutical organizations including company overviews, telephone numbers, addresses, web sites, and current product portfolios.

Pharmaceutical Executive: A pharmaceutical business and marketing publication that is published monthly. These are available at medical libraries and on-line at pharmexec.com

Med Ad News: A pharmaceutical business and marketing publication published 12 times a year. It may be available at some medical libraries. Engel Publishing Partners 609-530-0044.

F-D-C Reports ("Pink Sheets"): Current news information about the FDA and pharmaceutical R&D. These may be available at medical libraries ($$$ expensive).

Pharmaceutical Representative: The only newsmagazine solely for pharmaceutical sales representatives. Available from McKnight Medical Communications (rate $43.95 for 12 monthly issues 800-451-7838). They have a directory of regional and local Pharmaceutical Representative associations, which is also available on-line: www.pharmrep.com.

Medical Journals

The following are common and respected medical journals that can be found in medical libraries and many public libraries:

- *New England Journal of Medicine*
- *Journal of the American Medical Association (JAMA)*
- *Medical Economics*
- *American Journal of Medicine*
- *American Druggist*

pharmaceuticalsales.com resources

Below is the most extensive site listing available to a candidate doing research in the pharmaceutical industry:

- www.pharmaceuticalsales.com
  Anne Clayton's site offers numerous links to compliment your research, many of which are listed below. Feel free to send Anne Clayton a question on the free email help line.
- www.coreynahman.com Premier site for both prospective and experienced sales representatives. It is a one-stop shop for industry news, company information, drug information, career information, resume review, industry links, and more.
- www.cafepharma.com industry news, company information, drug information, career information, industry links, formulary coverage links, specific company and topic forums.
- www.businesswire.com
  News distribution
- www.mydrugrep.com
  Presentation examples, resources, drug information
- www.fdcreports.com
  Publishers of pharmaceutical news
- www.quintiles.com
  These very specific industry trends are used by the pharmaceutical industry (requires login).
- www.imshealth.com
  Industry insights, trend lines (requires login)
- www.pharmexec.com
  Web site of Pharmaceutical Executive Magazine
- www.pharmweb.net
  Source for industry news and links

- www.pharminfo.com
  Comprehensive information on prescription drugs
- www.smartbrief.com
  Set up your free daily updates on news in the pharmaceutical industry
- www.pharmalive.com
  A variety of research and education projects
- www.phrma.org
  Pharmaceutical Research and Manufacturers of America — List and links
- www.pharmrep.com
  Pharmaceutical Representative Online
- www.pharmalive.com
  Industry/company news and links
- www.eyeforpharma.com
  Industry news, events, channels, free e-mail newsletter
- www.fcg.com
  First Consulting Groug, provides industry news, public policy news links
- www.healthleaders.com
  Sign up for your free daily briefing
- www.wsj.com
  Wall Street Journal online, subscription required
- www.edgar-online.com
  Company business information, such as SEC filings
- www.fuld.com
  Links to industry specific pharmaceutical and biotechnology resources
- www.best-in-class.com
  Best Practices, LLC can help you gain access to the intelligence you need.
- www.biofind.com
  Biotech job and company information

Education

Interested in an education in pharmaceutical sales and marketing? There are several high quality programs available. Check the site's below to view their curriculums for more information. One can also use these curriculums at their College/University.
Be careful with many so called "Certification Programs" listed on the Internet.

- Pharmaceutical Marketing at St. Joseph's University
  www.sju.edu/PHARMACEUTICAL_MARKETING
- University of Mississippi
  www.olemiss.edu/depts/pharm_admin/index.htm
- Pharmaceutical Marketing at Rutgers Business School
  http://business.rutgers.edu/pharm-mba/default.htm
- Long Island University
  http://www.liu.edu
- Certified Medical Representative Institute (CMR). This is the only industry-recognized certification program and is generally for those already in the industry. Completing all the modules, which can take up to two years, is well worth the effort because it develops the representative's understanding of the role of pharmaceutical products in the treatment and prevention of disease; provides insight into the pharmaceutical industry, medical profession and health care markets. http://www.cmrinstitute.org
- SPBT, Society of Pharmaceutical and Biotech Trainers
  http://www.spbt.org

Chapter 5

Networking News

This chapter describes a unique way for self-marketing within the pharmaceutical industry. This method is the key to successful employment. Read this chapter and put the strategy into practice. Sending out the mass mailings of résumés and cover letters will yield little in the way of results.

You have probably heard the old adage, *"It's not what you know, it's who you know."* This expression refers to breaking into business and moving up the corporate ladder. Now, forget all about that old adage and relearn it the Anne Clayton way: ***"It's who you learn to know."***

This chapter will provide a sure-fire way for you to market yourself to the targeted environment. The "Anne Clayton Way" will be your primary strategy. Yes, you will still be checking the newspapers and responding to want ads, contacting recruiters and search firms, but these can not be your primary strategy. Remember, your going to differentiate yourself from the herd.

What you need to do is simple, and it works. It helped me into the industry over thirty years ago and has proven successful for thousands of candidates since I wrote the first edition of *"Insight"* in the spring of 1998.

YOUR GOAL:

- Become familiar with all the pharmaceutical representatives working in your geography, and more importantly, have them become familiar with you.

By following the strategy described in this chapter, you will accrue the following advantages:

- Obtain inside information about an opening before it is advertised (if advertised)
- Be known (and well thought of) by the employer before an opening even exists.
- Demonstrate your initiative and creativity to potential employers in your geography.
- Establish important relationships with individuals in the pharmaceutical industry.
- Possess detailed knowledge about the industry, the company, and the position.
- Demonstrate your detailed knowledge of the industry to representatives in your area.
- Learn the key individuals (District Managers) who do the hiring within your geographical area.

Okay, now you want to begin, so what do you do next? First, create your own database of current pharmaceutical industry professionals working in your desired geographic area. You can employ various means to accomplish this. Here are some suggestions:

Visit a physician's office. Typically, doctors' offices have from 25 to 75 sales representatives from the pharmaceutical industry calling on them on a consistent basis. Explain your desire to enter the pharmaceutical sales profession and ask if they will photocopy the business cards of all the Pharmaceutical Representatives who call on their office. Often, these business cards are filed together and can be easily accessed by an office secretary or nurse. First start with your own doctor, or the doctor of a family member (or friend of a family member). Finally, most common for most candidates, do not be afraid to walk into a physician's office cold. Be sure to tell them what you are doing and ask for their assistance. Your going to experience rejection, probably more rejection than success, but that is just part of being a salesperson. SMILE! Keep trying different offices until you get what you want. I suggest trying large medical buildings and starting at the top floor and working your way down. During this process, you're actually going to run into Pharmaceutical Representatives face to face while they are working the building. This will give you an excellent opportunity to express your interest in the industry, and ask if you can call them sometime (obtain their business card). So, always dress as if you were going to an interview (again, your interview best) and conduct yourself professionally.

TIP: *During your office visits, speak directly to the physician or nurse (if available) about recommending a specific Sales Representative for you to contact. Ask for a name that stands out as someone they like and consider an excellent Pharmaceutical Representative.*

When you contact each Pharmaceutical Representative, make it a point to inform them that the doctor specifically mentioned them as being exceptional or outstanding in their field. If possible, state exactly what the doctor or any member of the staff has said. This is a positive way to break the ice when you introduce yourself.

Apply these same successful strategies when you visit a hospital or retail pharmacy. Always ask for copies of their representatives' business cards. If you explain what you want to accomplish, most pharmacists are willing to help you. If your current work environment is a hospital, the hospital pharmacy and emergency room are also goldmines for Pharmaceutical Representative's business cards (maybe you also know a nurse or pharmacist that can assist you with this networking).

TIP: *Independent pharmacists, rather than large chain pharmacies, may be more likely to keep a file of business cards. They may be familiar with local representatives and be willing to share information.*

Another way to develop contacts is to call your State or City Pharmacist Association. Explain your desire to enter the pharmaceutical sales profession and ask if they will recommend a few contacts so that you can learn more about the industry. Many of these associations are located in your state's capitol. They may have regular meetings which you may be allowed to attend if possible.

Once you have collected your business cards, add them to the worksheets. Now you are ready to start making telephone contacts. I have some suggestions to help you ask questions during your initial contact that will produce your desired result. The goal of this phase is to gain job information, get to know pharmaceutical industry personnel, and make aware that you are a job candidate. Please read *Insight* entirely before you begin this networking phase.

Once you have the business cards of 15-25 representatives, make a few calls per day, perhaps two to five. Explain briefly who you are and the purpose of your call—that you are interested in pharmaceutical sales as a profession, and you would like to meet briefly to discuss it. Always ask the person if it is a convenient time for them, or if another time would be better. Let them know that you are willing to fit their schedule. The evening is best because representatives are out making sales calls during the day. Do not be shy!

Here is an example of how you might begin the telephone conversation:

"Hello, Ms. Young, my name is Janet Jones and I am interested in a career in pharmaceutical sales. Is this a good time to call you? I was given your card by Dr. Wellborn who suggested you would be a valuable resource because of your professionalism. I would like to talk about your career. When is the best time for you? I will work my schedule around yours."

Remember to conduct yourself professionally. As the saying goes, "You never get a second chance to make a first impression." Put yourself in your "Interview Mode" because this helps you prepare to be the best candidate for the job. Treat all contacts in your networking process as potential interviewers and as potential co-workers! Be upbeat, positive, and professional. If your contact will meet with you, then you have achieved your first goal. A personal meeting is more memorable, gives you greater opportunity to sell yourself, establishes rapport, and builds relationships. If some representatives decline contact, hang in there, its part of your process, don't take it personally, and keep networking.

Some contacts may decide they would rather not meet with you, but would be willing to give you time on the telephone. Be prepared for this situation. Ask when would be a good time to call back, and then during that follow-up call proceed with your discussion and questions as you would in a face-to-face meeting.

Many representatives will gladly share their time and expertise while there are others who will not. Respect their wishes and remain professional as you thank them for their time. Remember that rejection is common in sales at all levels. Never forget that you are a salesperson who is marketing yourself in this situation. At times, you will be turned down. Even a refusal adds to your knowledge base, which helps your career potential. Sales people know that there is a certain percentage of failure in their sales calls. Your persistence will pay off; you are going to get an offer!

Another situation you should prepare for is voice mail. You can use this to your advantage by being prepared ahead of time with a concise message. State your name, purpose of the call, and inform them that you will call again later. Here is an example of a voice mail message you might leave for a networking contact:

> *"Hello, Ms Young, my name is Janet Jones. I am interested in a career in pharmaceutical sales. Dr. Wellborn suggested that you would be best to provide some insight into pharmaceutical sales, and gave me your card. The purpose of my call is to discuss this with you. I will call again to speak directly with you. Thank you for your time."*

Note that you do not ask the contact to call you back. Take the initiative to make the connection yourself. You must attempt to reach the person, calling at various times of the day and evening, and leaving a concise message each time. Use your information to make notes on worksheets in the appendix. After you have tried to reach them two or three times (and left a brief message each time so they know you tried), it is appropriate to leave your number and ask for a return call. Here is an example of such a message:

> *"Hello, Ms. Young. This is Janet Jones calling. I would like to speak with you about the pharmaceutical industry, and have been unable to reach you after several tries. Would you please return my call at a time most convenient for you? My telephone number is 555-5555. If you get my answering machine, please let me know the best time for me to call you back, and I will do so. Thank you."*

Keep your messages brief and to the point. This helps you make a good impression. Your new network contact will sense that you are not likely to take up much time. If your contact wants to offer their time, he or she can certainly do so and will gladly call you back.

Use the same brevity and professionalism in recording your own outgoing message for your incoming calls. Avoid gimmicks, child greetings, your favorite rock/rap song or any background noise. Identify yourself by name, telephone number, and request that the callers leave a time for you to return their call. Here is an example of an outgoing message:

> *"Hello, this is Janet Jones, at 555-5555. Please leave your name and number and when it is a good time for me to return your call and I will do so. Thank you."*

Because you are asking people to call you back, be prepared for their call. The value of using the Worksheets and Profiles in the appendix is that you can find needed information quickly. You should have made notes of your previous contacts. It is perfectly fine to ask the caller to hold for just one moment while you locate your information. This also gives you a little time to take a deep breath and gather your thoughts for the call.

TIP: *Smile when you begin to speak. Yes, it sounds silly, but you will sound better on the telephone.*

Now that you are speaking to your contacts by telephone, you want to make an appointment to see them in person. Offer to meet at their most convenient time. Invite them to a breakfast or lunch meeting where you can talk one-on-one. Sales professionals are often too familiar with providing meals for their customers, and it can be a refreshing change to have someone buy them lunch. If they do not have time for a meal, perhaps a coffee/coke break would work better. Have them choose the restaurant or coffee shop that would be convenient for them. Have several locations in mind in case they want you to pick the place.

You have made your appointment! You are on course and networking the Anne Clayton way. Remember, this is your first interview with someone who can boost your career; be prepared. At this stage of the game, you will be controlling most of the dialogue. Review all of the information you have learned about the company and show your contact that you are familiar with their company. Your preparation will demonstrate that you are serious and committed. Your contact will not feel that you have wasted their time. On the contrary, they will be more likely to provide you with the information you want, and help you reach your goal (rapport with the representative) and even the future connection with a District or Regional Manager.

When you meet, bring your resume and other information you have collected about their company to show your dedication. Leave your copy and any mention of *Insight* at home, no need to give out your secrets. Write down various notes from the Profiles and your Worksheet regarding what you want to say and ask. Be friendly and enthusiastic. Remember this individual can be a critical part of your job search. They will be evaluating you, wondering if you would be a good candidate to work with, and one that they can recommend to their company. Most pharmaceutical companies pay a finder's fee or recruitment bonus to their own employees when a candidate they recommend is hired. This bonus can be between two and ten thousand dollars, which is less costly for the company than retaining a professional recruiter (headhunter). So, sales representatives are often on the lookout for good people!

The contact person with whom you are networking is representing their pharmaceutical organization. You are representing yourself. If you show up in attire that is inappropriate, your contact will probably conclude that you are not likely to demonstrate good judgment in their organization. Always dress the part (again, your interview best) in every networking situation.

Now, what kind of information do you want from your meetings and telephone calls with industry contacts? First, thank the person for meeting with you. State that you are excited about the career opportunities available in pharmaceutical sales and you would like to learn as much as possible about his or her job experience. You have two goals for the networking meeting. 1) Gain an understanding of the industry and this particular pharmaceutical organization. 2) Develop your relationship with the individual representative.

Getting to know a representative on the inside of the industry adds credence to the old adage that you have to know someone to get the job. The often-asked question by your competitors for the job will be: *"How did [your name] get that job with XYZ Pharmaceutical Company?" Answer: "She knew someone!"*

Twenty networking questions you might use are listed below. Write these down on a legal pad and enter a few of your own. You will not ask all these questions at one meeting, of course, but tailor them to your interests with this particular organization. Be sensitive to the other person; do not bombard them with closed-ended questions. Instead, include open-ended questions that will encourage them to discuss freely. Begin with questions that are more personal and show interest in the person. This will invite them to speak and builds rapport.

TWENTY SAMPLE QUESTIONS FOR YOUR INDUSTRY CONTACTS

1. What is your current job?
2. Why did you decide to enter a career in pharmaceutical sales?
3. How did you get your first job in pharmaceutical sales?
4. What educational background do you have?
5. What is your job experience?
6. How did you obtain your current position with XYZ Pharmaceutical Company?
7. What do you like about your current position?
8. What, if anything, about the position, do you dislike?
9. What is a typical day like in your territory? Who are your customers (doctors, pharmacists, hospitals, clinics, etc.)? How many customers do you have?
10. Who is your competition in the marketplace? How many competitors do you have for your promoted products? How does your product rank in sales versus the competition?

11. How are your customers receiving your products?

12. What differentiates you from your competition?

13. How does your company measure sales performance?

14. What kind of training does your company provide?

15. How is your company structured? What are the various divisions? How is your company's sales force structured (districts, regions, business units, etc.)?

16. What new products does your company have in development? What new products are expected in the next twelve months? What are they indicated for, and what advantages do they have over competing products?

17. What are some career options that you have within your organization that may be of interest to you?

18. Do you know of other Pharmaceutical Representatives with other companies I could contact? Do you have their telephone numbers, business cards, and addresses?

19. Is there a local professional association of pharmaceutical sales representatives? Whom could I contact to see about attending a meeting? Note: Some known Pharmaceutical Representative Associations listed at the end of the chapter, and some are listed on the website for Pharmaceutical Representative magazine at www.pharmalive.com.

20. I am very interested in a career with XYZ Pharmaceutical Corporation; can you notify me if anything comes available in the future that you hear about?

Conclude by thanking the individual for taking the time to meet with you. Ask if you may follow up with a telephone call to see if there are any positions open or possible opportunities in the future. Ask if they would contact you in the future if a territory even looks as if it might become available. It is to your advantage to know about it as soon as possible so you can respond quickly. *Be absolutely sure to send a follow-up letter or card to personally thank the individual for the meeting.* See the example thank-you letter provided at the end of this chapter.

Now, what do you do? Complete your notes, adding information you learned to the Profile section of Insight. Always send a typed follow-up letter within 24 hours (see example at end of chapter).

Pharmaceutical Representatives and Managers state that if a candidate does not show this simple courtesy they will likely be eliminated from the interview process. If your contact has provided you with additional names make those connections as soon as possible.

When you hear of an available position, move quickly and make contact with your network!

Express great interest in the position and ask for an interview. Get your resume to your contact person, and to the District Manager, immediately. Use U.S. Postal Service Express Mail or overnight delivery such as FedEx, which adds attention and urgency to it.

If you do not hear of any open positions right away, be patient. Your networking process will expand over time. Continue to make new contacts and meet more people each week, which will lead to a growing number of appointments each week. Be confident that you are building your own success and that over time you will gain the interviews and the job "offer" you are seeking. It may take several months or more of networking with your contacts. Some opportunities may come up even a year later. To maintain your relationship with your network, follow-up with telephone calls every four to six weeks. They will remember you and call you when there is an opportunity. With this strategy, you are placing yourself in front of other candidates. Only you can make it work. Stay focused and persistent. You will close the sale!

TIP: *Observe several Pharmaceutical Representative's performing their job in real situations with real customers. I refer to this strategy as the "Pharmaceutical Preceptorship" (described below).*

District Managers want to hire an individual who is knowledgeable about the position for which they are interviewing. In other words, they want to know that you have researched the job thoroughly, you know what is involved, and you are determined to get it. One way to demonstrate this is to show that experience on your resume. First, state clearly that you want to work in a pharmaceutical sales position. Objective: Entry level pharmaceutical sales. Next line list "Pharmaceutical Preceptorship." To achieve this, ask all of your networking contacts to allow you to accompany them for a day or even just a few hours as they go about their normal routine.

Not every representative will be open to this suggestion. If you are turned down, keep asking others. Be mindful that your acquaintance may say they need to check with their district manager first, and convey this understanding to your contact. Take whatever time is allotted for you. Yes, you will hear that it's against company policy (to have a candidate ride in the company car), against new HIPPA (health information privacy regulations) and numerous other excuses. You can meet the representative at a large medical building and easily make a few calls, and there is no regulations against a representative having somebody accompany them (take your "new hire" to work day). Settle on half a day, or one or two sales calls; try it with all your contacts, and go on more than one preceptorship so you can see different styles of how a representative works. If you are still in school, your holiday breaks and summers off are great times to accomplish this objective.

This is mandatory before any pharmaceutical sales interview. It will help you out as much as reading this book, to see first hand what happens on a daily basis. As you go through the day, observe everything you can about what the representative is doing, and why. Actually, you can pretend you are a trainee or perhaps the District Manager for a day! The "ride-along" (shadowing for a day or preceptorship) is very common, many companies make it a part of the interview processes, not only to be sure the candidates know exactly what's involved in the position but more importantly for feedback to the hiring manager from the Pharmaceutical Representative your riding with. No matter what the situation of spending time in the field with a Pharmaceutical Representative, I want you to take note of the following (this comes from being a District Sales Manager for 10 years).

1) How does the representative plan his or her day? Do they have an itinerary, call plan, or other means to plan their routing?

2) How they arrange their selling material before entering an office? Do they mention a specific goal or history for this physician there about to call on? What is Pharmaceutical Representative trying to accomplish on this call?

3) How they greet the office staff? Do they know their names? If not, do they attempt to learn and make note of names for future calls?

4) If the Pharmaceutical Representative is asked to wait, what do they do with their time? Revisit their daily plan? Catch up on paperwork? Build rapport, sell and interact with office nurses/receptionist? Read an old issue of *People* magazine?

5) How do they open their presentation with the physician? Is it enthusiastic? Is it engaging? Would it get your attention if you were a physician?

6) What material do they use to sell the product? The Sales Aid is a must. If they do use clinical studies, observe how they introduce the study (author, journal name, etc.) and draw out key points. If this Pharmaceutical Representative does not use a visual sales aid, clinical reprint or other materials, look for another rep to ride with!

7) How do they use the product samples to assist their selling efforts? Do they explain their value and usage to the customer? Ninety-Two percent of representatives fail to do this in a recent study. A sample for a patient is valued conservatively at $15-$75 (depending on the product). The physician will get the thanks from the patient for "giving" the sample out. A good Rep will remind the physician of how thankful a patient will be to them for the samples.

8) What questions do they ask the physician to learn their prescribing habits?

9) Do they emphasize the features and benefits of their product? Describe the dosing, side effects, or drug interactions to watch out for?

10) Do they gain commitment of the physician to try the product on some patients if agreed upon? Do you feel the physician will use the product?

11) Do they make some notes after the call and immediately plan for the next call? This will quickly show you a difference between the amateur and professional.

Now, here are your duties on the field ride-along:

Be on time! Be well-dressed, as for an interview. Offer to purchase lunch. Importantly, do not let your guard down. Be conversational but not too casual or familiar. As a rule, do not tell anything to this representative that you would not print on the top of your resume! Be a top notch professional every minute; again, your interview best at all times.

Take notes of what you observe during the day, perhaps after each call. Use your notes during an interview process for a particular company. You can refer to them when you meet the manager. For example, "I really noticed how Henry closed the call to gain commitment from the doctor..." Sometimes, a field ride may be part of the interview process, recommended by the manager. If this is the case, you will definitely need to discuss in detail the events of the day and your observations and conclusions. Another candidate vying for the same position my also be doing field travel. So be at your best and make the most of it. Ask the representative to put in a good word for you to the manager. You believe you would be an excellent fit this company and career opportunity with XYZ Pharmaceuticals. Follow up with a letter of thanks that evening to the Pharmaceutical Representative and send it via overnight delivery. See example letter at the end of this chapter.

Now that you are actively networking and researching the industry, you are likely to get to your next step—the interview! Chapter 6 promises many more *Insights* into this exciting stage of attaining your career goal.

[SAMPLE LETTER: FOLLOW-UP NETWORKING MEETING]

December 16, 2004

Janet Lynn Jones
1234 Summer Boulevard
Winter, PA 19123

Ms. Nancy Young
XYZ Pharmaceutical Company Inc.
1134 W. Emma
Milentz, PA 19126

Dear Ms. Young:

It was a pleasure seeing you today. I value your making the time in your busy schedule to meet with me.

Your position in pharmaceutical sales sounds exciting. I will call the contacts you gave me, and I have scheduled myself to attend the Philadelphia Representative Association meeting next month.

XYZ Pharmaceutical Company seems like an excellent organization. I believe your new product for cholesterol will be a huge success in an extremely competitive market. I would like to have the opportunity to interview with XYZ. I appreciate you informing your district manager of my desire to enter this industry with your company. Should any territories become available, please contact me.

As we discussed, I will call you in four to six weeks. In the meantime, please call me if any opportunities arise. My home phone is 555-5555. Again, thank you for your time and assistance. I am looking forward to working with you in the future!

Sincerely,

Janet Lynn Jones

[SAMPLE LETTER: FOLLOW-UP PRECEPTORSHIP]

June 4, 2004

Janet Lynn Jones
1234 Summer Boulevard
Winter, PA 19123

William Betz
XYZ Pharmaceutical Company Inc.
1134 W. Argonne Avenue
Milentz, PA 19134

Dear Mr. Betz:

I appreciate the time you spent this afternoon showing me aspects of your job with XYZ Pharmaceutical Company.

It was fascinating to see the consultative sales approach you use and how you schedule your day. Dr. Wellborn was interested in your new product for cholesterol and was eager to hear the points you made from the medical journal article.

Again, I would like to express my interest in any territories that become available with XYZ Pharmaceutical Company. I appreciate you informing your district manager of my determination to enter this industry. With your recommendation, I will forward my resume to him.

Thank you so much for your assistance. As we agreed, I will call you in four to six weeks to check on the status of any opportunities in your company. In the meantime, please call me if an opportunity develops. My home phone number is 555-5555.

Sincerely,

Janet Jones

pharmaceuticalsales.com representative association's reference:

Alaska Pharmaceutical Representative Association
P.O. Box 771753
Eagle River, AK 99577-1753
Phone: (907) 689-7736
Alternate Phone: Fax: (907) 689-7802
Steve Harris, president
Email: alaskapharmaceuticalreps@hotmail.com

Pharmaceutical Representatives of Stanislaus County, California
Phone: (209) 669-8301
Alternate Phone: (209) 869-2019
Mike Isola
Curtis Lineberger

SCPC (South Coast Pharmaceutical Committee, HIV specialists)
Orange Co., Long Beach and Palm Springs, CA
Phone: (949) 770-4489
Kimberly Murdock
Email: kimberly.murdock@abbott.com

Volusia County Pharmaceutical Representative Association, Florida
Julie McGuire, president
Email: VCPRA@aol.com

Atlanta Medical & Pharmaceutical Representatives' Association, Georgia
Phone: (404) 525-2110
Ray Thatch, president
Reno Odish, treasurer
www.ampra.com

National Association of Professional Pharmaceutical Representatives of Atlanta
P.O. Box 161902
Atlanta, GA 30321
Phone: (770) 621-5746
Jamal Grooms, president

Illini Pharmaceutical Representatives Association (IPPRA), Illinois
David Lee
www.ippra.org
Email: webmaster@ippra.org

NIMRA (Northern Illinois Medical Representative Association – Rockford, Illinois
Phone: (815) 227-4502
Todd Warda, president

Indiana Medical and Pharmaceutical Representative Association
10229 Lower Huntington Road
Roanoke, IN 46783
Phone: (260) 409-2610
Jack Young
Email: championwithin@aol.com

Topeka Pharmaceutical Representatives' Association
2787 SW Plass St.
Topeka, KS 66111
Tava Weidenbaker, president
Email: tavaweidenbaker@aol.com

Western Michigan Pharmaceutical Representative Association, Michigan
Phone: (616) 262-8861
Carolyn O'Grady
Email: cograd1@mccus.jnj.com

Metro Detroit Pharmaceutical Representatives Assoc., Michigan
580 Thornhill Ct.
Belleville, MI 48111
Phone: (810) 287-1499
Shannon Ostby
Email: sostby0427@aol.com

Kalamazoo Area Pharmaceutical Rep Assoc. (KAPRA)
Kalamazoo, MI
Margo Fitzgerald
Email: kazookapra@yahoo.com

Michigan Pharmaceutical Representative Society
815 N. Washington Ave.
Lansing, MI 48906
Phone: (517) 484-1466
Carmel Schwalm, chairwoman

PRIDE (Pharmaceutical Representatives in Detroit Excelling)
P.O. Box 4115
Southfield, MI 48037-4115
Phone: (248) 988-1061
Email: pridepharm@yahoo.com

Twin Cities Pharmaceutical Representative Association
1360 University Ave W, #130
St. Paul, MN 55104
Phone: (651) 690-2485
www.tcpra.com

Southern Oregon Pharmaceutical Representative Association
Phone: (541) 821-2391
Eugene Schulzke

Philadelphia Area Pharmaceutical Representative Association
Philadelphia, PA
Phone: (215) 801-5227
Jeff McGeary, president
Email: phillyrepassn@aol.com

Medical Representatives of Columbia, South Carolina
Phone: (803) 356-6786
Ruth Ann Alexander

Amarillo Pharmaceutical Representatives Assoc., Texas
Amy Duncan, secretary
Email: amy.duncan@spcorp.com

LAMPS (Longview and Marshall Pharmaceutical Sales Reps), Texas
Murry Hodge, president
Email: murhodge@cox-internet.com

Austin Pharmaceutical Representative Association, Texas
P.O. Box 696
Cedar Park, TX 78630
Phone: (800) 496-3772 ext. 87755
Stephen Blanton
Email: stephen.blanton@astrazeneca.com

Pharmaceutical Representatives Assoc. of Southside Hampton Roads Inc. (PRASHR)
Extreme Southeastern Virginia
Tom Cobin
www.prashr.org

CWPRA (Central Wisconsin Pharmaceutical Representatives Association)
Phone: (877) 202-2721 x4810
Alternate Phone: (866) 424-4260 x8115130
Cassie McLain, president
Jay Hutchinson, vice president
www.cwpra.com
Email: cwpra@cwpra.com

WWPRA (Western Wisconsin Pharmaceutical Representative Association)
www.wwpra.com
Email: wwpra@wwpra.com

pharmaceuticalsales.com recruiter reference:

Networking, as described in this chapter, should always be your primary strategy. When visiting a search firm's internet site, you should submit your resume. Follow that submission within a few days with a telephone call and speak to a specific recruiter at the firm. Then submit a thank you note and hard copy of your resume by mail. Use these web sites to post resumes, and learn about openings.

- www.sixfigurejobs.com
- www.horanmedsearch.com
- www.bioview.com
- www.bowdoingroup.com
- www.hotjobs.com
- www.monster.com
- www.medsearchusa.com
- www.amrjobs.com
- www.msajobs.com
- www.medzilla.com
- www.pharmhire.com
- www.pharm-jobs.com
- www.sandssearch.com
- www.medicaljobs.com
- www.greatsalesjobs.com
- www.vault.com

Chapter 6

The Interview

As you successfully apply the networking strategies described by pharmaceuticalsales.com, you will soon be reaping the desired result—Interviews. The chapter you are about to read describes what you should expect from the interview process and how you should prepare for it. This approach helps you to be at your best, with the greatest level of confidence. Included at the end of the chapter is a list of guidelines for professional attire that will have you looking and feeling your professional best as well. Follow these guidelines for dress for all your networking activities also.

Your first meeting is potentially the beginning of a long-term relationship; therefore, it is critical that you present a positive, winning image throughout the interview process. Initiate that relationship on your terms, and be the consummate professional.

Interviewing with pharmaceutical companies has its unique challenges. There are several different types of discussions you might experience with any given company. How you handle each of them is critical to your success. There will be a progression of meetings as you advance through the interviewing process. Be prepared for the various conversations you will have. Fortunately, your strategy will be essentially the same regardless of the type. However, there are some variations in how you must conduct yourself. Pharmaceuticalsales.com labels the different types of interviews as follows:

1. Screening Interview
2. Job Fairs
3. First Interview
4. Second Interview
5. Final Interview

Companies and District Managers will vary in how they conduct each step. They will also differ in the type of questions they ask and the manner in which they ask them. This fact underscores your need to be prepared for anything since you may or may not be given prior advice regarding the types of questions you will be expected to answer. For example, some interviewers may ask questions consisting of situations that occur in the day-to-day work of the Pharmaceutical Representative. In some cases, you will be given the situations in order to prepare for either a telephone screening or a face-to-face interview. The situational questions could be customer-related or company-related. Customer related situations would be challenges that come up with doctors, office nurses, and receptionists or gatekeepers. They could also be objections to your product, such as having a higher cost than your competitor has. Company-related situations are about working on teams with other representatives.

Because some companies are asking job-specific questions, it is important for you to study the answers in this guide. Also just as imperative is time in the field with several Pharmaceutical Sales Representative's to observe what they do (Field Preceptorships) as discussed in Chapter 5. Perform the preceptorship's early in your job search. Create a list of scenarios that you want to observe and use the situations Insight provides. Ask the representatives you talk and meet with how they would handle each one. You may add excellent and creative answers to your knowledge base.

Not every company will ask situational questions about selling pharmaceuticals. However, regardless of the situation or exact wording of the question, the interviewer is looking for evidence of whether or not you would be the right candidate for the job. Obviously, you have not had previous experience selling pharmaceuticals and the interviewer is aware of that. Initially they are looking for the way you think, how you sell, and what your skills are in different job competencies. Your answers should always include specific examples about how you were successful in similar situations, either current or past positions. This is critical. The interviewer will be looking for explicit behavior patterns and will ask if you do not provide them. One suggestion is to use a simple format to describe your accomplishments: Situation-Task-Action-Results. This is sometimes referred to as the STAR format of interview questions, or "situational" format. Even if the question is about selling to doctors or other aspects of pharmaceutical sales, your answer should include a similar personal experience and detail how you handled it successfully. Your answer would be complete by starting with a brief description of the actual situation, the task or goal to be performed, the action you took and the result of that action.

Regardless of the style of question or your answer, make every effort to demonstrate what you are saying. In other words, have proof of your success wherever possible, such as ranking reports, awards and recognition, sales data, etc. Also, be ready to show examples of your work, such as written memo's, presentations, plans, projects. This is important to do in the interview because it gives the manager confidence that you are telling the truth, and it demonstrates an important skill used by pharmaceutical reps—that of backing up your product claims with proof sources: visual aids and clinical reprints. Skillfully using your own proof sources as you answer questions will be an outstanding way to show your job skills. Some refer to a Brag Book for this purpose, but be sure to use it throughout your interview where it relates to the answers you are giving. Avoid paging through the brag book all at once.

Studying each question in this chapter will help you understand what the interviewer is trying to assess. Behind each question is an essential skill or behavior for successful performance on the job. The essential skills are "competencies," as listed and discussed in Chapter 2. To simplify the competencies, they can be condensed into three categories that you should keep in mind as you develop and rehearse your answers:

Achievement drive: results oriented, creative, confident, history of sales success

Strong work ethic: motivation, reliability, communication

Positive attitude: flexibility, teamwork, high energy

SCREENING INTERVIEW

Screening interviews are conducted, to put it bluntly, in order reduce the number of candidates after the unacceptable resumes have been removed from the stack. They are designed to identify the general qualities, or profile, of the desired candidate. These dialogues are often conducted by telephone, but also face-to-face. Usually the first twelve questions numbered in this chapter are covered in the session. Several characteristics distinguish the screening interviews from other types. First, it is usually brief and lasts about twenty to thirty minutes. Second, someone may conduct it other than the District Manager (such as a Human Resources Specialist at a Job Fair, Sales Trainer, or Hiring Agency). Finally, it is generally an identical set of questions for all candidates. A scoring system is used to determine who will advance to the first interview stage.

Screening interviews may not be scheduled ahead of time. You should be prepared for a call whenever you are actively networking. Keep your interview file close by and easily accessible at all times. Include your resume, job accomplishments, sales achievements, networking, and research notes that you have collected on each company.

TIP: *When the phone rings for a screening interview, feel free to ask the caller to wait just a moment, saying you would like to close the door, turn off the radio, get off the other line, let others at home know not to disturb you, or whatever. Take thirty seconds or so to gather your file and collect your thoughts. Then lift the receiver and thank the caller for waiting.*

If you have done your research and practiced your answers, you will sail past the screening step. Be sure to take notes. When you here, "Send me your resume", remember this can be a gentle way of getting you off the phone or a sincere request by someone that is genuinely interested in moving you on in the interview process. Either way, try to inject a few more questions on what skills the company looks for in a Pharmaceutical Sales Representative. Ask and write down the person's name, title, address, fax, phone, voicemail and email address if they will give it to you. Close by thanking them for their time and requesting a face-to-face interview when available.

When you complete this phase, send a follow-up letter, overnight mail. Emphasize your desire for the opportunity to demonstrate why you believe you will be a successful sales representative for the company.

JOB FAIRS

However, not a large fan of Job fairs, simply due to the large amount of candidates involved, they can be similar to screening interviews in that they are designed to eliminate lesser-qualified candidates. The interviewers are more likely to be Human Resource personnel, Sales Trainers, District Managers and Representatives from other geographic areas. These individuals are not empowered to hire you, but can make a good case either for or against you. Approach and follow up with them as you would any sales manager.

One advantage of the job fair is that you are face to face immediately with the company personnel. Take the opportunity to set yourself apart. If anything, they are excellent practice for you. The questions they ask will most likely be standard for each candidate that allows the interviewer to use a scoring system and classification of candidates. Again, close the interviewer on getting to the next step. Collect as many business cards as there are people from the company—meet everybody, and follow up with each person.

INITIAL OR FIRST INTERVIEW

This is the real thing. Congratulations! You are probably one of five or ten candidates invited for a full interview. This is your first meeting with the District Manager, and it is the opportunity for you to become the top candidate. You will be asked specific questions by the interviewer, and you must be able to ask your own questions. Volunteer as much information about yourself as you can, and always include successful scenarios.

Most companies will allow one hour for the initial interview. Be prepared to go longer—this will be good sign that you are serious candidate. Otherwise, the manager would not spend the extra time with you. Some companies will arrange for more than one interview at this stage. You may interview with more than one District Manager, Sales Trainer, Regional Field Trainer, or Regional Manager if they are trying to move quickly to fill the position or hiring numerous candidates.

Always conduct yourself professionally with every individual you meet during this process. Be relaxed and confident. If interacting with other office Administrative Assistants, converse briefly with them if you are given the opportunity, asking them topical questions such as who they are and what they do.

Have your own questions to ask the interviewer, but do not ever ask about compensation or benefits at the initial interview. There is more on this topic, including questions for you to ask, in Chapter 7.

SECOND INTERVIEW

Returning for a second interview means that you are considered a serious candidate. The questions asked will be more specific. There may be additional people involved, such as another District Manager or the Regional Manager. However, the second interview may be with the same District Manager. District Manager's will not hire or advance a candidate to the final step unless they usually see that candidate more than once. This allows the District Manager to confirm or challenge their conclusions made in the first interview.

FINAL INTERVIEW

Sometimes a third interview is necessary to answer a few remaining questions or to have someone else in the company meet you. You can be confident at this point that there are only about two candidates left. Sometimes this step takes place in a different setting, such as a restaurant, or hotel lobby. This allows the Manager to see how you conduct yourself in a less formal and controlled setting where you both can let your guard down. It permits them see more of your personality, and you to see more of theirs. This is where chemistry is important. So, be relaxed and confident. Be conversational but avoid controversial topics and chitchat. Be thoughtful, polite and positive in your comments at all times.

Always ask for the position. Review what has been agreed upon in your interviews to date, in terms of your qualifications. Ask if there is anything missing or still needed in order for the District Manager to reach their decision. If so, provide it. Either way, close for the job clearly and with determination. You must demonstrate your aptitude for sales! A sale is about closing the deal.

Your preparation for the interview includes the networking and research strategies outlined in Chapters 4 and 5. In this chapter, I will provide you the most common interview questions, and offers suggestions and examples of how you might answer each one. Give the finest response to every question based on your education, background, preceptorships, work experience, and the recommendations in this book. Learn the questions from this chapter backward and forward, because undoubtedly you will be asked some. Prepare your answers ahead of time and practice your responses until you are comfortable with every one. Remember, the more prepared you are, the more relaxed and confident you will be during the interview.

> **TIP:** *An excellent strategy is to video record the questions and your responses. Perform this with a cassette, MP3 player, etc. Listen to a question, pause the player and give your response to a video camera. Play back your answer and re-record it until you have reached perfection. You will have these things memorized in your words in no time, better here than your interview! Right? Be your own critic! On your video tape, note your non-verbal behavior—such as your posture, tone and the projection of voice. Do you look and sound confident? Dress the part, do you appear comfortable? These practice sessions will give you a profound advantage over other candidates. Now ask a friend to review your practice work also.*

As discussed in earlier chapters know as much as you can about the company and determine how you see yourself adding value in their environment. Walk slowly and stand up straight when entering the room. When greeting the District Manager, give that brief "raise of the head" accompanied by a warm smile. Begin by telling the District Manager that you have researched XYZ Pharmaceuticals, the industry, and the job of a Pharmaceutical Sales Representative. State early, you are extremely interested in this position. The District Manager, upon hearing such an aggressive opening, will often get right down to business. This is what you want, and now puts you on a more level playing field.

Sometimes you will discover that the interviewer is not exactly what you expected, or were looking for in a District Manager. I call it the "No Love Connection" interview, and it happens. Occasionally the interviewer is not as well prepared for the process as you are. When this is the case, you need to volunteer the answers you have prepared, even without being asked. Do this by weaving your accomplishments and strong points throughout the interview. Your confidence will show, and your skills and preparation shall be rewarded.

The interviewer is looking for initiative. Showing the strategy you used to network, research, and prepare yourself for this process is, in itself, evidence that you have initiative and are going to succeed. Make the conclusion for the interviewer to see that you will apply the same skills and abilities that you brought to the interview process to your new career. I suggest keeping your utilization and readership of *Insight* out of the discussion, take credit for *your* effort.

Insight has provided you the questions you will be asked. I have also included questions that you want to ask the interviewer. Always ask questions during every single interview, show your interest, and prove that you have done your homework. The more the District Manager speaks, the better the interview will develop. As you progress through the later stages, as in second and third interviews, ask more in depth questions. Why?

Your original goal was to market yourself. You have their interest, but is the company a good match for you—ask questions. Never, during any part of an interview process, bring up the compensation or benefits. Get the offer in a letter of offering in your hand first! There will be plenty of opportunity to discuss base salary, bonus, benefits and the dental plan after that.

TIP: *Before leaving the interview, be certain to obtain the interviewer's business card. You will need it for completing your follow-up correspondence (see sample letter at end of this chapter).*

The interview questions to follow are typical of what you should expect during an interview. The interviewer will use variations, but your responses will be appropriate and effective no matter how the questions are asked. Your preparation, including the industry and company-specific research, means you are ready for anything.

TIP: *You should never be asked certain questions. It is illegal for employers to inquire about certain areas of your life. However, you may volunteer any information you choose and the interviewer can listen to it once you bring it up, but they cannot ask for it. These questions include information about the following:*

- *marital status*
- *family*
- *religion*
- *age*
- *sexual preference*
- *race or national origin*
- *political affiliation*
- *arrest record; the exception is convictions*

- *emergency contact information*
- *type of military discharge*
- *health status*
- *height or weight*
- *to provide a photo*
- *children or the possibility of pregnancy*
- *spouse's vocation*
- *memberships in organizations, clubs, societies*

Since 1998, I have received countless emails stating, "I've been told I'm much too old for pharmaceutical sales. Companies just hire beautiful looking, young candidates." Since the 1964 Civil Rights Act, Title VII, it has been illegal to discriminate because of age. But rarely, it can still happen. When it comes to age, gender, religion, race, or even one's weight, there are biases, whether conscious or unconscious, that may come into play. You will not hear that, of course, if you are turned down for a position in any industry. You will possibly get a brief explanation, "We are going with a candidate with more experience." I assure you that this is going to be an exception if it does occur, and there is really no way to know. In reality, companies do seem to hire more sales representatives in their twenties and thirties. But this is the most common age demographic of the candidate pool—persons who have graduated, have a few years of work experience and are searching for a better career. When you network, and observe representatives working a medical building, you will notice Pharmaceutical Sales Representatives come in all ages, genders, races, sizes and shapes!

Also, I would contend that any group of high-end sales professionals, dressing their best, would look like a stylish crowd, so let us stop with the excuses and stereotypes. By following the strategies in this book and adding your dedication and hard work, you will have all the advantages to nail the job you want. During my twenty years of hiring, I hired numerous candidates in their forties and fifties because they bring a perspective to the job that younger candidates lack. This comes from what I call having experienced "life's firsts" (marriage, children, home, job, career, etc.). If you are an older candidate, you need to turn your age and maturity into your asset. Show off your experience, dedication, knowledge of this industry, appreciation of such an enjoyable, challenging and rewarding profession. And, your determinations to making this position a fantastic success for your career. Even at age 55 and older, you have many years you can offer an organization. This is probably longer than most tenure of the members in the hiring manager's current district.

THE MOST COMMON QUESTIONS FOR INTERVIEWING IN PHARMACEUTICAL SALES.

1) Why do you want to enter a career in pharmaceutical sales?

This is a fundamental question, and one you must be able to answer without hesitation. There are two parts to this question and it deserves a two-part answer. Why do you want to sell, and why in the pharmaceutical industry. State that you want and like to sell, and that you are successful at doing so. You possess the essential qualities of high energy, motivation, confidence, dedication, creativity, and organizational skills. Provide specific examples of situations that demonstrate one or more of these qualities.

Next, selling pharmaceuticals appeals to you because it is challenging and rewarding. The challenge lies in its technical environment (product knowledge), professional customer audience, and stiff competition. The rewards are based on your own individual efforts, which is just the type of environment in which you excel. Use the same examples you gave to illustrate essential sales qualities in the first part of your answer. Only this time, relate it to something you think you would do in your new position as a sales representative for XYZ Pharmaceutical Company.

TIP: *This question provides an excellent opportunity for you to describe your research into the pharmaceutical industry and specifically with XYZ Pharmaceuticals. Since you have networked with many sales representatives by this point, you can use specific examples from your conversations with them and real-life situations you have had in front of physicians. Use your answer to highlight your industry exploration. This will give you credibility when you say you want the job—you know what you are getting into and it is the perfect fit for you.*

2) Why do you believe that you would find pharmaceutical sales a rewarding career?

You know from your extensive research of the job and the company that you would find this profession challenging. It will be apparent to the interviewer whether you have done your homework. Answers such as "I have a friend that likes it" will not be sufficient.

You may include that you like being responsible for you own destiny. You are aggressive. You work hard. You will succeed based on your own merit. Include an example from a previous selling or business success. You may also include your knowledge of the career advancement opportunities, as described in Chapter 2. Communicate your excitement about the possibilities for personal and professional growth. State that you are willing to dedicate the time and effort to learn the business from the field sales position.

3) Why do you think you would excel at pharmaceutical sales?

This is a similar question to the two above, but by asking it, the interviewer is seeking more information. You should answer that you know what this position requires and you have those requirements. Give some specific qualities that you possess that are also critical for success in pharmaceuticals. For example, you have individual creativity—Pharmaceutical Representatives work alone and face unique challenges that require unique solutions. You possess excellent time management skills—a busy representative must plan and work efficiently. You have excellent business acumen, a skill that will help you target your most productive customers, which is efficient and productive. Again, you are indicating that you know what the position entails.

Also, be sure to include the fact that you will enjoy it. If you are doing something that brings great pleasure and confidence, you will naturally do it better. Being happy in your work is a principal indicator of success, and that makes you sure that you are pursuing the right position.

4) How long do you believe you would like to sell pharmaceuticals?

Be sure you relate to the interviewer that as long as you feel challenged and rewarded by the position, you feel your time is unconstrained. If career advancement is one of your goals, communicate that you desire to learn the industry "from the entry sales position up." You plan to use the opportunity to develop your strengths and assess your opportunities as you add value to the company, then realistically evaluate your career goals at that time.

5) Why do you want to change careers to pharmaceutical sales?

This question is looking for your conviction about what you want to do. Think about what attracted you to pharmaceuticals and why you started researching. Prepare an honest answer and convey your excitement.

The pharmaceutical industry has much to offer. You may be looking for growth. This industry has shown compelling expansion in the past and is poised to continue to do so in the future. You may want security. This industry is virtually recession proof. You may want prestige. This industry is one of the most sought-after and well-heeled industries in the world. You may be looking for a mixture of business and health care. You may desire professional, consultative relationships with your customers where you are the expert.

Perhaps you are more idealistic. You may want to be part of scientific discoveries and medical advances that alleviate suffering and improve people's lives. You want to offer solutions to real-life problems that physicians and patients face every day. Whatever the reason, deliver it with conviction.

6) What experience do you have that would lend itself to pharmaceutical sales?

If you have experience selling a product or service, this is the time to sell the interviewer on how you performed. If you have no previous sales experience, describe times in the past that you have sold an idea, a project, or a new way of doing things at your work or school. Sales experience is not essential for entering the industry. If you conduct research, then network with individuals in the profession and convey your determination to be successful, you will be conclusively more desirable as a candidate than someone with sales experience who has not prepared as effectively as you have.

7) How does your education prepare you for a career in pharmaceutical sales? Most any undergraduate college degree will easily lend itself to the industry.

Business, communications, marketing, management, education, language skills, psychology, biology, chemistry, pharmacy, nursing, and others, all enhance what you bring to this company. If your education is in science or health care, you are going to have to emphasize that you can "sell." If your background is sales, emphasize that you can learn the essential technical background needed to excel in this position.

Pharmaceutical sales are a union of science and business. Prepare your answers to incorporate your education into this union.

8) Why do want to work for XYZ Pharmaceutical Company?

The interviewer wants to know if you have done your homework. What are some unique characteristics of this company? Is it relatively large, small, or medium sized? What is its product line or area of medical specialty that you like? Are you excited about the current product line and the future possibilities of products to be released? Do you know anybody who works for the company? State that you are impressed with current pharmaceutical sales representatives that you have met through your networking, and that you would have an excellent working chemistry with the team.

TIP: *If you have done your research, you may even be more informed about this organization than the person on the other side of the table. See if you can surprise him with information he was not aware of, such as an experimental compound in development, or the latest quarterly profit figures. Managers will often be unaware of some details about their company because they are more involved with the day-to-day business of their district.*

9) What qualifies you to be a Pharmaceutical Sales Representative?

If you have obtained a four-year degree, are interested, have completed the research, networked with individuals, understand the position and the industry, and most importantly, want to do this job, you are qualified. However, the interviewer is looking for more. Emphasize to the interviewer that you want to make a long-term commitment to this industry based upon your research. You have devoted countless hours of time and energy towards obtaining your goal, which is employment in this business. You plan to be well versed in product knowledge, selling skills, and territory organization. You want to excel and will bring value to the company.

10) Are you currently interviewing with other pharmaceutical companies at this time?

You want to work in pharmaceutical sales. It is as simple as that, so be honest. State that your goal is to gain successful employment with a dynamic pharmaceutical company, and that you will persist until you accomplish your goal. Describe your networking strategy. Include that you are, or will be, interviewing with prospective companies as you push to uncover opportunities.

If this is your first interview, state that. However, if you are currently interviewing with other companies make it clear. Include companies by name, names of individuals, with whom you have met or interviewed, and a major product or two made by the other companies.

TIP: *Ninety percent of the candidates interviewing today cannot state what current products are being promoted by the firm they are interviewing with, much less the products of other companies. Think of the advantage you will create for yourself with this prospective employer by being versed on multiple companies in the industry.*

11) What are your greatest strengths?

Make sure that you can answer this question. It was probably used on the first interview in history. You will probably be presented with this question every time you interview in your working career.

Your strengths should be qualities that are in demand by pharmaceutical companies. You want to fit the profile of the successful representative by following the Anne Clayton' pharmaceuticalsales.com way.

- Self-motivated and self-disciplined: Your time management and organizational skills make you productive while working autonomously or with little supervision.
- Creative: You are able to differentiate yourself from other pharmaceutical sales representatives. You can create ways to access your "hard to see" doctors.
- Goal oriented: You do what it takes to get the job done, including making a few extra calls to physicians, hospitals, and pharmacies.
- Confident: Your background, qualities, and commitment will guarantee success in this career choice.
- Flexible: You are cooperative—you can take direction well, and work together as a team to reach corporate objectives.

12) What are your weaknesses? In what areas would you like to improve?

This question usually follows the one about strengths. Design your response so that ultimately your weakness is strength. Your interviewer will probably know what you are doing, but the fact that you have done the preparation to handle this difficult question will gain their respect. They are looking for your confidence under pressure. Many of your contemporaries will struggle with this question. Poor answers are ones that shift the weakness to another person, such as a previous manager, co-workers, or company policy. Be careful not to interject blame or negative comments about past employers and others.

Two examples of a good answer are as follows:
- Sometimes I have trouble compiling my paperwork in an enthusiastic manner. However, I do know that timeliness of reporting is important to my managers and my company, so I make sure I am always prompt with its delivery.
- Sometimes I have difficulty when other individuals do not display a positive attitude towards new ideas. I make it a point to stay positive, hoping it will influence other members of the organization or team.

13) Where do you see yourself five years from now?

From your research, you know that there are many opportunities in the pharmaceutical industry for a successful field representative: Management, Marketing, Sales Training, Sales Support, Communications, and Professional Education. Reiterate that learning the field sales position and becoming a proven performer within your organization is your primary goal for at least the next three years. After learning the business from this level, you will direct your goals so that you can grow professionally and contribute to the corporations' goals.

TIP: *During the initial phases of interviewing, most District Managers will delight in hearing that you are giving yourself three to five years to fully develop and demonstrate your abilities in your new territory. It is a sign of unrealistic expectations and poor knowledge of the job when a candidate places too much emphasis on upward mobility when they have not even entered the industry. Show your ambition in other ways—by researching, networking, preparing, and inter viewing with excellence.*

14) How do you feel about your current boss?

If you do not get along with your current boss, this is not the time to voice it. State that you have been managed effectively, provided guidance, and growth in your position. Specify that you have met your objectives, but do not talk about personalities and philosophies. As long as you perform your job, and reach or surpass your objectives, you feel just great about your current boss.

15) How do you feel about your current employer?

Again, never complain about your present position. State that the position has provided you with the ability to gain knowledge and grow professionally, but you desire a personal and professional challenge. Considering your research and career planning, the ideal career for you is in the pharmaceutical industry. Talk less about your current position and more about your decision to become a pharmaceutical sales representative. Keep your answer positive and career oriented. In other words, show that you are moving towards pharmaceuticals, not moving away from some other situation that you do not like.

16) What have you done that shows initiative in your present position?

Use a recent example in your present position, if possible, to describe the details of your current position. Your pharmaceutical research also provides an excellent response.

17) What are your immediate goals?

Your immediate goals are both professional and personal. Articulate that your number one professional priority is to achieve a career with a pharmaceutical company and begin contributing as a successful representative. Add personal goals, such as physical exercise, hobbies, family, if you would like to round out this response.

18) What are your interests, hobbies?

Choose activities that show competition, determination, motivation, creativity, or team playing. These attributes are the ones that fit the profile of success, and transfer well to the job. Leave out watching television, going to the movies, reading, and other sedentary activities. Studies have shown that executives that list sports among their extracurricular activities earn significantly more. Show you are a team player, enjoy a challenge, and are a person that is determined to succeed and various goals.

19) Describe a problem you have encountered in your current position?

The interviewer is really looking for a solution you created. Thus, you must not only describe a problem, but also describe a solution to the problem. Example: "A problem in my current position was that we were unable to reach some of the deadlines of our department. I overcame this by placing a large calendar in the break room with our deadlines marked in red. It was a clear reminder to the other office members, which in turn improved hitting our deadlines."

20) What have been some of your largest disappointments?

Describe a situation where you experienced disappointment and were able to learn and develop from it, thus turning it into a positive experience. Example: "As I began my job search in the pharmaceutical industry I found that it was taking too long to get my first interview. Since then, I have changed my approach and have become more aggressive at discovering opportunities. Therefore, I have become much more successful. I feel most disappointments can teach us something useful for the future."

21) How do you prepare your reports or paperwork in your current position?

Example: "I create my reports to communicate relevant information about my business. Not only for my manager and my company, but also for myself. I find they are more useful when I write them down as soon as I complete a sales call. I make sure that my reports are prompt, organized, and detailed, yet concise."

22) Have you ever had to deal with a difficult person at work? How did you handle this?

If you have never done so, then say that and be finished with the question. If you have, describe a situation in which, though you did not agree with an individual, you where able to work through the assignment or task to complete the project. It is more important to cooperate with individuals so that the work atmosphere remains productive.

23) Do you feel you are treated and compensated fairly at your present position?

Never complain about your present position, boss, company, duties, etc. The interviewer wants to know you are a positive force. Simply answer, "Yes."

24) What is your largest accomplishment in your present position?

If you have received any awards or acclamations, mention them. Bring documentation of any recognition that you have been awarded, and show it to the interviewer. Leave a copy at the end of the interview. Describe a work situation that you resolved with favorable results, or a creative solution you used with a difficult customer. Although the question may be worded specifically to address your present position, take license to expand to other jobs or to extracurricular or community accomplishments, as well.

> **TIP:** *Use your answers to lead the interviewer to other areas you would like to present about yourself. Find a way to bridge to another topic or example that you know is a positive attribute for you. If you rely on the interviewer to ask the question, it may not be asked, and you will lose an opportunity to say something important about your successes.*

25) What do you dislike about your present position?

You may want to choose some minor and menial aspect of your job. It is a good idea to pick something that deters or distracts from the business. Office chatter is a good one, waiting on people who are late, or being stuck in traffic. Be sure to include what you do to deal with the problem. Paperwork is always a good thing to dislike. Just be sure to include that because you dislike it, you are sure to complete it in a timely and accurate way.

Conclude by saying that you have been satisfied with your present position, but you desire to accelerate your growth in pharmaceutical sales.

26) Do you feel you have been evaluated fairly?

Again, never complain about current or past positions. The interviewer is not looking for someone who is unhappy in relationships with an employer, regardless of who is at fault. Do not complain about anything or blame anyone. A simple "yes" is appropriate.

27) Give me an example of one of your best sales.

If you are currently selling a product or service, use a sale in which you encountered objections, misunderstandings, or a lack of customer interest, and how you overcame these obstacles. If you are not currently selling a product or service, detail the way you have gone about marketing yourself through the interview process. Describe, in detail, how you have set goals, strategies, networked with individuals, and kept records. Compare the interviewing process to a sale. Express in either situation how rewarding your sales activity and accomplishing your goals was. Example: You have felt rewarded by your increased knowledge of the pharmaceutical industry and the people who work in it. You are confident you will be successful.

28) Give me an example of a sale that you missed, and how you could have handled it differently?

Failure is universal in sales. A good salesperson thrives on it. It is common for sales professionals to experience this, and the interviewer wants to know how you will respond to it when it happens again. Give an example, be honest, state what you learned in the process, and how you tried to correct the situation. If you have no sales experience, use a business or office situation in which you created a solution and benefited from a past failure. Either way, convey your excitement over challenging sales situations, customers, and the thrill of achievement.

29) How do you go about selling your product?

Describe your sales cycle and approach to the customer. Do you initially use telephone contacts, direct mail, or any type of advertising? Be competent in your description of your sales process and how you differentiate yourself from your competition. Example: You telephone all customers within two weeks of their purchases to check their satisfaction with your product or service. This process has led to many repeat purchases of your product line, and improvements in your service.

30) Do you believe you are able to handle the pressure of sales quotas?

Yes. State that you find the challenge of sales quotas motivating. You enjoy being responsible for your own destiny. You work hard and want to be recognized and compensated according to what you accomplish.

31) How do you handle rejection in your sales position?

Whether in the sales position or your current career search you must often experience some rejections before success. Rejection is an opportunity to get to know your customer better. It forces you to make changes in your approach. Creating innovative solutions has provided ways that have allowed you to move closer to your customers and understand them better.

32) What things do you and your current manager disagree on?

State that you and your manager rarely have disagreed on issues, and that your relationship has been very productive within your organization.

33) How are you motivated in your position?

This question tells the interviewer what you will be like to manage. You are motivated by a job well done. Your own accomplishment and success feeds you. Besides being self-motivated, you thrive on recognition from within your company, comments from your superiors with periodic performance reviews, and financial rewards (commission, bonuses, etc.). Also, state that you gain a sense of satisfaction by achieving personal goals. Example: To be in the top 10% of your company's sales force.

34) What things detract from some of your initiatives?

With this question, make a negative a positive. For example, you may occasionally overachieve. While good for the business, it can be better to keep a balance between your work and relaxation. You find that you are more productive when you take an occasional break to refocus.

35) How have you differentiated yourself from your peers both outside and within your organization?

Embellish the successful attributes of a salesperson: ambition, determination, organization, energy, self-motivation, ability to handle rejection, targeting the correct customer base, teamwork, etc. Give an example of a situation in which you excelled. Was there a time when you went the extra mile to help a customer? Perhaps your forte is personal rapport and relationship selling, or maybe you have a unique talent that you incorporate into your sales approach, such as cooking, fishing, or athletics?

36) How were your grades in college?

If they were admirable, bring an official transcript from your college or university to present to the interviewer. Your answer should focus on the fact that you will learn product knowledge quickly, and communicate that information to your customer. If grades were not praiseworthy, fault it on working while attending school (if appropriate), extracurricular activities (sports), or finally, youth. Move on to illustrate recent successes in your career, continuing education, seminars, or training classes.

37) What is your current salary?

Answer briefly and to the point, and then stop talking. Do not exaggerate. From your research, you know the starting salary range for a pharmaceutical sales representative. Avoid discussing what salary you may require until you have been made an offer. Likewise, avoid the temptation to ask anything about salary or compensation.

38) Can I contact your current employer, or co-workers?

"No" is an acceptable answer. You would not want to jeopardize your current standing within your present organization. Do offer references, both business and personal, and contact information for co-workers if acceptable to you.

TIP: *Do not bring pre-written reference letters. They are not of value to a prospective employer and may be insulting to the interviewer, especially if they are overstated (which most of them are). If it is appropriate in your situation to provide references, bring them typewritten on a separate sheet of paper. Provide both personal and professional references; usually three of each is appropriate. Give complete names, titles, addresses, and telephone numbers. Be sure to have permission from the individuals on your list and keep them posted when you give out the list.*

39) When I call your references, how will they describe you? What would your boss say about you?

List some of the qualities that you have demonstrated for your referenced individuals. For example, they would say that you are determined to enter pharmaceutical sales, are creative and motivated, have a strong work ethic, are honest, reliable, good sense of humor, great salesperson, etc. Again, be sure you contact every one of your references before you list them. Let them know about your career search.

40) How much are you willing to travel? Are you willing to relocate?

Various positions or sales territories require that you travel, especially in the pharmaceutical industry. Even if you do not have to stay overnight to work your territory, you will surely have to travel to meetings and training activities from time to time.

Your foremost consideration at this stage of the game is to obtain the job offer. Once you have an offer letter, you can decide if the particulars of the position (travel, relocation, salary, benefits, commission structure, or management style) are satisfactory for you. Do not eliminate yourself from the process before receiving the offer you deserve. Always indicate that you are willing to travel and relocate for the right opportunity.

41) What do you expect to earn in the first year?

Never discuss salary until you have the offer in your hand. If you have done your research, you know the compensation level you can expect. Again, do not eliminate yourself by quoting too high, or even too low, a figure. State that you are confident that you shall compensated fairly for your efforts and you are looking forward to receiving an offer.

42) Describe what you believe a typical day, as a Pharmaceutical Representative, would involve?

This is your ideal question. Because of your networking, your field preceptorships, and other research, you are an expert at this question. Example: "Typically, an office based Pharmaceutical Representatives will start the day by stocking the trunk of the car with literature and samples. S/he will have a detailed plan for the day of where to go and who the contact is. A salesperson will call on 7-9 physicians to make detailed sales presentations. This may include visiting several pharmacies to gather information about prescribing habits and to check product supplies. Additionally, stopping at a hospital or clinic to reach physicians may be an alternative to their offices. The professional representative will assess how physicians are reacting to their product, present new information, leave samples, and get a commitment from the doctor for increasing prescriptions of the medication. During the office call, talking with the nurses, secretaries, and other office staff is an important part of communications. Be sure to add a real-life example: "When I was observing Maria Sanchez for a day, we went to a new physician in the area and…."

43) How many hours a week do you feel it will be necessary for you to get your job accomplished as a Pharmaceutical Representative?

No correct answer here, so again, you have to cover all the bases. Some District Sales Managers pride themselves on working nights and weekends, and leaving voice and emails throughout the weekend. Others pride themselves on their excellent planning and time management that allows them to work a smart 40 hours per week. You must mesh the two stating you plan your time effectively but as always, projects and deadline's will demand that extra effort to get the job done. Ask the District Manager what is typical in their sales district?

44) How could you target the customers (physicians) in your territory in the most efficient way and still achieve maximum sales results?

This is a very advanced question and, if asked, means you are a serious contender. The more insight you can show about the job, the better. Answers that come from your own successes and networking are best, but we have included a few examples.

"Targeting" means choosing which doctors you are going to visit to make your sales presentations. This is your customer base. These doctors make up your call plan, as discussed in Chapter 2. Obviously, you cannot see all of the specialists in your territory. Many companies use call plans that are developed by the company or by consultants using sophisticated marketing data. Your call plan is then provided to you. However, it is usually not set in stone, and you are responsible for refining it based on your own observations in the field. The following answers are applicable to this process, and to the process of developing your own call plan.

First, match the product class to the physician's specialty. Example: You would call on a gynecologist more frequently to sell an oral contraceptive agent than you would to an internal medicine or general practice physician.

Second, evaluate the physician's practice size. Is their office busy? Do they see many patients of the type that would use your product? You can determine this by the number of patients waiting to be seen, number of support staff in the office (nurses and receptionist), or how full the appointment book is for the week. You would increase the number of calls to these physicians to promote their prescribing. This is "call frequency" and it is dependent upon the number of times you would normally call on that customer in a given period, referred to as "call cycle." Call cycle is the length of time you spend covering all locations in your territory one time. The company usually sets the call cycle. It can range from two weeks to two months, depending on territory size and sales strategy.

TIP: *Familiarize yourself with the terms such as targeting, call plan, call frequency, and call cycle. Review Chapter 2 for more information.*

For efficiency, plan your appointments by geography in your territory, and for the best times to see doctors without having to wait too long. Avoid walking in at busy times of the day. You will get to know this as you work a territory, and become more efficient as you learn about each customer and how the office runs.

45) What aspects of pharmaceutical sales do you feel are most vital to success in this field?

You can take your pick of the following suggestions or build your own list. The more relevant to your experience from discussions with your networking contacts, the better you will be. Examples: building customer relationships, being an expert on your products and the competition, listening for what the physician wants in a product and positioning your product accordingly, prompt follow-up, self-motivation, organization, creativity, determination, product knowledge, professionalism, targeting, and above all attitude.

46) What is the worst thing you have heard during your networking about XYZ Pharmaceuticals?

From current representatives and competitors of XYZ I have heard that you are very well respected and a difficult company to obtain a sales position, due to your thorough interview process, which I admire.

47) Tell me a story?

First, ask what would the interviewer like to hear a story about, your professional or personal life? Always leave out the forbidden areas of interviewing (marriage, religion, age, etc.). This shows the interviewer that you are thinking through the question and your answer. If about your personal life, reference a time when you demonstrated qualities such as your tenacity, or dependability. If your choice is personal, chose some qualities such as your ability to take direction (from management) and willingness to go the "extra mile" to complete the job.

48) On a scale of one to ten, where do you rate yourself?

Go with an eight to nine, noting that one should always be striving to increase their competencies, skills, and education.

49) What was the last book your read?

Most important here, is that you actual read the book, because the follow up question could kill the interview if you have not. Arrive at a response that will differentiate you from the mass of other candidates (in other words, stay off the bestseller list). Choose a book that strives for self-improvement, and again, do not mention *Insight*.

50) Let us pretend your product is a pen. Sell it to me.

Begin by probing the interviewer for requirements he or she is looking for in a pen. For example, "Why are you looking for a pen?" or "What are you looking for in a pen?" Listen and clarify the answer, then provide features and benefits of the pen that satisfy the stated need. Close the sale by asking for the business.

<u>Feature</u>	<u>Benefit</u>
• Round	• Easy to hold
• Shirt Clip	• Easy to find during daily activities
• Retractable point	• Will not leave marks on clothing
• Refillable cartridge	• Will provide years of service
• Smooth writing tip	• Effortless writing

Explore any reason that he or she would not want to use this pen. Close with, "How many would you like to order today?"

51) Let us pretend your product is XYZ Aspirin. Sell it to me.

Again, be certain to investigate what the customer would like to see (and if they currently use) an aspirin product in their practice. Listen, clarify, provide features and benefits, check for any questions or objections, and then ask for the business.

<u>Feature</u>	<u>Benefit</u>
• Low cost therapy	• Patient has more money for other things
• Pain relief in thirty minutes	• Patient can quickly resume normal activities
• Proven medication	• Doctor can prescribe it with confidence
• Low incidence of side effects	• Doctor will not be bothered by telephone Calls from patients about side effects

Next prompt for acceptance: "Doctor, is there any reason you would not prescribe XYZ aspirin for your next patient with mild pain?" Then close: "Will you prescribe XYZ aspirin to all of your patients today with mild pain?"

Of course, there are many ways you could finesse or alter the above selling situations. This is short and to the point. Each describes what you should explore first, listen carefully, present features and benefits, urge for acceptance, and close.

> **TIP:** *Clip and save prescription drug advertisements from magazines. Medical journals are the best source for this information. Find an advertisement for a medication manufactured by the company with which you are interviewing. Bring the article to the interview and make a sales presentation to the interviewer based on the advertised product. Use the advertisements as your sales "visual aid," and make a product presentation as if you were talking with a doctor. Be sure to practice ahead of time, and ask for coaching from an experienced pharmaceutical representative, if possible. Get the commitment from "the customer" to prescribe your "product."*

Note: Sometime the company will give you some sales aids to help with your presentation, but if the product is a significant product, go to their website (sometimes specifically for the product, not just the company) and pull up the main features and benefits that are stressed in the promotion. Print these out for your presentation and practice. In addition, call a few pharmacies, speak to a few pharmacist, learn what the cost is for a prescription to the consumer (you can check online pharmacies with NABP certification), and ask the pharmacist who are the largest competitors in this therapeutic class of drugs.

Open your presentation by asking the interviewer (physician) what they use for treating this disease or condition. Use the pharmaceuticalsales.com inc. algorithm™ to assist you on the next page. Usually its one of three things, efficacy (how well it works), safety (low amount of side effects) and/or price (what it cost the patient). After you have determined this, then focus your features of your product that reach this need. You will always come across some objection in role-play (just to see how you handle them). Take your time, take a deep breath, and ask them to explain a little further how this fits into their (the physician's) treatment decision. The more they (interviewer or physician) speak the better. Finally, summarize, from what features and benefits the physician desire, and how your product accomplishes this. Then ask them to try the product (a trail) on the next 5-12 patients. Make sure you gain some closure here (demonstrating your aptitude for sales), for this is the most important part of the exercise, asking them to use your product.

52) What interests you least about the Pharmaceutical Sales Representative position?

Example: "I have done plenty of networking in the area of pharmaceutical sales, and I have not encountered anything I consider as negative. Some Pharmaceutical Representatives that I have networked with have commented about waiting to see physicians, or the paperwork, or parking. I understand that these are all parts of the job, and there is a positive way to manage it, such as using downtime in waiting rooms to increase my product knowledge."

53) Respond to a physician stating, "Your product is too expensive."

"Cost is a common objection in sales, and is relative to the perceived value of the product. I believe with excellent product knowledge and persuasive selling skills, I would highlight the features and benefits of the medication over competitive therapies, and increase the value of the product in the physician's eyes. The best medication at the best price—that's a bargain!"

54) How do you believe you would develop your knowledge of a physician's needs in prescribing a drug therapy?

The interviewer is not looking for any one specific answer, but wants to see your poise, confidence, and sales skills. Obviously, if you have not worked in pharmaceutical sales, you will not have detailed answers. However, your industry research will give you some solid answers.

Example: "Listening, as in all sales, is the tool to uncover the needs of the customer (physician). Often, the customer will volunteer information, or offer open-ended questions that help me clarify my comments to increase his knowledge. I may also assume that many needs are common to many physicians and begin by addressing one specifically."

55) How would you deal with an angry receptionist or nurse in the physician's office, who was preventing you from seeing the physician?

In this situation, it is best to exhibit empathy. If an office is busy, as is common, it may mean that you have to return at a more suitable time. State that you understand the situation and request a better time for you to call back that day or that week. Sometimes, as in all sales, a client may take out their job frustration on a sales representative. You will show great sales maturity when you can diffuse such a situation and not take it personally. You are developing a long-term relationship. The customer is always right!

56) Tell me about a time you have failed.

This question and many like it are seeking information about what may appear to be negative answers. Be aware of the concept of "balance" during an interview. If an interview is going very well and the interviewer is beginning to believe you are a qualified candidate, he or she may start looking for balance. They will do this by looking for the human side of you, and this is a step forward. Your response helps them avoid concluding that you are "too good to be true," which could create a letdown for the manager after you are hired. It is okay to be human with your answers, and provide an example of when you feel you have failed. Make it a job-related answer, not personal. Also, incorporate how you dealt with the failure and how you learned to turn it into success.

pharmaceuticalsales.com inc sales algorithm™

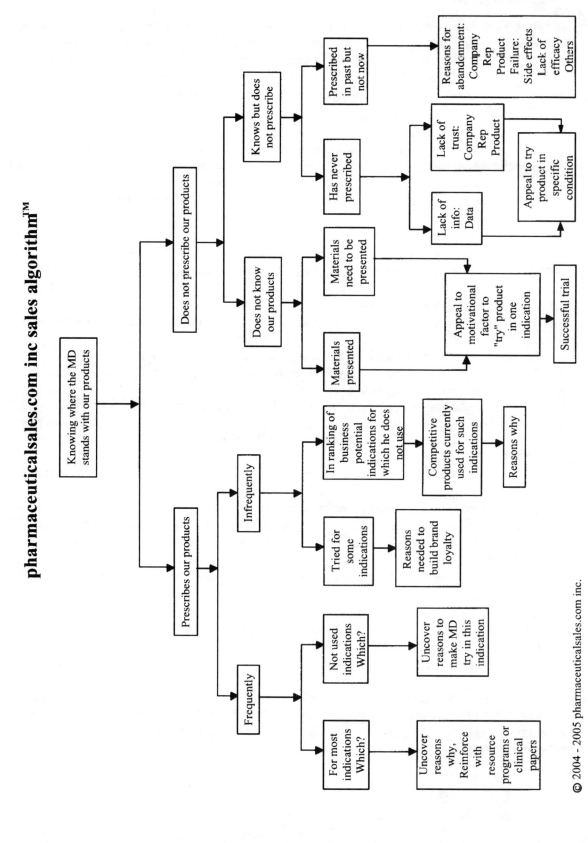

57) How would you differentiate yourself among the many sales representatives calling on the same doctor?

This question is seeking creativity and familiarity with the daily role of the sales representative. First of all, use something about yourself that already makes you stand out—sense of humor, clinical or technical expertise, an avocation that can be shared such as cooking or golf. Then choose a solid skill necessary for top performance such as product knowledge—you will set yourself apart by providing value; also mention your excellent follow through on commitments, questions, etc.

58) How do you handle change on the job?

This question is looking for a healthy attitude towards the only constant in any pharmaceutical position—change! If you do not work well with change, you are interviewing for the wrong job. To answer this question successfully, as with all your responses, include an example of when and how you were confronted with a change and the way you handled it. Common changes you will encounter in pharmaceuticals (and almost any sales role) can vary from realignments in territories, to new products or products being pulled from the market, sales teams, managers, computer systems, sampling regulations and even company mergers. Your best attitude is that change is healthy and good; your approach is to always discern what you can and cannot control; always take a long-term view; set a good example for your colleagues by keeping them on track, too. Successful representatives stay focused on goals and opportunities. This requires flexibility and resilience; qualities that are also crucial for managers. You will be remembered for your abilities to work successfully in a constantly changing environment.

59) What would you do to get more time in front of busy doctors?

This is a good question to test your knowledge of the customer. Nine out of ten sales calls last less than two minutes. That job fact is not likely to change. You will need to follow two different directions with your answer. First, acknowledge that you know sales calls to physicians are less than two minutes and some are actually only a few seconds. This is not the end of the world, however, because doctors do everything quickly. They spend short periods multi-tasking, and are used to getting and giving information quickly and clearly. You must always be prepared to deliver your sales messages in the same manner. That takes excellent product knowledge and lots of practice. Try to extend the time of the call by presenting information the physician needs; this requires knowledge of that doctor's specific needs for their clientele, or by asking an engaging question on the disease or therapy you would like them to focus on at that time.

60) Sales representatives spend a good portion of the day behind the wheel. What would you do with that time?

This question will assess your organization and planning skills, self-motivation, and self-improvement skills. The obvious answer is listening to product or sales motivation tapes to educate yourself on the job, products, and selling skills. A good example would be CMR courses (Certified Medical Representative). You should include the obvious, but also set yourself apart by including this approach: efficient management of the territory to reduce windshield time. By taking time to plan each week and each day, you will know where to go and when to make best use of your own time and cut down on time spent in traffic.

61) How do you balance your work and family or non-work activities?

This question is looking for planning, setting goals, and prioritization. The pharmaceutical sales position requires 8-10 calls per day plus planning time, follow-up letters and memos, administrative reporting, etc. Your time selling is only part of the situation. For many representatives, this means working at home in the evenings at the expense of family or personal time. You will probably already have your own strategies for managing your off time. In addition, make the point that you prioritize what you need to do versus less critical activities. Though selling time is top priority, you also take advantage of downtime during the day to complete tasks. You do this by bringing materials such as clinical reprints to study while waiting in offices. You use your computer at lunch to complete memos or reports. You keep current with tasks so you do not fall behind. Therefore, you are free to enjoy your family time without being burdened by unfinished work.

62) How do you develop relationships with your customers?

The best approach is understanding and trust. Personal relationships are built on these precepts just as business and customer relationships are. Learn as much as you can about your customer's business, and about them personally; this is the best way to understand and address their needs. To develop trust, you always keep commitments and you provide objective information. That may mean including the negative aspects of your product. You do not emphasize negatives, but fair balance is especially important with pharmaceutical products. Your customer knows there are downsides to virtually all medications and still prescribes them. They need to know what to watch for and this will go a long way to gain their trust. In your answer, include an example of how you learn about your customers (what questions you ask, research you do, etc.) and a time when you gave fair balance about your product in a sales presentation.

63) How do you work on teams?

This question can take many forms, but the answer is always regarding how you work with others and manage team conflict. It is vital for Pharmaceutical Representatives to work well on teams because so many products are co-promoted by other representatives, divisions within your company, or even by other companies. This requires excellent communication and coordination. Your answer must include an example of how you demonstrated team skills:

• Respecting the differences in others.

• Knowing that not everyone approaches the job the same way.

• Discovering each person's professional goals on a team.

• Knowing each person's family history, brothers, sisters, parents' occupation, etc.

• Recognizing their goals are often not the same, and may even conflict, with the job.

• State how you develop a common team goal on which to focus.

• Recognizing individual goals including establishing dialog and agreed upon methods of communication such as meetings, email, voice mail, time line's and conference calls.

• Your ability to resolve conflict.

• Always try to use specific situations.

64) What do you think is the most important factor for success as a Pharmaceutical Representative?

This question is looking for your level of knowledge and understanding of the position of pharmaceutical sales. As a side note, people generally answer this with an aspect of the job that they themselves do well. This is not necessarily a conscious process, and most managers are not aware of this connection. For the manager in the know, however, this question can be a way to identify what you consider your strength to be. There is no silver bullet answer for this one. Safe answers would be any of the core competencies listed in this guide. For example, "focus on results," or "positive attitude," or "knowledge of your products and customers" would be fine. As you give your answer, preempt the next logical question by also explaining why you chose that factor as the most important. Give an example of how you demonstrated that behavior in a current or previous job.

65) What do you expect the hardest part of being a Pharmaceutical Representative will be?

This question is looking for job knowledge first, and whether you know enough about the job to imagine what the biggest challenge would be. It also gives an indication of where you might have a developmental requirement that the manager will want to address in the future. That is not necessarily a negative—just more information the manager needs for the decision. Everyone has strengths and weaknesses and the manager seeks to identify these in serious candidates. The safe answers is, "access to the doctor," but follow your answer with ideas or what you would do to gain access to the doctor. Insight has previously provided answers to this question.

66) If a competitor moves your samples, what should you do?

Consult the nurse or office manager, whoever is in charge of the drug sample closet. State that your samples have been moved and ask for their suggestions as to what to do about it. Do not jump to conclusions that it was a competitor, even if you believe that is the case. Allow the office personnel to offer information since it may have been the staff or the doctor who moved your samples. Do not explicitly badmouth a competitor. This strategy will often result in the office personnel taking your side and providing a solution that will help you sell the most. It will also allow you to have more selling time; your professionalism will be highly regarded.

67) A nurse or physician gets angry with you and says they are too busy to see you. What do you do? Because this is a long-term relationship, you should remind yourself that everyone is allowed to have a bad day at the office. In a professional tone, agree that their schedules can be hectic and offer to return
- a more convenient time. Although you may have already been waiting a long time, showing poise in this situation makes you very welcome in the office. Being confrontational will aggravate the customer. When offering to return, you can often end up having more time with the doctor because they will remember that they made a commitment to see you later. You should also try to set an actual appointment. Appointment or not, it will be harder for them to turn you away the next time. Of course, when you return, you would remind them that they had suggested this was the best time to come back.

> **TIP:** *You may be asked to describe what you would do in a very specific on-the-job situation for which you have no basis for an answer—because you are not yet a Pharmaceutical Rep. You can remain calm, buy time to think, and appear very professional. As a preface or introduction to your best guess answer, you will score extra points by starting off with the honest truth—that you are not sure how to answer an industry-specific question. The interviewer and you both know that you are not a Pharmaceutical Sales Representative and have no actual first-hand knowledge of the job. Therefore, you might begin the answer as follows, "As a new Representative, I may not be certain what to do in this situation. I would consult my manager or trainer if necessary before getting back to the customer with a correct response. Because you asked, here is one approach that I think would work, given the scenario you are describing." Then continue with your best response to the scenario.*

68) After meeting a doctor for the first time, and introducing yourself, what do you do next?

This question is looking for customer focus and selling skills. To answer it, describe the steps you take to understand the customer and establish trust. Even before establishing product needs, what is the best way to serve that individual in the long-term relationship? Determine the personality of the physician (such as talkative and friendly versus technically oriented) and use the correct approach. Once you learn the right tactic, you will want to know more about the physician's practice of medicine in the areas of your products. Ask a series of questions (sales probes) to see what they prescribe for the various disease states for which your products are indicated. Why do they make those choices? Answers may include efficacy, side effect profile (safety), price, managed care recommendations, etc.

Only after that process will you know the best manner and which specific information to present on your products. Always state that you will add any suggestions from your trainer/manager to your selling techniques.

69) What would you do after entering a doctor's office for the first time then you are informed the physicians does not see Pharmaceutical Representatives?

The manager is looking for your thought process as you evaluate and plan in this situation. This is more important than the specific answer. Focus your answer on how you would gather information and determine a course of action.

First, you have to know why you went into that office. Based on your pre-call planning (from prescription data, notes from previous representatives, etc.), is this a valuable target? Are you prospecting a potential target just because you are in the area? Next, you should get more information from the office to better plan your strategy for this doctor. Inquire about the policy. Have they seen representatives in the past? Is this a new policy? Why did it change? Are there any suggestions they will offer in terms of how to best reach the physician? Ask about when and where the doctor makes hospital rounds. Ask how he prefers to obtain information about drug products, and how he meets his continuing medical education requirements.

Once you leave the office, decide whether this physician can have an impact on your territory and what actions are appropriate to gain access to them. You should tap into your resources—ask experienced representatives, successful representatives, and your manager for ideas and tactics they have used. This may include seeing doctors outside the office, such as at the hospital. You may decide to provide product literature, clinical reprints, studies, and samples without seeing the doctor—using creative ways to call attention to it. You may also use mailings, educational programs, and entertainment events. On the other hand, you may discover that this physician has a very low potential for your products and remove them from your call list. Either way, research and due diligence are required on your part.

70) During your first month on the job, you meet with a doctor who just recently switched to a competitor's product. How do you persuade them to come back to your product?

This is simple! Go back to the basics. Approach this doctor as you would any new customer and understand why the physician switched. Was it efficacy, safety, price, MCO recommendations? It may be as straightforward as the lack of a sales representative calling on them to provide needed services such as starter samples and updated information on the product. You will have to gain the physician's trust that you will take good care of your new client.

71) When presented with a last minute, unavoidable change to your itinerary, such as preparing for a new product launch, what planning, and coordination would you undertake?

This comes down to solid time management to make sure that you meet your commitments. You may have to work extra hard for a week making extra calls to cover your territory and keep up with new responsibilities. State that you are willing to make these calls in the early morning or evening if appropriate. Use time in the car and during one or two evenings or weekends to study. You may possibly even see some physicians on a Saturday morning. The interviewer wants to know how you can handle a little work pressure, so show them that it would not faze you, that you have the commitment to your territory, and product knowledge to be a top performer. You would also talk it over with your manager and other team members to assist in setting appropriate goals and priorities.

72) You go to one of your regular physician's office and are introduced to a new physician in the practice. How do you approach the new doctor?

Introduce yourself with a handshake and present your card. Then use the same approach as any new customer—probe to develop an understanding of the doctor's preferences in how you can best be of service to her with her specific interests, personality, or behavioral style in mind. Understanding the doctor may include researching information regarding her background, when and how she prefers to see reps, and her attitude towards your products. Then go into a sales presentation that describes features and benefits, and reply to her concerns or objections, and when ready, close the sale.

73) A doctor tells you he will not prescribe your product because its cost is $40 more than your competitor's product. What do you do?

The obvious answer to the cost objection is to clarify misunderstandings the customer may have on this issue including managed care formulary and reimbursement data. If the doctor has this information correct and you are dealing with a true cost objection, the next step is to outweigh it using patient and physician benefits of the product as well as with the service you provide. The cost of a product is relative to its perceived value. Highlight the features and benefits of this product as compared to the competition to demonstrate that while your product may cost more in the short term, it is ultimately a more cost effective way of treating patients overall.

74) It is your first week on the job. How do you get to see the doctors who are a priority?

At this point, the list of priority doctors is based on a territory analysis list. First, plan your day to have all the tools and supplies necessary to be effective. Next, map out the most efficient route to make the best use of your time. Consult your counterparts and manager for any advice as to the office protocol of these priority doctors. Once at an office, introduce yourself to the nurse or receptionist presenting them with your card and the name of your products. Probe for office protocol and any other information that would be important, and then ask specifically to see the doctor. If it is not possible to see the doctor at that time, arrange the best time to return and follow through exactly as agreed upon.

75) You are on a team with four other sales representatives. For the past few weeks, you have done all the planning of lunch meetings with the doctors. In your opinion, your teammates are not doing their share of the work. What do you do?

This common question is similar to "How well do you work on teams?" First, bring it to the attention of your teammates and get their perception of the situation as you work out a solution. It may be a simple matter of asking for more help from them. If that does not bring about a resolution, the next step would be to take it to the attention of your manager for advice. There may be something going on that you are not aware of which is preventing the others on your team from assisting you with lunch meetings. Realize that you may have set a higher standard of expectations for yourself. Lead by example.

76) Why are you thinking of leaving your current position?

This question is looking for what motivates you and your level of knowledge about the Pharmaceutical Rep position. Include positive statements that indicate your desire for challenge, increased responsibility, achievement, professional and personal growth, compensation for your effort, etc. Your answer should convey that you have done extensive research and discovered that the job of pharmaceutical sales is the ideal fit for you. For example, "Though there are many aspects of my current position that I enjoy, I have found that my skills and abilities are best suited to pharmaceutical sales. I desire the challenge for professional and personal growth within the industry and particularly with XYZ Pharmaceuticals."

77) Are you working at the last organization listed on your resume?

This is easy if the answer is, "Yes." If not, answer the question honestly, with confidence and in a matter-of-fact tone. Today's economy has brought about many job changes. Being "between jobs" does not carry the stigma it once did now that we operate in a constantly changing business environment. An example of an answer could be, "I was one of nine individuals not retained with the organization. Our profits did not meet expectations. There were many cutbacks within all departments. Due to my tenure, I was not retained." Then stop and allow the interview to move forward from there.

78) Will you have a tough time becoming acquainted with a new industry after being with the same organization for a while?

Not at all, I have worked for several different managers and interacted with numerous departments during my time with ABC Incorporated. I am very flexible and learn quickly. I know I can contribute to your sales team from the start."

79) You have had numerous positions over the past four years. How do I know that you will stay at XYZ Pharmaceutical Company?

Job changes are always good if they involve and increase in challenge, responsibility, or compensation. Show the benefit and progress of your career moves. Some factors may have been out of your control. Examples are acquisitions, mergers, layoffs, relocation, etc. Be confident, direct, and honest in your reply. For example: "With each new position, I have progressed in achieving my career goals. Over the past several months, I have redefined these goals due to extensive research, networking, completing pharmaceutical preceptorships, etc. I know that pharmaceutical sales are exactly where I want to achieve these goals and XYZ Pharmaceutical Company is the company in which I will excel."

80) How long have you been looking for a pharmaceutical sales position?

Here is an opportunity for you to describe your research and extensive knowledge of this industry. If you are interviewing with another pharmaceutical company, disclose where you are in the interview process (second, third, final interview, or offer stage). This response will evoke the competitive nature in the interviewer. Keep the time you have been looking as short as possible because managers may feel that you may have been passed over for a particular reason.

81) You seem like a great candidate, why haven't you secured an offer in the industry to date?

This is a hardball question. It is meant to see if you can be thrown off your game. There is no right or wrong answer. Remain confident. Display your knowledge of the industry and companies with whom you have interviewed. Include offers if you have had any. For example, "I have had an offer with ABC Pharma, but the geography and the timing were not right for me. The position you have available is perfect, and I am ready to make a commitment to your organization."

82) How did you do on your last performance review? What strengths and areas of improvement did you manager observe?

This is a repeat of "tell me your weaknesses." Choose and explain the steps you took to improve yourself. Examples may be that you are impatient with the others in your department, or you tend to take on too much. You have remedied this by gaining a better understanding of other people's work habits, developing time lines and new tactics of time management. If you have copies of excellent past performance reviews, show them, and leave a copy at the conclusion of your interview.

83) Tell me about the best manager you have ever had?

This is time to give the most praise, because a hiring manager wants to see that you can interact well with management. Explain your position, how you followed your manager's direction, how management monitored your progress, and gave the appropriate praise and comments.

84) Tell me about the worst manager you have ever had?

Using the same strategies in discussing your weaknesses, avoid stating that you have ever had a bad manager. "I have learned from all of the managers I have had in my professional career. If I had to pick a particular competency in a manager that could have been demonstrated better, it may have been enthusiasm and keeping our team motivated."

85) Describe in one word what selling means to you.

Many different words can be used, but stick to the request for one word. Suggestions are value, challenge, satisfaction, integrity, relationship, or success.

86) How is your driving record?

This question is a practical matter for the company to determine eligibility for hire. It is asked in the screening interview and is always a question on the employment application. Your driving record will always be part of the background checks. Some companies will run the background check before making an offer, while others will make the offer first, contingent on the background checks. Since driving is a requirement of the job, and you will drive the company car, the insurance requirements demand that you have a good record. Moving violations are usually no problem unless you have a license suspension or revocation on your record. However, DWI and DUI's in the past three to four years may eliminate you from consideration for many companies. The best way to answer this question is to know what is and is not on your record. Include in your answer only felony or misdemeanor convictions, which is normally all that is requested. Citations such as moving violations can be requested. If you do not know what your record shows and you suspect there may be something there, find out. Know what your record states and the state's laws in terms of how long infractions remain on your record, and always be straightforward. When required, admit your mistake, what you have learned from it, and that your record since then has been impeccable.

87) Have you ever had any financial difficulties?

When you fill an application, usually you sign a release for an employer to check your credit history. One must under the 1972 Fair Credit and Reporting Act. So, do not try to avoid this one, be up, with no lengthy details. "Filling bankruptcy is something that was not a pleasant experience, but I have learned much through the process and I am well on track to an excellent credit rating.

88) Your product and price is very similar as a competitor. How would you sell your product?

This is when it comes down to relationships. A person buying from people applies in pharmaceuticals just as any other sales venture (relationships). Give examples of how you develop rapport, provide excellent service, follow-up, call frequency to establish physician habits, the value you add, and that you close for the business. Often, this business goes to the sales representative who both earns the right to ask for it and does ask for it.

89) A doctor says that she is going to stop writing prescriptions for your drug and is switching to the competition. What do you do?

This question, like many of this type, is looking for your selling skills. While this is at first, a bad situation to encounter with a customer there is a positive aspect. Because the physician bothered to let you know she is switching products, it indicates a trusting relationship and is an invitation to talk about it. The doctor has probably heard something negative about your product, and now needs reassurance to rebuild confidence in you and your product. You will no doubt have a detailed discussion beginning with asking all the questions and listening well. Collect all the concerns, objections and misunderstandings the doctor may have before going off on a tangent. Use your best listening and probing skills with non-defensive posture and verbal tone. Once you have all the information, you can address it.

90) What do you expect is the most difficult or challenging part of being a Pharmaceutical Representative?

This question is seeking your knowledge of the Pharmaceutical Sales position and if you have the skills and confidence to be successful. There is no right or wrong answer here, but "physician access" or "time with the physician" is a solid answer. Do not wait for the next question, "What would you do about it?" Answer that question at the same time.

91) What would you do to gain access to "no see" physicians and spend more time key physicians?

This will be a common question since it is the biggest challenge you will face. Practice your answers before you interview. Some of the obvious responses are:

- Contact the doctor at hospital displays.
- Invite him to educational programs.
- Discover how they spend their free time.
- Offer to entertain the doctor and a spouse or guest (within company guidelines).
- Always provide new information and value on your calls.
- Have other "hard-to-see" doctors give you a recommendation.
- Call on the doctor with increased frequency to better your chances of getting in.
- Develop rapport with the staff and make a "friend" who will give you the inside track.
- Acknowledge this challenge will be met with creativity, persistence, and patience.

There are no "magic answers," every doctor is different. State that you would take a long-term view of this situation to develop a specific plan of action for the less available physicians in your territory. You know that even doctors with a "no see" policy will see certain sales representatives who offer them value, and whom they respect. You may consider writing to the doctor and asking for a one-time meeting that will take no more than five minutes of their time. Promise that if you do not provide value to his expectations you will not ask him again. When you do get access, always request permission for the next meeting before you leave. Finally, know that your relationship skills are critical and you must show genuine concern and interest in the physician. Show confidence and believe in your ability to influence that customer.

92) A doctor is resistant to trying your product. What would you do?

Physicians "buy" like any other group of individuals. Some will respond quickly and try whatever is new. These "early adopters" are mostly focused on effectiveness of the product. Others are cautious and wait for information from those who did try it first. These "late adopters" are more focused on safety (side effects). The majority of physicians are in between these two extremes. Once you know you are dealing with a late adopter, you can approach him or her accordingly. In addition to rapport building, probing, and the listening skills that you would always use, this doctor may respond if you narrow the product to a specific patient type. Gain commitment for that patient only. Discover which doctors he associates with, either professionally or personally, who prescribes your product. Knowing that other doctors prescribe your product may give him the confidence he needs to try it.

93) Your counterpart is having problems with his day-to-day responsibilities. His sales results are showing it and affecting your share as well. What do you do?

If you are an experienced sales representative, you should offer your assistance in a positive manner. Maybe something you know, or a way you approach your position, can help this individual. This shows your competencies around "teamwork." If this has failed and you feel that the individual is harming your district sales, then it is a concern that you will want to address with your manager in an appropriate manner.

94) You have spent all of your month's expenses on a luncheon with three doctors and their staff. Just before the lunch, one of the staff members says that two of the doctors will not be there. What do you do?

You have to be flexible and creative in this situation. Obviously, you are going to follow through on your commitment. On the bright side, you will have more time with the doctor who is there. Next, you can leverage the situation with that doctor and the staff by asking what they would suggest could be done about meeting with those who did not join your group. Never simply excuse it. Create urgency or mild tension by reacting in a serious manner. Let them know you are out on a limb financially to provide this lunch. This will put them in the position of trying to help you out. They may offer to schedule appointments with the missing doctors to make up for it. If not, ask for an appointment or another way of accessing those doctors when they return.

95) Why should I hire you?

This is a typical "tough" question, but it is a great opportunity when you get it. Being prepared with more information will help you answer this by asking for the job. By this point in the interview, you may have already asked the manager what he or she is looking for in an ideal candidate. If not, this is the time to ask. You will show confidence in your demeanor by looking right back at the interviewer and asking, "To help me focus my answer, what are you looking for in the ideal candidate?" Then tailor your full response to his or her "hot buttons." In general, you will hit the core competencies for the job. For example, "I have demonstrated the drive to achieve (as evidenced by previous sales success); I have shown you that I am creative, persistent, self-motivated, and a fast learner. I have thoroughly researched the industry and this company and know what the position requires. I am excited about the challenges ahead and am confident that I will be a successful member of your team. I want the job! Is there anything else you need to know in order to make me the offer? Great!"

96) Describe yourself in one word.

This question is not as important as it sounds. The intention is to see how you think on your feet. As long as you maintain composure and deliver a one-word answer, you have succeeded. Keep a word in mind so you can deliver it without hesitation. Pick something you can back up with specific examples of when you demonstrated that aspect or behavior. Here are some ideas:

Creative	Persistent	Consistent
Sincere	Determined	Competitive
Motivated	Energetic	Tenacious

97) Since you do not have sales experience what makes you believe you will be successful in pharmaceutical sales?

Your answer should begin by stating the only indicator of future success is past performance. Then make the case for success in sales by demonstrating that you have succeeded in professional and personal endeavors that translate into sales. Many roles and responsibilities will transition well—anytime you had to convince another person on a course or action, way of thinking, for example. Or anytime you have taught something, made a presentation, worked in groups or on teams, debated a point successfully, completed a project, you have developed the competencies for success in sales.

98) Do you know the name of the CEO of our company?

Make a note of before each interview by visiting the appendix and double checking the company website. .

99) We are a rather small pharmaceutical company here at TDB Pharma, with only one product, and a couple in research and development, versus some of the big Pharma companies with 3-5 products selling

over a billion dollars a year, and hundreds in development. Why would you want to work for TDB Pharma?

I have always enjoyed a challenge, and the ability to be unique in the marketplace. With TDB though many physicians are not yet aware of the company and its products, I see that as a benefit, for they are interested in something new. In addition, I enjoy the fact that the salesforce is small and there is not two to three other representatives calling on the same physicians and having the same territory. The territory is mine, my challenge, and therefore, will be my success.

100) How comfortable will you be with co-marketing XYZ's new product *CuraFlu* with ABC Pharma (for example)?

Many times different companies will be selling the same drug. However, only one company has developed the product and received FDA approval, but the product may need more "sales power" than some companies have (headcount). Looking through the Appendix, and you will see numerous examples where a listed drug and in parentheses, another company is mentioned (co-marketing agreement). State that with most sales efforts, the more "voice" that is available for the marketing, the more success the product will have. An additional 300-500 representative can often make or break a product upon launch (with the first six months being critical).

101) There are numerous candidates for this opening with pharmaceutical sales experience, why should I hire you for the position?

State that you have the core competencies by which to succeed in this position (refer again back to the core competencies earlier in the book). You have a demonstrated record of accomplishment in your education, prior employment. You have the advantage of training me at the level that XYZ pharmaceutical wants their representatives to obtain. I have acquired any bad habits, or dissatisfaction in the industry that needs to be changed.

102) How does a Pharmaceutical Representative differentiate between a sales call and a sample drop?

Often when the physician is in need of your samples for their patients and having an extremely busy day, the nurse or receptionist will suggest that they just have time to sign your form (or computer). In this case, you actually just leave samples (sample drop), and witness the signature versus when you spend a few minutes talking to the physician about your product, features, benefits, indications, dosage, side effects, etc., (this is a sales call). Respect the physicians/nurse/receptionist request, show you are a professional, smile, and suggest gaining more time on your next visit.

103) In your education and prior positions, do you have any examples where you have had to learn technical information?

Most of us have had some science, statistics, and math courses in our education, develop this for your answer. State that you enjoyed this type of coursework and this is one strong attraction of pharmaceutical sales. If you have been in a position where you have learned technical features and benefits of your product, you may use that.

104) During your sales presentation, what do you feel is most important, the opening or the close?

While it is always vital to gain a physicians interest during a sales call in "the opening", there are many other aspects that are just as vital. Understanding misconceptions, answering objections, presenting clinical data, therapeutic and price comparisons, etc. After covering these issues with proficiency, then a Pharmaceutical Representative can ask a physician for their commitment to use your product, (close the sale). Closing the sale is always the most important factor in sales, great openings mean nothing if a Pharmaceutical Representative never asks for a commitment (the close). Just as your interview, your final "close" (asking for the position) is far more important than your initial comments (though vital, not too many candidates are been hired for a great greeting).

105) How do you respond to me if I told you, your sales presentation today was terrible?

First, ask the interviewer to expand on their statement. They did say "if", correct? Do not loose your composure, then state, "I would have to ask what areas of my sales presentation was there a problem?" This is something that you are going to face in the field with your manager quite often. After a sales call (and we hope they state it more tactfully) a District Managers job is to analyze your performance, coach you, and improve your selling skills. If this is a valid concern, it gives you a chance to revisit your presentation, and address any misconceptions they may have about your statements. Often, this is just a ploy to test your nerves, hang in there.

106) How would you rate me as an interviewer?

If the interview has gone well in your eyes, state though it has been slightly stressful I feel excellent, I feel I have been able to demonstrate to you my competencies that are required in pharmaceutical sales. If the interview has not gone well, now is your time to revisit the area were you may felt that you were not at your best. State, "Very well, but I would like to revisit the topic of…." If the District Sales Manager was poor, keep it to yourself.

A NOTE ON THE PSYCHOLOGICAL TEST

Though not very common in pharmaceutical interviews, I have heard of some organizations using a third party (to screen candidates) using some of the many available psychological tests. The tests usually are written test, sometimes over the phone, and other times, face-to-face. Be ready for the common statement, "There is no right or wrong answer, just answer the questions how you feel." When you take a test such as this, put yourself in your "interview best" mode. The "corporate way" are the answers you want to give, not your "personal feelings or preferences." I am not telling you to be dishonest, but picture yourself as the #1 Pharmaceutical Representative in the company (which you want to be), and answer the questions from that viewpoint. Ask yourself, "What has my networking, research, preceptorships, and education taught me? What is the most professional way I would act or select in this situation? What you would like to see in response to the questions if you were the employer? Approaching these tests with this in mind will get you through this requirement successfully, if presented.

PROFESSIONAL ATTIRE

Your efforts in networking, research, and resumes have met with success. You have just been called for an initial interview with the District Manager of XYZ Pharmaceutical Company. It is time to get dressed. You scrutinize your wardrobe for the perfect look, one that says, "I am the qualified individual for this position." Why are your attire and appearance more important than your attributes, skills, and abilities? Because there is that one hurdle that you must cross with every new encounter—the critical first impression.

Sociologists use the term "halo effect" to describe the first 30 seconds of a meeting. In those first 30 seconds, people generally make up their minds about you. They decide whether they have just met someone who is competent, genuine, and "on top of it" or not. Your dress is a nonverbal communication as to what you think about yourself, your attitude toward business, your goals, and how well you regard the other individuals with whom you are meeting. Right or wrong, decisions about your ability and character are based upon the interviewer's response to your appearance. It is assumed that anyone who can handle personal details well will be just as meticulous with the details of the job. Thus, your goal is to create the halo effect for yourself. Professional attire, an engaging manner, a firm handshake, and an air of energy and vitality will set the stage on which you will perform to your highest level.

Beyond first impressions, the way you dress indicates your sense of professional judgment and establishes your credibility. While you are selling yourself orally during your interview nonverbal communication, including attire will either reinforce what you are saying or undermine your own words.

Recent college graduates may not yet own expensive business attire. Shop for deals on wool fabric suits, but spend the extra money to get it tailored to fit correctly. You can get away with a lesser quality suit by wearing higher quality accessories, such as shoes and ties. The hiring process for pharmaceutical sales may require two or three interviews. Be prepared with two interview suits, if possible. If not, accessorize with ties, shirt styles (men keep it all white), and shoes for a slightly different look. Finally, make sure your suit is clean and freshly pressed.

Putting time, energy, and expense into your professional appearance will always pay you back. Think of it as an investment in yourself and your career. You will command authority and assume credibility beyond that which you currently possess. "Looking the part" is critical during the interview process. The interviewer will begin to visualize you in the job instead of just another interviewing candidate. Never underestimate the power of the first impression. Meticulous attention to your appearance will put you at an advantage.

Many recruiters will tell you to construct the "brag book", a binder or portfolio that contains your resume, performance reviews, letters of recommendation, sales awards, any letters or recognition, etc. Please do not consume and control your interview by paging through one of these brag books. Yes, have one for a reference but let the interviewer control the interview and ask the questions. I cannot tell you how many "brag books" I had the pleasure of being put through in 20 years of management (similar to home movies). Often by the time the candidate was done, I was finished also, never conducting the interview.

The following are guidelines for women followed by those for men.

WOMEN'S GUIDELINES FOR INTERVIEWING DRESS

- No outfit is more effective for an interview than the matched suited skirt. Research has shown the most successful colors are black, navy, and gray, and you should pair it with a high-necked white or ivory silk blouse. Pantyhose should always be lighter in color of your clothing. A medium-healed pump is safest. Shoes should be well polished, clean, and darker than the suit.
- Practicality dictates that a woman may carry a purse as well as a briefcase. You must manage both comfortably when shaking hands, sitting down, etc. A briefcase only is quite acceptable, as is a nice leather portfolio. A leather portfolio is good for note taking during the inter view, but a new legal pad will do just fine. You will need a briefcase for your interviewing files and materials, and it should be leather and the best you can afford. Avoid company names or logos on your accessories.
- Your hair should be neat and off the shoulders in a manageable style. Avoid bows and complicated styles. Your hair should draw attention to and complement you face.
- A touch of makeup is appropriate. Light makeup will enhance a woman's professional image. The goal is to wear makeup without looking made up.
- Nails should be short and rounded. The only appropriate nail colors are clear or natural; a French manicure is also acceptable and distinctive.
- Jewelry should be simple and professional; avoid anything that will draw attention away from you. Gold or silver chains are smart. If worn, lapel pins should be elegant. Earrings lend authority and professionalism, and should be small and simple, no bigger than a quarter. Dangles or hoops are inappropriate.
- Wear a nice analog style watch (not digital) because analog watches project more of a traditional/formal business appearance versus a sports/digital watch; a wedding ring, if married, with or without the engagement ring. No other rings.
- Use a fine gold or sterling pen.
- There should be no perfume or fragrance. Many individuals have chemical sensitivities that can be aggravated by hair spray or perfume.

MEN'S GUIDELINES FOR INTERVIEWING DRESS

- The two-piece wool business single-breasted suit is the foundation. Research shows that the most authoritative colors are dark blue and dark gray. These two colors look good on everyone. Use a traditional, conservative style versus a European designer one. The fit is more important than the quality of the wool, so spend your money on the tailoring. Button the top button while standing or walking, unbutton it when sitting. Your jackets pocket flaps should always remain out of the pockets.
- Shirts should be solid white and all cotton for interviews. Use a straight collar instead of a button-down collar for the conservative, slightly more formal look. Avoid collars with snaps or ones that require collar pins. Your shirt should be professionally laundered, and starched for a crisp look. Pens go in the coat pocket, not the shirt pocket.
- Wear a new, fashionable conservative silk tie. Choose a solid colored tie that complements, not matches, your suit. Good colors are maroon, crimson, or navy blue (except with a navy blue suit). Patterned ties such as stripes, foulards, or small dots are acceptable. Avoid paisleys, prints, club ties, insignias, or depiction of any identifiable cartoon, or other characters. Skip the pocket-hand kerchief. The bottom point of the tie should line up with the middle of the belt buckle. Do not wear a tie clasp or a pin of any kind.
- Avoid wearing an overcoat; it is cumbersome to handle.
- Avoid monogrammed belt buckles, or designer initials and monograms anywhere. A plain black leather belt will complement the navy or gray suit.

- Shoes should be good quality and newly polished. A laced, plain-toe or wing-tipped oxford is best. Tasseled loafers can project casualness. Error on the conservative side. Black and cordovan are appropriate colors. Socks should be over-the-calf or long enough to cover your legs when sitting or if your pant-leg rides up. Do not cross your legs during an interview. Use a solid colored sock in black for black shoes and in navy for cordovan shoes. In some areas of the United States, cowboy boots are not out of place for business wear, but are best avoided for interviewing.

- Hair should be short and neat. Beards and mustaches are a means of self-expression and identity. However, for the most professional look, be clean-shaven during your job search. You can always grow it back later.

- Wear a nice analog (not digital) wristwatch. Do not wear rubber sport watches. Never look at a watch during any interview. The only ring should be a wedding band, if married. Avoid other rings, bracelets, lapel pins, or other jewelry. Cuff links are fine if they are simple, plain gold. Use a pen of excellent quality and keep it handy in your coat pocket.

- Your briefcase should be professional, leather, well-polished and dark colored. A leather portfolio is especially valuable for taking notes during the interview. You will need a briefcase for the interviewing files and materials you have collected. Avoid company names or logos on your accessories.

- Men's fingernails should be short and rounded, clean and buffed to a shine. Trim and clean the cuticles for a detail-oriented look.

- There should be no cologne; avoid anything with a fragrance. Chemical sensitivities apply to many people.

[SAMPLE LETTER: INTERVIEW FOLLOW-UP]

October 26, 2004

Janet Lynn Jones
1234 West Drive
Salestown, MA 41124

Patrick Vick
District Manager
XYZ Pharmaceutical Corporation
1220 Burgess Avenue
Maplewood, MA 43128

Dear Mr. Vick,

Thank you for the opportunity to discuss the Sales Representative position with XYZ Pharmaceuticals. It was a pleasure meeting with you today.

I am excited about our conversation and am especially impressed with the autonomy given to each sales representative and the challenge that it offers. You are looking for a determined self-starter with a successful sales background. I am looking for a company that rewards individual effort.

A career in pharmaceutical sales at XYZ pharmaceuticals is an excellent match for my skills and career objectives. I really want this position; for I know that, I can make a significant contribution to your sales team.

Thank you again for you time and consideration. I look forward to hearing from you soon.

Sincerely,

Janet Lynn Jones

Chapter 7

Your Questions

This chapter provides you with ammunition and questions you could ask during the various stages of the interviewing process. Why should you be asking questions? The point to having your own questions to ask is twofold. First, you will demonstrate your preparation, awareness of the position, and communication skills. Second, you need to evaluate the person and company that you are considering joining, perhaps for your entire career.

There are two main questions. (1) Is the organization the best for you? (2) Can you work with, or for, this individual? You must answer each other's questions during the interview process to move forward and result in your employment.

This chapter offers twenty-five questions that are appropriate for you to ask the interviewer. Pharmaceuticalsales.com has listed the questions in the chronological order of the interview process. Avoid asking questions that are easily answered with a little independent research, such as visiting the company websites. It should be a given that you know basic information at least, such as the product names and indications. Change the style to match your own, and have fun with it!

Many of the following questions are similar to those you may have already asked in your networking. If you are already aware of information from your pharmaceuticalsales.com networking phase, interlace it into your interview process. As discussed in Chapters 4 and 5, presenting your knowledge about the company demonstrates preparedness and drive. For example, instead of asking the District Manager, "How many territories are in your district," use that piece of information as a lead-in to another question: "I understand there are twelve territories in your district (information from your networking). How does the open territory's performance compare with the other territories in the district?"

TIP: *Every interviewer usually concludes by saying, "Do you have any questions for me?" Prepare five to ten important questions that you want answered. It is completely acceptable to refer to your notes during the interview.*

SCREENING AND INITIAL INTERVIEWS

1. What qualifications and qualities are you looking for in the ideal candidate?
This is a critical question and must be the first one asked! Do not wait to ask it! The sooner you get the answer from the interviewer, the better job you can do tailoring your own statements to what the manager wants to hear. It uncovers the manager's "hot buttons," or the key characteristics in a job candidate. Ask this at the start of, or early in, the interview and repeat it for every different person with whom you interview. The answer is significant, and should guide you as you match your own qualifications and qualities to those the manager is looking for. Emphasize your attributes that respond to the stated requirements.

2. How did this position become available with your company?
The answer could be that it was opened due a promotion, transfer, expansion, or termination

3. I have completed many hours of research on a career in the pharmaceutical sales industry and your company. I am extremely interested in this position. When can we meet to discuss it in detail?
This is a solid close for the initial interview process. Be sure to mail a follow-up letter within 24 hours.

TIP: *Often, initial screening interviews are accomplished over the telephone. Be free of interruptions. Turn off call waiting by pressing 70 before the scheduled interview time. Have all information, notes, and questions in front of you.*

4. What is the geography of this territory?

Examples may be rural or metropolitan, certain cities, towns, or zip codes. The interviewer's answer may give you an opportunity to state that you are familiar with some of the various areas. Example: I attended school in Bryn Mawr, PA., and am very familiar with the area.

5. What are the major accounts in this territory? Who are the key customers?

This answer will tell you who brings in the most business in the district. Possibilities may include an individual or a group of specialists who are considered to be "thought leaders." These are the experts in a given specialty, and are highly respected by other physicians in the area. Their importance is due to this significant influence. Pharmaceutical companies assign responsibility for calling on these thought leaders to their best and most experienced representatives. Other examples could be a large university-based teaching institution that has an influence in the area, or perhaps a large retail pharmacy chain that is dominant in the district.

TIP: *One purpose of asking questions is to gain information. Another reason is to discover what is important to the interviewer. When you uncover something of significance in your interview with the District Manager, refer to that item in your follow-up letter. This demonstrates that you listen and comprehend what is important to your customer.*

6. What type of physician specialties do you target?

Examples: family practice, internal medicine, surgery, pediatrics, dermatology, psychiatry, allergy and immunology, rheumatology, obstetrics, oncology, and urology. A growing number of physicians concentrate their practices on pain management as well.

7. How many territories and representatives are there in this district?

Districts may average seven to twelve representatives. Regions may have five to seven districts. This is information you may already have from your networking contacts with a representative from this company.

8. What are the various divisions of the sales force?

Different pharmaceutical companies are similar in some ways and vary greatly in others. One area where they differ is in the structure of the sales force and the various divisions or groups within it. This answer gives you the sales specialties and challenging directions in which your career could go. Examples include a Hospital Sales Force, Diabetes Specialists, National Account Team, Managed Care Account Representatives, Governmental Affairs, and many others.

9. How is this territory performing to budget? How does it rank in the district?

You need to know the current state of the business in what may be your new territory. Is the territory operating at 10% below budget or 20% over budget? Whatever the answer, your goal is to improve upon it.

10. What is the total sales revenue of this territory? How many prescriptions are being written in this territory?

With this question, you are asking how many dollars worth of sales you will be responsible for when you take over the territory. The quantity of prescriptions is also significant because your goal will be to increase both dollar sales and prescription volume.

11. Describe the training program for new representatives to continue education and development programs.

You want to choose a company that is committed to training and development. You realize the importance that skills and education are to your success and career advancement. This question will communicate your desire for a continuous educational cycle throughout your career.

12. Are there any products that have been submitted to the Food and Drug Administration (FDA) for marketing approval or which are in Phase III of development?

From your research, you may already know the answer to this question. If so, mention what you know and ask if there is any news on how the product is coming along. Asking shows that you are seeking information on the company's future over the next several years. You want to choose a company that has a full pipeline of new products in the near future. It means the company is more stable and can withstand competition from other brand name and generic manufacturers. If a product has been submitted to the FDA, it is close to approval and may be launched to the market soon. If a product is in Phase III of development it is in final stages of human research and may soon be submitted to the FDA for the approval process. The FDA approval takes one to two years.

13. What products are in early stages of development (Phase I and Phase II)?

This answer provides you with a longer-term picture of the company's future. Phases I and II are conducted in the initial R&D process for newly discovered compounds. Phase I is conducted in the laboratory and in animals. Phase II begins small-scale safety testing on humans. District managers may not be aware of products in early development.

14. Which therapeutic areas or specific diseases does the company target for new product development?

Companies will specialize, much as physicians do, by concentrating their R&D efforts on a limited number of diseases. Are the targeted therapeutic areas (such as cardiac diseases, depression, or diabetes) similar to current treatments, or is the company expanding its research into other possible solutions? Do they have a focus for research? Does it match their product line? This question will uncover the general direction, or strategy of the organization.

15. Does the company co-market with another pharmaceutical company?

Co-marketing (also called co-promoting) is an agreement between two companies to promote the same product at the same time. Co-marketing usually involves a trade-off in which each company takes on one of the other company's products, though not necessarily at the same time. Example: XYZ Pharmaceutical Company is co-marketing a new antibiotic from Widget Pharmacia. Next year when XYZ Pharmaceutical Company introduces their new diabetes agent, Widget Pharmacia will co-promote it in return. This question can give you insight into how aggressive the company is in hitting the bottom line. Are they willing to use co-marketing arrangements to meet sales and profit objectives?

16. I like what I have learned about the company, and I have demonstrated that I can contribute and will add value. I want this position. What is our next step in the process?

This is a good closing question to get yourself to the next interview, but it is aggressive and should be used at or near the end. This helps you assess the interviewer's interest in you and moves you forward in the process. Be firm and convincing. Watch for the manager's reactions.

TIP: *Always use a strong close at or near the end of each interview. It gives the interviewer confidence that you will close in a sales call, too. It will also give you immediate responses as to how you rate with the interviewer. When you close, use a question like the one above, accompanied by a confident statement that you WANT THE JOB.*

SECOND AND/OR FINAL INTERVIEWS

The following questions are appropriate for more advanced, or second and third interviews. You are now a serious contender for the offer, and you should ask more in depth questions. These hit harder and are designed to give you the information you need to make the best decision when you receive an offer. You need to know where you are in the interviewing process and what is still ahead of you. Alternatively, how many interviews does it generally take to get the job? This information helps you plan and enact your strategy.

17. May I contact the previous Pharmaceutical Sales Representative that occupied this territory?

This is a risky question. Ask why the territory is open before asking to contact the previous representative. If the territory is open due to a termination, do not bother asking if you can contact him or her. If the previous representative was promoted within the company, the district manager would probably welcome you to contact him or her. If the previous representative left the company voluntarily, the district manager could answer either way. Regardless of the answer, it is a smart question to ask and shows you are thorough about your research. You take seriously your decision to join a company with which you plan to spend a long career.

18. May I contact any representatives that report to you?

As in the previous question, you want to gain more understanding about this company and your decision to work for it. You need to be confident that this is the one for you. Contacting other representatives is a good way to gain this insight. Ask them why they work for the company, what their level of satisfaction is, and what their goals are (see networking questions in Chapter 5 for more ideas). In addition, by asking this question you will gauge the manager's self-assurance in his or her managerial style. Ask yourself if this is the right person to help you achieve a successful career.

TIP: *Be sure you know as much about a company as you can before joining it. Always speak to the previous representative (as discussed in question 17) and at least one representative that currently reports to the district manager who would be hiring you. Do this before accepting a position with any organization.*

19. How would you describe your management style and that of the company?

This is an invitation for the interviewer to speak. Listen as the manager describes his or her own style and management philosophy within the organization. Is this is a good fit for you?

20. How does the company measure sales representatives' performance? How is it rewarded? What percentage of total compensation is base salary versus bonus?

This answer should provide insight into the sales tracking mechanism that is used (see Chapter 2 for more discussion of sales tracking). You will also hear about the commission plans, bonus structure, field promotions, merchandise awards, and incentive trips. You want to discover how much of your total compensation is at risk depending on sales performance. Remember that your compensation is mostly a fixed base salary.

21. How long do you believe it would take your new Sales Representative to generate significant results in the territory?

This answer tells you how quickly the manager expects to see results, and how he perceives the learning curve.

22. How do you evaluate your sales representative and how often?

This question offers insight into the manager's style of presenting feedback. Good managers will give frequent and consistent criticism or advice in addition to routine performance reviews, which are either semiannual or annual. You need to know what to expect in terms of suggestions and recommendations.

23. With excellent performance, how long should a new Sales Representative expect to gain experience in his or her territory before being eligible for promotion?

You will communicate a desire to climb the corporate ladder with this question. If you do not have that desire at this point, that is fine, but it opens the door for the manager to relay some career success stories of individuals or themselves within the organization. The answer tells you what you can expect for you or other representatives.

24. Describe the typical career path for your Sales Representatives.

The key to this question, as opposed to the previous one, is that you are asking about the potential advancement for the person who stays in sales throughout his or her career. As discussed in Chapter 2, field sales are a career that is challenging and rewarding. There are many opportunities for promotions and advancement other than entering sales management or a home office position. This answer will vary. You may hear about increasing levels of recognition, salary, prestigious titles, and additional district, regional, or national responsibilities.

25. Considering what I have learned in our interview process, plus my research and networking within the industry, I know I can make a strong contribution to your district and your organization. I want this position. May I do the job for you?

This is your final statement. The wording should match your style, but deliver it emphatically. The purpose of the close is twofold. First, you need to clearly communicate that you want the job. Second, you want to uncover any lingering objections or questions the interviewer may have. This may be your last chance to make your case. Although it has been known to happen, you will probably not get an offer or rejection on the spot. However, you should get some valuable comments. You will most likely receive a "qualified" maybe, pending an interview with another final candidate, reference checks, or simply the need for further consideration.

TIP: *When you touch the door knob or cross the threshold to exit the room, turn back to the interviewer and state it one more time: "Thank you for your time. I want to do the job for you." Use your own words, but say it with conviction!*

Chapter 8

Decisions, Decisions

Congratulations! You have just completed your interviewing process. You have networked, researched, studied, prepared, interviewed, and followed-up with a letter. Only few things can happen next: you will receive an offer, be turned down, or asked to return for another interview.

As you await the District Manager's decision, you will probably be contemplating the following thoughts: What will he or she say? How should you respond? What will you do if the answer is no? What if you get the offer but do not want the job? What if you want a better starting salary? As these questions suggest, there is still plenty of work ahead for you no matter what the decision.

THE REJECTION

First, let us examine the bad news—you are turned down for the position. It is important to remember that it is not the end of the world; it happens to everyone. If you respond to this unfortunate situation correctly, it will turn out to be a positive experience for your career.

How should you reply? It is natural to be disappointed. However, it will serve you well to remain positive and courteous. Continue the same professionalism and determination that got you to the interview in the first place. Be persistent with the interviewer until you get direct comments about your interview. Find out what you can do to improve your qualifications or interviewing techniques in the future. Ask the interviewer for honest advice. Ask for one or two key strengths that he or she feels you possess. What are essential areas in which you could improve and how? In other words, accept the opinion from a manager who has spent time getting to know you. If it is honest advice, it will be valuable for you.

Usually, the position will already have been offered and accepted before the runners-up are contacted. However, it can happen that a candidate receives multiple offers, accepting employment with one company and then, within weeks or months, accepting another. Thus, the same position may be open again. Alternatively, a different territory in the same district could become available, and since you have already been through the interview process, you can state your interest. Therefore, it is important to keep the door open for yourself. Tell the interviewer that you still want the job, and if their top-choice candidate does not work out, you are willing to make a commitment. Communicate that if any other sales territory becomes available, you would like to be considered for that job as well. The benefit to the manager is that he or she will not have to go through the entire hiring process all over again if they can call you and make an immediate offer.

TIP: *Tell the Manager that you will call back in three months to check for any potential new openings. Be sure to schedule it on your calendar and make the call regardless of your job situation at that time. If you already have an offer or are working with another company, explain that you just wanted to follow-up on your commitment.*

Even a rejection should be followed with a letter of appreciation to the interviewer. An example of a letter you might use for this purpose is at the end of this chapter.

The Offer

Next, the good news! You have an offer for the position you want. Congratulations! Now you are ready to accept, decline, or negotiate.

Regardless of your intention, I suggest that you not respond immediately with your decision. You have worked long and hard for this offer and your work has been rewarded. Take some time to think about it. Ask for at least twenty-four hours or more to consider it, sleep on it, and discuss it with your spouse or significant other. The company has kept you waiting. It is acceptable to ask for as much time as you need to make your decision.

It is also important to request a letter of the job offer. This letter describes everything that the organization is proposing to you. You can review it and make sure that no misunderstandings exist before you make your decision. This strategy gives you time to think about the details of the offer and review other offers you may have. You will also demonstrate to your potential new employer that you are mature and serious about your decision. Furthermore, you have been patiently waiting for the decision from them. They will understand giving you time to make a thoughtful decision—and will appreciate your request.

If the offer meets your requirements and you want the job, accept it. If you would like more money, take this opportunity to ask for it. For example, "I am looking for a base salary of $53,000. What flexibility do you have in your offer?" If you are struggling with whether to ask for more, some quick calculations may motivate you. Consider that even a modest increase ($500 to $1000) in your starting salary accumulates from year to year. Over a 20 year career, compounded annually, this could easily add up to over $25,000. Because all future increases are based on a percentage of your current salary, all your subsequent raises will be larger. In addition to the financial motive, negotiating for more money demonstrates your desire to achieve more—an excellent trait for a sales person. This also builds your negotiating skills. Try it!

You are all set with your start date, yet there are more questions. Should you suspend your job search immediately? The logical response is yes, however, I believe that such a decision may be premature.

Consider this scenario: You are excited about accepting the offer and want to get underway with your new job. During your job search, you have followed the strategy outlined in *Insight*. All of your efforts with other companies are still paying dividends. Ironically, the week after you accept your offer, a company with which you previously interviewed calls because of an unforeseen vacancy. The vacancy is actually a better fit for your interests and the complete package is significantly more attractive. This situation is rare but it can and does happen. In your excitement over your new position you think that it would be unethical to continue the interview process, and politely inform the company who called that you are not interested. My advice is to reconsider all your options and make the best decision for you and your family for the long term.

Because of scenarios such as this one, we urge you to keep your options open as much as possible. It is not disloyal to leave a job in which there is no mutual benefit. Over time, it may be worse to stay in a job where you are not 100% committed. Integrity and professionalism are always paramount and lead to a more satisfying career. Be sure that you do not alienate yourself from the organization, sales managers, or human resources executives that you may want to work with in the future. A word to the wise: The old adage, "It's a small world," applies to the entire pharmaceutical industry.

TIP: *Consider all options with professionalism and courtesy. You will always benefit.*

Finally, the remaining possible outcome is that the decision has not been reached and more time is needed. This may occur for several reasons. First, the company may have decided not to fill the position after all. In an ever-changing and complex business environment, such as the pharmaceutical industry, this may occur when a company is in a state of flux due to a merger, product sell-off, acquisition, or a change in corporate strategy or direction. Another reason for a delay may be that the District Manager and Regional Manager are not completely satisfied that they have considered all the qualified candidates. They are still searching. If this is the case, you will probably not be told that you are still considered a viable candidate.

Finally, they may simply want to bring you back for another interview. There may be someone else in the organization for you to meet before making the final decision. The purpose of this may be to get another person's perception about you and whether that person agrees that you are a fit for the company.

Regardless of the reason for a delay, your strategy should remain the same. Continue to be upbeat, positive, and emphatic about your desire and commitment to the position and the company. Do whatever it takes in terms of additional interviews or company contacts. Follow each contact or telephone call with a brief note. Offer to call every week or so for updates on the process. Thorough communication will demonstrate your commitment and sales abilities. The manager is also interested in keeping you interested during the period of delay. A good manager knows keeping you excited and positive about the job until a final decision has been fully implemented benefits their corporation. The manager wants you to know that you are his or her number one choice. This is motivating for you and helps keep any candidate's energy level high.

[SAMPLE LETTER: FOLLOW-UP TO 'REJECTION']

August 4, 2004

Janet Lynn Jones
631 Any Street
Anytown, USA 54321

Bill Franklin
District Manager
XYZ Pharmaceutical Company
12345 East Drive Way
Newark, NJ 01234

Dear Mr. Franklin,

Again, thank you for the opportunity to interview with you and XYZ Pharmaceutical Company. I know that I can make a significant contribution to your team.

If a position becomes available in the near future, please contact me. My home telephone is 5555555. As we agreed, I will contact you in three months to discuss future opportunities.

Sincerely,

Janet M. Jones

Conclusion

Your Commitment

Anne Clayton wrote and published *Insight* with the confidence that it would empower you to fulfill your goal of breaking into a rewarding career in pharmaceutical sales. As you follow the strategy that you have just read about, Anne would like you to keep in mind these words of encouragement:

- It is common to receive rejections during your networking and interviewing process.
- Not everyone will be as determined in meeting his or her own goals.
- Be persistent and resolute; set yourself apart from those who will become discouraged or quit after being turned down by one or two companies.

You are learning and applying a process or method. These skills are valuable to you regardless of the outcome of each individual contact or interview. Your experience with this challenging process helps you grow and become better with every effort you make. Thus, as in all sales professions, even in rejection there is progress and advancement toward your goals.

Once you have reached your goal, live up to your promises to the interviewer and the company. Continue to apply the diligence and determination you showed during your job search. After you have accepted the offer, continue to differentiate yourself from the other candidates your company has hired who may be your new co-workers and peers. You have set a high standard for yourself throughout the interviewing and candidate selection process that will now provide momentum for your success throughout your career.

Upon accepting the offer, begin by sending brief letters to your new manager and any other managers, directors, and human resources personnel with whom you had contact during the hiring process. State that you are excited to be aboard and looking forward to meeting your professional career goals and the business goals of your new company.

Apply yourself diligently during the various training programs in which you will participate. Professionalism at all times is the rule. Bear in mind that the quality of your performance is always important, and you must continue to make your mark by excelling in your initial training.

Continue your research and networking; these skills will always enhance your career. However, focus on getting to know the sales representatives, managers, companies, and products in and around your territory, rather than uncovering job prospects. You will encounter many opportunities to meet other sales representatives as you move about in doctor's offices, hospitals, clinics, conventions, meetings, and seminars. Use these occasions to introduce yourself and learn more about your new colleagues. Ascertain what they are doing that can be helpful to you. Talk about your work habits and practices, not about your sales messages and strategies on your particular products.

Do representatives from other companies seem satisfied with their organizations, or do they complain about their work, their managers, or their products? This information provides insight that can be used to promote your product over a competitor's, or find possible job candidates for your own company. Frequently, you may receive financial gains for your referrals.

As you have learned in your research and networking process, some metropolitan areas have professional associations for pharmaceutical representatives. Find out if one exists in your area and check into it. Joining a professional organization opens new doors and enhances your own career as people learn who you are.

You have learned valuable skills that will be practical throughout your career. Work hard, be your best, and always differentiate yourself from your competition and your peers.

Best of Success!

APPENDIX
Company Profiles

The following *Company Profiles* and *Worksheets* will complement your efforts and save you countless hours of research time (and numerous trips to the library). Since 1998, my research is one of the immeasurable values of ***Insight into a Career in Pharmaceutical Sales***. I, Anne Clayton, was the first author to offer the candidate a specific book about entry into pharmaceutical sales in 1998. Since then, I devote time almost ever day to clipping articles, reviewing annual reports, visiting websites, making countless phone calls to my network working in the industry, reading industry publications and press releases to keep this information as pertinent as possible. No other single resource is available to have you quickly, yet thoroughly prepared for a pharmaceutical sales interview. These purpose of these company profiles is to offer you the depth of information that will help you prepare for any networking contact and the interview process. In fact, I contend that many employees (including your interviewer or District Manager) may not be aware of their company s history and product pipeline to the degree as contained in these profiles.

I have profiled the top fifty companies based on annual revenues. Thus, not every pharmaceutical company is in this profile section. You will find as you read the profiles that in many companies the sales force size is relatively small (sometimes less than 100 representatives for the United States). While this may appear to mean limited opportunities for employment, these smaller pharmaceutical concerns offer similar professional and personal growth so in no way exclude them during your search.

Use this Appendix as a tool to record your notes and organize additional information (i.e. contacts, press releases, etc.) on a specific company as you progress through the interview process. Set up a Worksheet and file for every company that you have contact with, from Abbott to Wyeth. You can cut out, print or copy the company profile and place it in your file if desired. Record all your networking meetings and contacts; update your file with each new contact, meeting and phone call. Include any new information you collect based on other research from internet sites, library, etc., as described in Chapter 4. Keep your file handy in order to be prepared for unexpected phone calls from any organization, whether it is a networking phone call, screening interview, or face-to-face interview. Bring your file to your interview to reference if needed and to show your efforts. Transfer some of your own notes on a legal pad for quick review before going in. Differentiating yourself from the competition is so easy by being prepared!

Once you are obtain an interview, immediately revisit your file and the company s website (for e-book readers place your cursor on the website addresses within the company profile and press control CTRL and right click your mouse). Under the investor relations tab, view any recent annual reports, SEC (Securities and Exchange Commission filings), and press releases over the last twelve months. As always, feel free to email me to see if I have any additional information. when a new addition of ***Insight*** is released, you may request that I email you the most recent appendix of company profiles. I will do this at no charge, but please keep a copy of your receipt and confirmation email for proof of your original book purchase. This will bring you up to date on any significant changes since publishing of this Sixth edition of ***Insight.***

I suggest even that after you obtain your offer and are working in the industry, keep abreast of the other companies by using this same method. You will become a valuable asset, knowing what company has which product, or what competition may be coming in the pipeline to compete with your product.

CONTRACT SALES ORGANIZATIONS

You will also find a list of names, addresses and contact information on the top Contract Sales Organizations (CSO s) in the following pages. Many great employment opportunities exist with these companies.

RANKING PHARMACEUTICAL COMPANIES

Other than listing by sales revenues, sales growth and sales force size (as in Chapter 1), I do not provide or believe anyone should try to "rank" pharmaceutical companies. In other words, I do not qualify or recommend any specific company over another to choose as your employer. It is not the name of the company you work for or the specific product you sell that makes your position rewarding. These both may change and can change often throughout your career. Regarding compensation, top companies consistently track salaries and bonuses paid by other companies in order to remain competitive and retain top sales people. I do not recommend leaving one company for another just to gain a couple of thousand dollars in base pay or bonus. That fantastic bonus plan you hear about from a friend in the field may sound great but the following year after you have made your switch, your former company's plan may change and be even better. Therefore, I caution representatives considering moving to another company for financial reasons. The individuals (District Manager, Regional Manager, Director of Sales, Training Managers, and District Members) you work with can be a huge factor in making your position a positive or negative experience. If you are well satisfied with those individuals and your career is progressing, stay put. So again, *Insight* and Anne Clayton do not offer any rankings or ratings for companies within the pharmaceutical industry. Often I receive emails with candidates with two "offers" and the candidate asks which company I would choose. I always reply with the question, "How do you like the people?" Make your decision based on that—you will be the most successful when you enjoy the people you work for and with.

GET FUTURE UPDATES to the company profiles free of charge!

As a client of Anne Clayton, you are your name, your email address, and a copy of your receipt and purchase confirmation that you received when you placed your original book order. I will send an E-book version of *Insight's* Profiles back to you via email.

ABBOTT LABORATORIES
100 ABBOTT PARK ROAD
ABBOTT PARK, IL. 60064
847.937.6100
ABT
abbott.com
ross.com

Summary: Abbott Laboratories is a global company producing medications, nutritional supplements, and products used in hospitals and laboratories. The pharmaceutical division develops antibiotic, anti-infective, antihypertensive, oncology, thyroid, and other medications. Ross Products, a division of Abbott produces nutritional products and pharmaceuticals. Tap Pharmaceutical Products Inc. is Abbott's joint venture with Takeda Chemical Industries Ltd. of Japan.

History: Wallace Abbott a medical doctor established the Abbott Alkaloidal Company in a Chicago in 1888 to sell his formulations. The company went public in 1929 and by the mid 1930's opened branches in South America, Mexico and Britain. *Erythocin* was introduced in the early 1950's and currently Abbott is the #1 generator of erythromycin in the world. The 1960 has brought such products as *Selsun Blue* shampoo, *Murine* eye drops, and various infant formulas. The late nineties brought approval for *Norvil, Gabitrol, Zemplar,* and *Flomax* (the number one product for benign prostatic hypertrophy). Product approvals in 2000 include *Biaxin XL, Depakote ER* and *Mobic.* In 2000, Abbott acquired the Knoll Pharmaceutical division of BASF. Knoll Pharmaceuticals has brought significant product additions with products that include *Synthroid,* and *Meridia.* In 2003, the FDA approved Abbott's rheumatoid arthritis treatment *Humira.* Numerous analyst forecast sales in 2006 for *Humira* to reach over $1 billion. 2003 brought Abbott announced that it will spin off its global hospital products division into a separate company and brought the sale of the *Rythmol* product line to Reliant Pharmaceuticals.

Annual Healthcare Revenue: $17 billion

CEO: Miles D. White

Sales force: 4,000

Major Brands: *Biaxin* >$1.1 billion antibiotic, *Depakote* antiepileptic agent, *Dilaudid, Vicoprofen* narcotic analgesics, *Flomax* benign prostatic hypertrophy (with Boehringer Ingelheim), *Ensure, Glucerna, Enfamll, Pedialyte* and *Similac* infant formula's and nutritional supplement's (Ross) *Isoptin, Hytrin, Mavik, Tarka* hypertension, *Humira* rheumatoid arthritis, *Kaletra* HIV/AIDS, *Meridia* obesity, *Mobic* osteoarthritis (Boehringer Ingelheim), *Omnicef* antibiotic, *Oxycotin* for chronic pain (with Purdue), electrolyte formulation, *Precedex* sedative, *Synagis* viral prevention, *Synthroid* thyroid hormone, *TriCor* cholesterol agent, *Zemplar* bone disease, *Zyflo* asthma.

Near approval: *Atrasentan* cancer, *Clivarine* deep vein thrombosis, *Humira* additional indications, *Dilaudid CR* pain, *Hextend* hypovolemia, *Prolyse* ischemic stroke, *Simdax* congestive heart failure, *Xopenex* bronchospasm, *Vicodin CR* for pain.

ALTANA Pharma
210 Park Avenue
Florham Park, NJ   07932
973.514.4240
AAA
Altana.com
Fougera.com

Summary: Altana Pharma U.S. is the North American subsidiary of Altana Pharma AG, a leading worldwide pharmaceuticals concern with over a 130 history in developing, manufacturing and marketing pharmaceutical products. Together with more than 10,000 employees, spanning the globe Altana generates roughly $2.6 billion in annual sales – of which nearly $1.8 billion comes from the pharmaceutical operations. Altana Pharma U.S. is one division of Altana Inc. In addition, a division by the name of Fougera is a producer of topical dermatological and ophthalmic pharmaceuticals. The Altana Research Institute, a genomics-oriented research center, was established in Massachusetts. Altana Pharma U.S. oversees the development, launch and marketing efforts in the therapeutic areas of respiratory and gastrointestinal agents.

History: Since its founding back in 1873, when Dr. Heinrich Byk opened a small operation named Byk AG in Berlin, which, patented and marketed *Euphyllin* (theophylline) in 1907. In 1917, the company merged with the companies of Paul Gulden and Ernst Lomberg, becoming known as Byk Gulden. In 1941, Dr. Herbert Quandt, took majority control of the company and served as its first chief executive officer. Dr. Quandt was also very instrumental in entrepreneurial growth of automaker BMW. Nearly 35 years later, Dr. Quandt, along with Hans Graf von der Goltz and Eberhard von Heusinger, formed Altana AG, based in Bad Homburg, Germany. The company established its U.S. subsidiary, Altana Inc., in 1984. In 2002, in an effort to create unity, the company changed its pharmaceutical unit's name from Byk Gulden to Altana Pharma. Currently, Susanne Klatten, Dr. Quandt's daughter, remains the majority shareholder of Altana AG over sixty years later.

Annual Healthcare Revenue: $1.8 billion

CEO: Dr. H.C. Nikolaus Schweickart

Sales force: 300

Major Brands: Altana: *Protonix* for gastrointestinal and esophageal diseases (with Wyeth), **Fougera**: *Foilpacs, Nitro-Bid, Surgilube, Swim-Ear, CroFab, DgiFabi* topical preparations.

Near approval: *Soraprazan* is an acid pump antagonist, *Alvesco, Roflumilast* for asthma,

AKZO NOBEL N.V.
ORGANON INCORPORATED
375 MOUNT PLEASANT AVENUE
WEST ORANGE, NJ 07052
973.325.4500
AKZOY
organon.com

Summary: Established in 1994 Akzo Nobel operates in various different business segments, including pharmaceuticals, chemicals, and coatings. The companies' health-care segment includes Organon Inc. (the pharmaceutical division) Organon Teknika (hospital supplies), Intervet (veterinary products) and Diosynth (pharmaceutical raw materials). The pharmaceutical division includes hormone products, central nervous system treatments, atherothrombosis treatments, contraceptives, fertility treatments, and autoimmune disease agents. The chemical operations produce pulp and paper chemicals, base chemicals, surfactants, polymers, and catalysts. The coatings division makes paints, industrial coatings, and resins. In 2001, Organon announced moving their headquarters from the Netherlands to the United States, which is the units' largest market.

History: Alfred Nobel not only invented the blasting cap in 1863 but the beginnings of this organization. The "Nobel Prize" was first awarded in 1901 (and annually since) is named after the company's founder. The Akzo side of the company traces its origin to a German coatings developer, and a Dutch rayon maker. In 1929, these two companies merged operations creating Algemen Kunstzijde-Unie. Akzo acquired Nobel in 1995. In 1996, *Remeron* was first launched. *Follistim, Mircette* were approved in 1997. In 2001, Akzo Nobel agreed to acquire Covance Biotechnology Services, Inc. for 190 million. In addition, the FDA approved *Nuvaring*. *Arixtra* was launched in 2002. Akzo announced plans to develop and market *Asenapine* in 2004, with Pfizer.

Annual Healthcare Revenue: $3.8 billion

CEO: G. C. Wijers

Sales force: 1100

Major Brands: *Antagon* hormone therapy, *Arixtra* thrombosis following surgery, *Cyclessa, Desogen/Marvelon, Gracial, Implanon, Mercilon, Mircette, Nuvaring* contraceptive agents, *Follistim* infertility agent, *Orgaran* thrombosis, *Remeron* depression.

Near approval: *Andriol Testocaps* male hormone replacement, *Ariza* depression, *Asenapine* for schizophrenia and bipolar disorder, *Hextend* hypovolemia, *Implanon* a contraceptive, *Orgaran* heparin-induced thrombocytopenia, *Xyvion* estrogen agent/post menopausal complications.

ALLERGAN, Inc.

2525 DuPont Drive

IRVINE, CA 92612

714.246.4500

AGN

allergan.com

Summary: Allergan, Inc. headquartered in Irvine, California, is a technology-driven, global health care concern provides eye care and specialty pharmaceutical products. Allergan develops and commercializes products in the areas of eye care pharmaceutical's, ophthalmic surgical devices, contact lens care, movement disorder, and dermatologicals. Allergan research includes the areas of glaucoma and retinal disease, cataracts, dry eye, psoriasis, acne, photo damage, movement disorders, pain, metabolic disease and various types of cancer. Allergen's has more than 150 patents securing its future as a specialty pharmaceutical company.

History: Founded in 1950, Allergan became a public company and in 1970, merged with SmithKline Beckman in 1980, and re-established as an independent company again in 1989. Products include eye and skin pharmaceuticals, ophthalmic surgical equipment, contact lens cleaners, and intraocular lenses. The company's skin care products include acne and psoriasis treatments. 1989 brought the approval of *Botox.* 1996, brought the approval of *Alphagan,* which is now the second leading agent for the treatment of glaucoma. In 1998, Allergan added 225 scientists to its global research and development team to bring to market its specialty products. *Alocril* was launched in 2000, as was the acquisition of developmental compound *Epinastine* from Boehringer Ingelheim. New indications for *Botox* and approval for *Lumigan* were gained in 2001. In 2002 *Botox Cosmetic,* gained approved and Allergan entered into an agreement with EntreMed Inc. to develop treatments for age-related macular degeneration (a leading cause of blindness). Currently, United States sales contribute approximately 50% of Allergen's total global revenue. In 2003, *Restasis, Zymar* and *Acular LS* obtained FDA approval and Allergan entered co-marketing agreements for *Finacea* and *Elestat* (from Berlex and Inspire Pharmaceuticals respectively).

Annual Healthcare Revenue: $1.3 billion

CEO: David E. I. Pyott

Salesforce: 1325

Major Brands: *Acular LS* for ocular pain*, Alphagan, Alphagan P, Lumigan* glaucoma (market leading treatment), *Botox, Botox Cosmetic,* neuromuscular disorders, skin wrinkles, blepharospasm, type VII nerve disorders/cervical dystonia, *Finacea* for roscea (with Berlex), *Tazorac Gel/Cream* acne/plaque psoriasis treatment, *Restasis, Zymar Elestat* chronic eye disease's.

Near approval: *Androgen Tear* chronic dry eye, *Avage* psoriasis, *Botox* expanded indications, *Brimonidine X* glaucoma, ocular hypertension, *Epinastine* eye allergies*, Gatifloxacin* anti-infective agent, *Lumigan Memantine* for glaucoma, *Phakic Intraocular Lenses* for refractive surgery, *Vitrase* severe vitreous hemorrhage.

AMGEN INCORPORATED
1 AMGEN CENTER DRIVE
THOUSAND OAKS, CA 91320
805.447.4587
AMGN
amgen.com

Summary: Currently Amgen is the world's largest biotechnology concern. Amgen develops and markets therapeutic products in four medical areas: hematopoiesis (blood cell production), inflammation and auto-immunity, neurobiology, and soft tissue repair and regeneration. Over 25% of the company's revenues are devoted towards research and development. *Epogen* and *Neupogen,* currently account for most of the company's revenue. Amgen has nearly a dozen new products under development. In addition to its own product portfolio, Amgen licenses products and technologies from and to other companies.

History: A group of devoted scientists to develop health care products based on molecular biological technology formed Amgen (as Applied Molecular Genetics) in 1980. In 1983, Amgen cloned the human protein erythropoietin (EPO), which stimulates red blood production in the body. The company formed a joint venture with Kirin Pharmaceuticals of Japan in 1984 to develop and market EPO. Amgen and Kirin also collaborated on recombinant human granulocyte colony stimulating factor (G-CSF), a human protein that stimulates the body's immune system to withstand bacterial infections. Amgen established a marketing arrangement with Ortho Pharmaceutical Corporation (Johnson & Johnson) in 1985 and created a link with Roche Holdings in 1988. In 1989, the FDA granted Amgen a license to produce *Epogen* (brand name of EPO) and *Neupogen* (brand name of G-CSF). In 2000, Amgen received approval for *Neupogen SingleJect,* and purchased Kinetix Pharmaceuticals in a stock transaction valued at $170 million. In 2001, *Aranesp* gained approval. In 2002, Amgen completed the acquisition of Immunex for $16 billion, and leading product *Enbrel* and *Neulasta* was launched. 2003 brought approval of *Enbrel* in a once weekly dose, collaboration with Tularik Inc. for oncology agents, and strategic alliances with Serono SA for foreign marketing rights.

Annual Healthcare Revenue: $5.5 billion

CEO: Kevin W. Sharer

Sales force: 400

Major Brands: *Aranesp, Epogen* (*Procrit* by J&J, marketed to oncology market) >$3 billion, anemia treatments, *Enbrel* >$1.4 billion, rheumatoid arthritis (co marketed with Wyeth). *Kinerat* for rheumatoid arthritis, *Neupogen, Neulasta* >$2 billion, recombinant human granulocyte colony-stimulating factor, as an adjunct to chemotherapy, *Neupogen SingleJect* for neutropenia in HIV.

Near approval: *Cinacalcet HCL* for secondary hyperparathyroidism, *Enbrel* plaque psoriasis, Wegener granulomatosis ankylosign spondylitis, *Epratuzumab* non-Hodgkin lymphoma, *KGF* oral mucositis, *LyphoCide* non-Hodgkin lymphoma, *Neupopeg* reduction in the duration of neutropenia, *Neulasta* breast cancer.

ASTRA ZENECA
1800 CONCORD PIKE
WILMINGTON, DE 19850
302.886.3000
AZN
astrazeneca.com

Summary: Therapeutic arenas include anti-infectives, cardiovascular agents, gastrointestinal agents, pain control drugs, and agents for respiratory disease. Astra has research operations in Sweden, United Kingdom and United States, and subsidiaries in 40 countries. The United States is Astra's largest market. In 1999, Astra AB and the UK's Zeneca completed their merger and Astra Zeneca was born, with world headquarters based in London. Zeneca has pioneered and developed many breakthrough products including beta-blockers, anti-cancer medications, anesthetics and cardiac medications. AstraZeneca will have leading therapies in areas of gastrointestinal, anesthesia, oncology, respiratory and cardiovascular medicine.

History: Astra began in 1913 when a group of physicians and pharmacist formed the company and became its inaugural stockholders. Among this initial group of individuals was Hans Von Euler, who won the 1929 Nobel Prize in chemistry. During the 1930's research and development became the primary focus of the corporation. In the late forties, the company began marketing *Xylocaine* (lidocaine). *Xylocaine* sales soared in the fifties and Astra broadened production and licensing globally. Astra continued expansion through the seventies, including new leading products such as *Seloken* for heart disease. Astra paid $820 million in 1994 for a 50% interest in a joint venture with Merck to market Astra products in the United States. In 1998, Astra Merck was combined with Astra's wholly owned subsidiary Astra USA, Inc. to form Astra Pharmaceuticals L.P. Zeneca has a similar history to Astra. Zeneca has grown by bringing important new medicines to society. Zeneca has been instrumental in hormonal treatments for particular breast and prostate cancers, along with a very broad oncology line. *Atacand HCT* for the treatment of hypertension was approved in 2000. *Arimidex* was approved in late 2000. *Accolate, Atacand HCT, Nexium* currently known as the most successful launch of a pharmaceutical agent in the industry, *Toprol XL, Entocort EC,* and *Zomig ZMT* were all launched in 2001. *Prilosec* was recognized as holding the position of the largest selling branded pharmaceutical product in the world. In 2002, AstraZeneca received approval for *Faslodex* and *Iressa*. In 2003, *Crestor* was launched. In addition, *Prilosec* was approved by the FDA for OTC status and *Zomig* was approved in a new nasal spray formulation.

Annual Healthcare Revenue: $17.8 billion

CEO: Tom McKillop

Sales force: 6,000

Major Brands: *Atacand* hypertension, *Diprivan* anesthesia, *Crestor* hypercholesterolemia, *Entocort EC* Crohn's disease, *Faslodex* breast cancer, *Naropin* anesthesia, *Prilosec* >$4 billion, *Nexium* >$3 billion antipeptic ulcer agents, *Pulmicort* asthma, *Rhinocort* allergic rhinitis, *Seroquel* >$ billion an antipsychotic, *Xylocaine* anesthetic agent, *Accolate* asthma, *Arimidex, Casodex, Iressa, Nolvadex, Tomudex, Zoladex* oncology agents, *Cefotan, Merrem* infections, *Zestril* >$1 billion, hypertension, *Zoladex* prostate cancer, *Zomig, Zomig ZMT, Zomig Nasal Spray* migraines.

Near approval: *Cerovive* for stroke, *Exanta* new class of an oral anticoagulant, *Merrem I.V.* hospital acquired pneumonia, *Naropin* pediatric pain management, *Seroquel Granules, Seroquel Sustained Release* for schizophrenia, *Tomudex* colorectal cancer, *Symbiotic* asthma, *Zomig Nasal Spray* migraines.

AVENTIS PHARMA
ROUTE 202-206
P.O. BOX 6800
BRIDGEWATER, NJ 08807-0800
908.231.4000
AVE
aventis.com

Summary: Aventis Pharma currently operates four business units. Aventis Pharma AG, the prescription pharmaceutical division, Aventis Pasteur, the human vaccine business, Aventis Behring the plasma protein business, and Dade Behring the diagnostic business. In 2002, Aventis divested of Aventis CropScience and Aventis Animal Nutrition, focusing primarily on the core business of pharmaceuticals.

History: Founded in the mid 1800's by a chemist in the actual German village of Hoechst. Hoechst expanded into fibers, plastics, and petrochemicals in the 1950's. In the seventies, Hoechst acquired majority control of Roussel Uclaf of France (pharmaceuticals, perfumes). In 1987, the company purchased Celanese forming Hoechst-Celanese. In 1995 the company was renamed Hoechst Marion Roussel after the purchase of Marion Merrell Dow. Ewing Kauffman started Marion Laboratories in 1950 within his home's basement, in Kansas City, Missouri. Marion's sales in the seventies reached $116 million; products included *Carafate, Cardizem, OS-CAL* and *Gaviscon.* In 1989, the company merged with Merrell Dow. Rorer (RPR) was created in 1990 with the combination of Rhone-Poulenc's pharmaceutical operations and the Rorer Group. In the early fifties, Rorer developed an immensely successful product that is still successful today, *Maalox.* In 1995, Rhone-Poulenc purchased Fisons for $2.6 billion. Late 1999 Rhone-Poulenc SA shareholders approved their companies' merger with Germany's Hoechst AG to create Aventis SA. In 2001, Aventis entered partnership with Altana AG to develop asthma agents. Product approvals in 2001 include *BenazClin Topical Gel, Carac, Lantus, Lovenox,* and *Tripedia. Late in 2003,* Aventis and Avalon Pharmaceuticals formed an oncology research collaboration. Aventis looks forward to the approval of *Ketek* in 2004.

Annual Healthcare Revenue: $17.6 billion

CEO: Igor Landau

Sales force: 5200

Major Brands: *Actonel* Paget's disease, *Allegra* >$1.9 billion, allergies, *Capaxone* multiple sclerosis, *Nasacort AQ* allergies, *Amaryl, Insuman, Lantus* (currently one of the leading insulin treatments on the market) all for diabetes, *Lovenox Arava* rheumatoid arthritis, *Azmacort* asthma, *BenazClin Topical Gel* acne, *Carac* keratoses, *Delix* antihpertensive/antianginal agents, *Cefrom, Claforan* and *Rulid* anti-infectives, *Helixate, NexGen, Kogenate FS* hemophilia A, *Lasix* edema, *Lovenox* >$1.5 billion, thrombosis, *Penlac* onychomycosis, *Synercid* pneumonia, *Taxotere* >$1.1 billion cancer, *Thymoglobulin* allograft rejection, *Trental* vascular disorders, and numerous *Vaccines.*

Near approval: *Azmacort HFA* asthma, *Alvesco MDI* for asthma, *Cariporide* coronary surgery, *Dynepo* anemia due to chronic renal failure, *Exubera* (with Pfizer) first inhaled insulin formulation, *Flavopiridol* cancer, *Glulisine* diabetes, *Giliadel* malignant glioma, *Hexavac* preventative vaccine, *Ketek* (first in class) antibiotic, *Menactra, Pentacel* vaccine's, *Intal HFA* bronchospasm, *Sabril* pediatric epilepsy.

BAYER CORPORATION
400 MORGAN LANE
WEST HAVEN, CT 06516
412.394.5500
BAY
bayer.com

Summary: Bayer Corporation operates six main segments producing over 8,000 varied products. Bayer's largest segment, HealthCare has four divisions, Animal Health, Biological Products, Consumer Care and Diagnostics. Other business segments are the Crop Science (animal health and crop protection), Chemicals (base and organic chemicals, polyurethane's, solar cells, dyes, food preservatives, fragrances), and Polymers (fabrics, films, plastics, rubber). The Bayer Corporation in the United States is Bayer's largest worldwide subsidiary, accounting for about 23% of sales. In November of 2003, Bayer announced that it plans to sell its Bayer Chemicals division and part of its polymers business by 2005.

History: Friedrich Bayer established the organization in 1863. Dedication to research fueled Bayer's growth above its original synthetic dye business, leading to the introduction of such breakthrough compounds as *Bayer Aspirin* (1897) and synthetic rubber in (1915). During World War I, the United States seized Bayer's American operations and trademark rights, offering them to Sterling Drug. After W.W.II Bayer promptly began rebuilding entering a joint venture with Monsanto Chemical Company, forming Mobay in 1954. In 1967, Bayer purchased Monsanto's share in the organization. In the sixties Bayer augmented its offerings in dyes, plastics, and polyurethane's, and the company built factories globally. The company grew with various acquisitions over the next 30 years including Miles Laboratories *(Alka-Seltzer, One-A-Day Vitamins)* in 1978. The company integrated its United States holdings under the name of Miles Inc. in 1992. In 1996, Bayer introduced its first genetically engineered product, *Kogenate.* Bayer regained American rights to the Bayer brand (known for its Aspirin trademark) and the Bayer logo in 1994 when it purchased the North American business Sterling Winthrop from SmithKline Beecham for $1 billion. Over seventy-five years later, the company returned to its original name, Bayer Corporation. Sales of antibiotic *Cipro* had reached over the $1 billion mark by 2000. During 2001, Bayer signed an agreement with Memory Pharmaceuticals to develop an agent for dementia. In 2001, product approvals include *Avelox, Cipro I.V., Cipro Oral Suspension, Nimotop* and *Viadur.* In 2002, Bayer acquired Aventis CropScience division for $7.3 billion. In 2003, *Cipro XR* was granted approval and *Levitra*, the first competitor to *Viagra* (Pfizer) was launched in September.

Annual Healthcare Revenue: $8.8 billion

CEO: Werner Wenning

Sales force: 2400

Major Brands: *Adalat* angina, *Avelox* anti-infective, *Cipro, Cipro XL* >$1.7 billion, infections, *Levitra* for erectile dysfunction (with Glaxo SmithKline), *Kogenate* hemophilia A, *Nimotop,Viadur* prostate cancer.

Near approval: *Avelox I.V.* antibiotic, *Cipro OD* urinary tract infections, *Gamunex* for immune deficiency, *Repinotan* ischemic stroke.

BERLEX LABORATORIES, INC.

SCHERING AG
340 CHANGEBRIDGE ROAD
PO BOX 1000
MONTVILLE, NJ 07045-1000
973.487.2000
SHR

berlex.com

Summary: Berlin based Schering AG product areas include prescription pharmaceuticals, diagnostic imaging agents, radiopharmaceuticals, and agricultural chemicals. Schering AG secures approximately 30% of the world's fertility control and hormone therapy. Therapeutic areas include dermatology, diagnostic imaging, female healthcare, multiple sclerosis, therapeutics and oncology. Schering AG operates as Berlex Laboratories in the United States.

History: Schering AG acquired Cooper Laboratories in 1979 for entry into the United States market. North American pharmaceutical operations are under the Berlex name. Berlex is a leader in magnetic resonance imaging agents, leukemia treatment, and estrogen replacement therapy. In 1986, Berlex entered the oral contraceptive market with *Levlen* and *TriLevlen.* In 1990, Berlex expanded into biotechnology with acquisitions of Codon and Triton Biosciences. 1991 brought the introduction of *Betapace.* In 1993, the first interferon multiple sclerosis therapy *Betaseron* was introduced. *Climara* and *Ultravist* were launched in 1995. In 1998, *AcuTect* and *NeoTect,* radiopharmaceuticals were launched.. The acquisition of Diatide Inc. and Oris/Cis Bio International strengthened the radiopharmaceutical therapeutic segment in 1999. In 2000, Schering AG acquired Mitsui Pharmaceuticals Inc. of Japan. Currently Schering AG is the world leader in contrast media market share. Also in 2000, *Levulan* was introduced. Product approvals in 2001 include *Campath, Yasmin, Mirena* and *Finevin.* In 2002, Schering relocated the management of the pharmaceutical division from Berlin to Montville, New Jersey and *Leukine* was acquired from Immunex. 2003 brought *Climara Pro*.

Annual Healthcare Revenue: $4.7 billion

CEO: Hubertus Erlen

Sales force: 1,100

Major Brands: *AcuTect, Iopamiron, NeoTect, Magnevist, Feridex, Ultravist* radiopharmaceuticals for diagnostics, *Betapace* cardiovascular agent, *Betaseron* multiple sclerosis, *Fludara, Campath* oncology agents, *Climara Climara Pro* estrogen patch, and once weekly dosage form, *Finevin, Levulan* dermatology products, *Leukine* leukemia, *Mirena* intrauterine contraceptive device, *Quadramet* for cancer pain, *Levlen, Tri-Levlen, Levlite,* and *Yasmin* oral contraceptives.

Near Approval: *Angeliq, Avaden* osteoporosis, *Betaseron* additional indications, *Endometrion* endometriosis, *Fasudil* angina, *Flucis* imaging agent, *Leukine* additional indications, *Refludan* heparin induced thrombocytopenia, *Imavist* cardiac imaging agent, *Menostar* transdermal estrogen patch.

BIOGEN IDEC
14 Cambridge Center
Cambridge, MA 02142
617.679.2000

Biogenidec.com

BIIB

Summary: Biogen Iden's products and development programs address the therapeutic areas of oncology, immunology, neurology, dermatology and rheumatology. The merged company will focus on developing treatments for cancer and autoimmune and inflammatory diseases. Its product roster includes Idec's best-selling *Rituxan*, a monoclonal antibody. Biogen contributes *Avonex*, and *Amevive*; and royalties from alpha intron licensing deals with Schering-Plough and other licensing arrangements. Biogen Idec hopes the combined pipelines of its predecessors will yield the next breakthrough in autoimmune therapies.

History: In November 2003, Biogen Idec Inc. was formed from the merger of two of the world's leading biotechnology companies, Biogen, Inc. and IDEC Pharmaceuticals Corporation. This combination has resulted in a fusion of complementary biotech strengths in various therapeutic areas, research and development capabilities, manufacturing expertise, global infrastructure, and financial position. Biogen Idec intends to continue its growth through discovery, development and commercialization of its own innovative products and through strategic alliances as the partner-of-choice for biologics development, manufacturing and marketing. In 2002, *Zevalin* was launched. 2003 brought the launch of *Amevive*.

Annual Sales: $1.5 billion

CEO: James C. Mullen

Salesforce: 380

Major Brands: *Zevalin* for non-Hodgkin's lymphomas, *Amevive* for moderate-to-severe chronic plaque psoriasis, *Rituxan* >$1.4 billion (with Genentech) for non-Hodgkin's lymphomas, *Avonex* >$1 billion for multiple sclerosis

Near Approval: *Rituxan* for rheumatoid arthritis and other indications, *Antegren* for the treatment of multiple sclerosis and Crohn's disease.

BIOVAIL CORPORATION
2488 DUNWIN DRIVE
MISSISSAUGA, ON L5L 1J9 CANADA

416.285.6000
BVF
biovail.com

Summary: Biovail Corporation is a full-service pharmaceutical in the United States that brings over six proprietary drug-delivery processes. Biovail applies its proprietary drug delivery technologies to many successful drugs already on the market. Teva Pharmaceutical USA handles Biovail's generic agent's sales in the United States. The Canadian pharmaceutical unit operates under the name, Crystaal. Chairman Eugene Melnyk owns approximately 20% of the company.

History: Since incorporation in 1977, Biovail's technologies have been used to develop over 18 products, which have generated in excess of $400 million in worldwide yearly sales. The firm applies its numerous timed-release drug-delivery systems to existing drugs that treat hypertension, asthma, and arthritis, among other disease states. 1999 brought the acquisition of *Verelan* from Mylan Laboratories. 2000 brought the purchase of privately owned DJ Pharma in the United States, which significantly grew Biovail's United States infrastructure by adding over 300 representatives. In 2001, Biovail Corporation acquired *Cardizem* from Aventis for $410 Million. Biovail also secured agreements with GlaxoSmithKline whereby Biovail has worldwide marketing rights to a once-daily version of *Wellbutrin*. Additionally, Biovail has acquired GlaxoSmithKline's *Zovirax.* Currently Biovail has over 17 products on the market in the United States, and over 20 agents in the pipeline. Biovail acquired *Teveten, Teveten HCT* from Solvay in 2002. Finally in 2002, Biovail Corp. acquired Pharma Pass LLC and its French company Pharma Pass SA for a total of $190 million. Pharma Pass Develops oral controlled release technologies and formulations. 2003 brought approval of *Wellbutrin XL* and *Cardizem LA*, and acquisition of *Ativan* and *Isordil* from Wyeth.

Annual Healthcare Revenue: $788 million

CEO: Eugene N. Melnyk

Sales force: 600

Major Brands: *Ativan* antianxiety, *Cardizem, Cardizem LA* hypertension/angina (with Reliant Pharmaceuticals), *Cedax* anti-infective, *Isordil* cardiovascular agent, *Dura-vent, Rondec* allergies/decongestant, *Teveten, Teveten HCT, Tiazac* for hypertension, *Wellbutrin, Wellburin XL* (with GSK) depression.

Near approval: *Buspirone* anxiety, depression/smoking cessation, *Metformin* type 2 diabetes, *Tramado* pain, *Citalopram* depression.

BOEHRINGER INGELHEIM CORPORATION
900 OLD RIDGEBURY ROAD
RIDGEFIELD, CT 06877
203.798.9988
boehringer-ingelheim.com

Summary: This Ingelheim, Germany concern obtains about 96% of its net sales from prescription pharmaceuticals. The business units include human pharmaceuticals, consumer health products, animal health and contract manufacturing. Boehringer is privately owned with no publicly available traded stock. The prescription business focuses on products for the respiratory, cardiovascular, gastrointestinal, rheumatology, oncology, urology, and virology therapeutic areas. Over the counter medications, include the cough/cold market, analgesics, and vitamin and mineral products.

History: Boehringer Ingelheim was founded in Ingelheim Rhein in 1885 where world headquarters is still located today. The chemical business segment is the oldest of the companies units. In the fifties Boehringer Ingelheim began its work in the animal health area. Products in this area focus on antibiotics and vaccines. In mid nineties, Boehringer Ingelheim acquired US company, Fermenta, Ben Venue Laboratories and Nobl laboratories to strengthen its pharmaceutical presence. In 1997, the company launched *Mobic, Flomax* (with Abbott), *Viramune* and *Combivent.* In 1998 a new unit, Industrial Biopharmaceuticals was formed which is responsible for the contract manufacture of biotechnology products. The company is continuing research in therapeutic areas of cardiovascular, airway, and metabolic diseases. Also included are central nervous system, oncology, virology, immunological and inflammatory diseases. In March of 1998, Boehringer Ingelheim and Glaxo Wellcome PLC reached an agreement to co market, *Miracles* worldwide. In 2000, *Cafcit* received approval and Boehringer Ingelheim announced that it would provide its HIV/AIDS drug *Viramune* to developing countries free of charge. In 2001, Boehringer signed an agreement to co-market *Spiriva* (with Pfizer). Product approved in 2001 include *Berodual Non-CFC MDI,* and *Micardis HCT.* 2003 brought and agreement with Lilly to comarket *Cymbalta.*

Annual Healthcare Revenue: $7.1 billion

CEO: Rolf Krebs

Sales force: 1700

Major Brands: *Actilyse* myocardial infarction, stroke, *Atrovent, Combivent* bronchospasm, *Caficit* apnea in premature infants, *Aggrenox* stroke, *Catapres* hypertension, *Micardis* (with Abbott) hypertension, *Mirapex* Parkinson's Disease, *Flomax* (with Abbott) benign prostatic hypertrophy, *Mobic* (with Abbott) rheumatoid arthritis, *TNKase* acute myocardial infarction, *Viramune* HIV infections.

Near approval: *Actilyse* immediate stroke treatment, *Cymbalta* urinary stress incontinence (with Lilly), *Epinastine* ocular allergies, *Atrovent Non-CFC-MDI* bronchospasm, *Pritor HCT* hypertension, *Respimat, Spiriva* pulmonary disease/chronic obstructive pulmonary disease (with Pfizer), *Tipranavir* HIV infection.

BRISTOL-MYERS SQUIBB COMPANY
MEAD JOHNSON
345 PARK AVENUE
NEW YORK, NY. 10154
212.546.4000
BMY
bms.com

Summary: This New York City pharmaceutical concern established in 1989 has products in therapeutic categories that include cardiovascular, anti-infective, anticancer, anti-AIDS, nutrition and wound care products. Bristol-Myers Squibb has increased research and development and has many new compounds in the pipeline including antihypertensive, antimigraine, and antitumor agents. Bristol-Myers Squibb is the number one producer of oncology medications in the pharmaceutical industry. Sales by Bristol-Myers Squib's Oncology Therapeutics Network exceed over $1 billion annually.

History: William Bristol and John Myers founded Clinton Pharmaceutical in New York, in 1880's (renamed Bristol-Myers in 1900) to sell pharmaceuticals. Mead Johnson was purchased in the sixties (drugs, infant formula's) and Zimmer in the early seventies (orthopedic products). The companies acquired several biotech concerns in eighties, Oncogen and Genetic Systems. In 1989, Bristol-Myers purchased Squibb for $12.7 billion. Fellow New Yorker Dr. Edward Squibb founded Squibb in 1850's. Developments included ether and chloroform. By the middle 1970's sales reached over $1 billion. Products such as *Capoten* and *Corgard* became market leaders among the cardiovascular segment. In 2000, BMS announced that it would divest its Clairol beauty care business and Zimmer orthopedics division to concentrate solely on the pharmaceutical segment. *Vaniqa* was approved in 2000. In 2001, BMS purchased the pharmaceutical unit of DuPont for 7.8 billion. DuPont brings key products such as *Sustiva, Coumadin,* and *Cardiolite* to the BMS portfolio. DuPont Pharma was formed in the early nineties by DuPont and Merck Pharmaceutical. Product approvals within 2001 included *Glucophage, Glucophage XR, Levaquin* and *Videx EC.* 2002 brought approval of *Metaglip* and *Plavix* for the additional treatment of acute coronary syndrome and *Abilify.*. 2003 brought approval of *Pravigard Pac* (*Pravachol* and buffered aspirin), and agreements with Sequenom Inc. for genetics discovery collaboration. In addition *Ovcon 35* the first chewable oral contraceptive received FDA approval (to be marketed by Warner Chilcott).

Annual Healthcare Revenue: $18.1 billion

CEO: Peter R. Dolan

Sales force: 4400

Major Brands: *Abilify* an antipsychotic, *Avapro* hypertension, *Cafcit* (Mead Johnson) injection for apnea of premature infants, *Coumadin* venous thrombosis, *Cardiolite* radio pharmaceutical, *Innohep* deep vein thrombosis, *Levaquin* antibiotic, *Ovcon 35* chewable oral contraceptive, *Pravachol, Pravigard Pac* >$2.2 billion, cholesterol agents, *Taxol* >$1 billion, *Paraplatin* anticancer agents, *Metaglip, Glucophage Glucophage XR, Glucophage IR* and *Glucovance* >$2.6 billion for type II diabetes, *Videx, Zerit* and *Sustiva* HIV products, *Tequin* respiratory infections, *Enfamil,Viactiv* (Mead Johnson) nutritional products, *Plavix* >$1.8 billion, for prevention of stroke, *Vaniqa* unwanted facial hair.

Near approval: *Aripiprazole* schizophrenia, *Atazanavir* HIB/AIDS, *Definity* contrast imaging agent, *Entecavir* hepatitis B, *Erbitux* cancer, *Glipizide* type 2 diabetes, *Garenoxacin quinolone antibiotic, Irbesartan* heart failure, *Reyataz* for HIV, *Zerit ER, Zerit Prolonged-Release* HIV-1 infection.

DAIICHI PHARMACEUTICAL CORPORATION
11 Philips Parkway
Montvale, NJ 07645-1810

877.324.4244

www.daiichius.com

Summary: Daiichi Pharmaceutical Corporation was founded in 1915 as Japan's first research based pharmaceutical company. Daiichi Pharmaceutical Co., Ltd. has established its first subsidiary in the U.S. - Daiichi Pharmaceutical Corporation. The vision in the U.S. is to make Daiichi a premier clinical research and sales & marketing driven pharmaceutical company. In the U.S., Daiichi will focus in specific and specialized therapeutic areas through the development of innovative products that improve patient's lives. Daiichi will focus on three core therapeutic areas, oncology, anti-infectives, and internal medicine specialties. In 2003, Japan represents 75% of global sales.

History: 1982 Daiichi Pharmaceutical Company established in the United States focus on developing relationship with U.S. pharmaceutical industries and supporting existing bulk fine chemical business in the U.S. 1989 DPC began to establish medical development organization *Floxin* was first launched in the U.S. by Johnson & Johnson. 1996 *Camptosar* was launched in the U.S. by Pharmacia & Upjohn, co-promoted by Daiichi Pharmaceutical Company. In 1996, Daiichi and Pharmacia & Upjohn (now Pfizer) agreed to co-promote *Camptosar*, initially developed by Daiichi Japan and Yakult Honsha Co., Ltd., for the Japanese market. In 1997, *Levaquin* was launched in the U.S. (by Johnson & Johnson). In 1998, *Floxin Otic* was approved for market. 2000 brought *Evoxac*. In 2002, Daiichi celebrated its 20th anniversary in United States marketplace.

Annual Healthcare Revenue:

CEO: Tadashi Suzuki

Sales force: 376

Major Brands: *Floxin* anti-infective, *Evoxac* for dry mouth with Sjögren's syndrome, *Camptosar* for cancer, *Levaquin*>$1 billion antibiotic.

Near approval: *Evoxac* for additional indications, *Exatecan* expected to be the world's first oral taxane derivative for cancer,

EISAI INCORPORATED
GLENPOINTE CENTRE WEST
500 FRANK W. BURR BLVD.
TEANECK, NJ 07666
201.692.7710
ESALY
eisai.co.jp

Summary: Incorporated in 1941, Eisai now supports more than 7000 employees worldwide. Business segments include agrochemical products, bulk pharmaceuticals, diagnostics, vitamins, prescription pharmaceuticals, veterinary products, food additives, and a full range of pharmaceutical production equipment. Eisai now operates a global network of research facilities, manufacturing sites and marketing subsidiaries. Eisai develops, manufactures, and distributes prescription and OTC pharmaceuticals, diagnostic products, and pharmaceutical production equipment around the world. Prescription drugs account for a majority of the company's sales. The drug maker has alliances with such pharmaceutical giants as Johnson & Johnson and Pfizer.

History: Established in 1941 in Japan, Eisai was first to synthesize and commercially produce vitamin E, along with the production of various other bulk chemicals. As recent as 1981, Eisai USA was established for chemical and pharmaceutical machinery sales. In 1995, the prescription pharmaceutical company was established in the Unites States with headquarters in New Jersey. 1997 developed and brought approval of *Aricept*, which is currently the number one prescribed Alzheimer medication in the world. 1997 Eisai Incorporated opened an 85,000square-foot, production, research and development facility in North Carolina. In 1999, Eisai's *Aciphex* was approved for marketing. Eisai and Neurogenetics Inc. announced in 2002 the extension of an agreement involving Alzheimer disease targets using human genetics. In July 2002, Eisai acquired exclusive rights to promote Pfizer's *Cerebyx.* In 2003, Eisai announced the doubling of its United States sales force (from 250-500 representatives) and submitted new formulations of *Aricept* for approval to the FDA.

Annual Healthcare Revenue: $3.8 billion

CEO: Haruo Naito

Sales force: 400

Major Brands: *Aciphex* >$1 billion, ulcers (comarketed with Janssen), *Aricept*

Near approval: *Aciphex* helicobacter pylori infection, *Aricept* vascular dementia, *Cleactor* pulmonary embolism, *E2000* spasticity, muscle relaxant, *E7155* magnetic resonance imaging contrast medium, T-614 rheumatoid arthritis.

ÉLAN PHARMACEUTICALS

7475 LUSK BOULEVARD
SAN DIEGO, CA 92121
800.859.8587
ELN
elan.com

Summary: One of the first pure drug delivery concerns, Élan of Ireland has transformed into a fully integrated pharmaceutical researcher, developer and marketer. Products are prescription pharmaceuticals. Research facilities are in Ireland, the United States and Israel.

History: Incorporated in 1969, Élan's first product was *Tetrabid,* marketed by Organon in the United Kingdom. In 1989, Élan produced *Cardizem SR* with Élans proprietary release technology for Marion Laboratories of Kansas City. 1996 Élan announced the acquisition of Athena Neurosciences of San Francisco. Athena provided several agents in development for neurology in addition to a specialized neurodiagnostic testing service through its subsidiary, Athena Diagnostics. In 1998, Carnrick Laboratories was acquired, which included *Skelaxin.* Élan also acquired Neurex Corporation, Ligand and Dura Pharmaceuticals to compliment its United States presence. In 2002, with accounting misappropriations, Élan put a plan to restructure its businesses, assets and balance sheet to create a new smaller Elan that will focus solely on neurology, pain and autoimmune diseases. In June of 2002, Elan launched *Frova.* In July, Elan sold Athena Diagnostics Inc, as part of the recovery plan and a cost reduction, which reduced headcount by over 1000 employees. In June of 2003, Elan announced the sale of its primary care business unit to King Pharmaceuticals for $750 million. The transaction included pharmaceutical products, *Sonata, Skelaxin* and Elan's 400 member primary care sales force and management. In July, the company agreed to sell its stake in Ligand Pharmaceuticals and Elan Transdermal Technologies. In December of 2003, Elan announced it intends to focus on delivery technologies and acute care business.

Annual Healthcare Revenue: $1.4 billion

CEO: Kelly Martin

Salesforce: **200**

Major Brands: *Frova* migraine, *Maxipime, Azactam* antibiotics, *Myobloc* cervical dystonia, *Zanaflex* spasticity, *Zonegran* epilepsy.

Near approval: *Antegren* Multiple sclerosis (with Biogen), *Prialt* chronic pain.

ENDO PHARMACEUTICALS
100 Painters Drive
Chadds Ford, PA 19317
610. 558.9800
ENDP
endo.com

Summary: Endo Pharmaceuticals is a specialty pharmaceutical company who specializes in the research, development, sales and marketing of branded and generic prescription pharmaceuticals primarily used in pain management.

History: In the 1920's Endo, a family-run business was established in Manhattan, New York. In the fifties one of the gold standards of pain relief *Percodan* is developed. In 1969, DuPont acquires Endo Pharmaceuticals. The seventies had brought *Percocet,* a leading medication for moderate to severe pain even today. DuPont and Merck form and independent joint venture, known as the Dupont Merck Pharmaceuticals Company in 1990. In 1994, DuPont Merck re-establishes Endo as a separate entity within the organization, named Endo Laboratories and serves as DuPont Merck's generic products division. Endo Pharmaceuticals Inc. was born, as a separate entity one again in 1997, due to a management buyout from key executive from DuPont Merck in 1997. *Lidoderm* a topical patch for pain of neuropathic pain is launched in 1999. In 2000, Endo Pharmaceuticals purchases Algos Pharmaceuticals company and becomes a publicly traded company.

Healthcare Revenue: $400 million

CEO: Carol A. Ammon

Salesforce: 325

Major Brands: *Lidoderm* topical patch for neuropathic pain*, Percocet, Percodan, Zydone, Morphine Sulfate ER Tablets* all for moderate to severe pain.

Near Approval: *Propofol IDD-D I.V.* Induction and/or maintenance of anesthesia, *Depomorphine, Oxymorphone ER, IR, DepoMorphine* all for moderate to severe pain, *Lidoderm* additional indications, *Chronogesic* sub dermal 90 day pain management system, *Oxycodone Extended Release* for chronic pain.

FOREST LABORATORIES INCORPORATED
909 THIRD AVENUE
NEW YORK, NY 10022
212.421.7850
FRX
frx.com

Summary: Based in New York City with operations throughout the United States and Europe, Forest develops and manufactures name brand, generic prescription and OTC pharmaceutical products. Forest Laboratories has subsidiaries in the United Kingdom and Ireland.

History: Incorporated in 1956 Forest products are marketed principally in the United States and western and Eastern Europe. In the United States Forest operates three sales divisions (Forest Pharmaceuticals, Forest Therapeutics, and Forest Specialty Sales). In the mid-eighties, *Aerobid* was approved. 1996 Forest bought *Tiazac* for hypertension. In 1998, Forest Laboratories launched *Celexa,* an antidepressant that accounts for some 60% of total current sales. The company's generic products are marketed directly by its Inwood Laboratories, Inc. subsidiary. In 1999, Forest promoted over 25% of their sales force due to expansion. In 2000, Forest's sales force was expanded by 70%, *Infasurf* and *Zanidip* (licensed from Recordati of Italy) were launched. In 2001, sales of *Celexa* grew by 67% to over $700 million. In 2002, the FDA approved *Lexapro* and *Lexapro Oral Solution.* Forest continues to convert *Celexa* patients to *Lexapro*, the single isomer version of *Celexa*, due to its superior therapeutic profile, and lower price. *Namenda* was approved in 2003.

Annual Healthcare Revenue: $2.2 billion

CEO: Howard Solomon

Salesforce: 2300

Major Brands: *Aerobid/Aerobid-M, Aerospan* asthma, *Benicar/Benicar HCT* (with Sankyo Pharma) hypertension, *Celexa, Lexapro* >$1.5 billion for depression, *Monurol* urinary tract infections, *Namenda* moderate to severe Alzheimer's disease *Tiazac* hypertension, *Infasurf* respiratory distress in infants, *Cervidil* obstetrical care.

Near approval: *Acamprosate* alcohol dependence, *Campral* for alcohol addiction, *Dexloxiglumide* for irritable bowel syndrome, *Lexapro* additional indications, *Licofelone* osteoarthritis, *Lercanidipine* hypertension, *Neramexane* for central nervous system disorders, *Oxycodone-Ibuprofen* narcotic analgesic combination.

FUJISAWA HEALTHCARE, INC.
Three Parkway North
Deerfield, IL 60015-2548
847.317.8800
FJSPF
fujisawa.co.jp

Summary: Fujisawa is involved is a dynamic array of products and services, including divisions in Ethical Pharmaceuticals, Consumer Products, Medical Equipment and Supplies, Home Medical Care and Industrial chemicals. Research focuses on the therapeutic areas of immunology, inflammation, cerebral metabolic diseases and anti-infectives. In late 2003 Fujisawa Pharmaceutical CO. LTD. stated it is discussing with Yamanouchi Pharmaceutical Co. Ltd. A possible merger that would create Japan's second largest drug maker.

History: Founded in Osaka, Japan in 1894, Fujisawa Company has offices, plants, and research facilities spanning Japan, North America, Europe and Asia, employing over 7500 individuals worldwide. Consumer Products include OTC drugs including cough, cold, gastrointestinal, analgesic and anti-inflammatory agents. Medical Equipment and Supplies segment provides many diagnostic and research reagents, including dentistry and medical checkups. Chemicals and Animal Health Products include industrial chemicals as well as antibiotic feed additives. Fujisawa is a leading Japanese pharmaceutical concern with a history of strong research and development. Through Fujisawa's overseas subsidiaries and licensing agreements, the company is able to offer a broad range of pharmaceutical products worldwide. Currently the Ethical Pharmaceuticals division accounts for nearly 90% of total revenue. In 2000, Fujisawa signed a development and marketing agreement with CV Therapeutics Inc. to gain the North American rights to CVT-3146, a second-generation heart stress drug. In 2001, Fujisawa launched *Protopic Ointment.* In 2002, Fujisawa and Aventis Pharma Ltd. formed an alliance to market the injectable streptogramin antibiotic *Synercid* in Japan.

Annual Healthcare Revenue: $3 billion

CEO: Hatsuo Aoki Ph.D.

Sales force: 300

Major Brands: *AmBisome* antifungal, *Adenoscan* cardiac imaging agent, *Cefzon* antibiotic, *Prograf* prophylaxis of organ rejection, *Protopic Ointment* dermatitis, *Rescula* glaucoma.

Near approval: *Atrisone* acne, *Micafungin* fungal infections, *Prograf* additional indications, *Protopic* atopic dermatitis in children, *Zindaclin* acne.

GENENTECH
1 DNA WAY
SOUTH SAN FRANCISCO, CA 94080
650.225.1000
DNA
gene.com

Summary: Genentech, Inc. is a biotechnology concern using human genetic information to manufacture and market pharmaceuticals. Genentech focuses on cardiovascular, pulmonary, oncology, and metabolic and autoimmune diseases. The company is a world leader in the manufacture of biopharmaceuticals, producing many products used for clinical research through a variety of fermentation and proprietary purification processes. The Founders Research Center, the world's largest biotech research facility was opened in 2001.

History: Genentech Inc. was founded in 1976 by venture capitalist Robert A. Swanson and biochemist Herbert W. Boyer. In the early 1970's Boyer and geneticist, Stanley Cohen forged a new scientific field labeled recombinant DNA technology. In 1978 Genentech cloned human insulin, which was licensed to Eli Lilly and Company and marketed in 1982. In 1979, human growth hormone was cloned and *Protropin* human growth hormone for children was granted approval to market. In 1986 Genentech's alpha interferon was licensed to Hoffmann-La Roche, Inc for treatment of hairy cell leukemia. In 1987, Genentech received approval to market *Activase*. In 1990, Genentech and Roche Holding Ltd. of Switzerland completed a $2.1 billion merger where Roche now owns 59% of Genentech's stock. In addition, that year the company received approval to market *Actimmune*. In 1993 *Nutropin* was introduced, and Factor VIII for hemophilia-A was licensed to Bayer. *Nutropin AQ* was released in 1996. *Rituxan* was approved in late 1997. In 2000, two new products from Genentech emerged, *TNKase* and *Nutropin Depot.* In 2001, Genentech's approvals included *Cathlo Activase.* In April 2002, Genentech received approval for *Nutropin AQ Pen.* June 2003 brought approval of *Xolair*.

.**Annual Healthcare Revenue:** $2.7 billion

CEO: Arthur D. Levinson PhD.

Sales force: 700

Major Brands: *Cathlo Activase* restores function to central venous catheters, *Herceptin* breast cancer, *Nutropin AQ, Nutropin Depot, Nutropin AQ Pen* and *Protropin* human growth hormone, *Activase, TNKase* myocardial infarctions/acute massive pulmonary embolism/acute ischemic stroke, *Tracleer* pulmonary arterial hypertension, *Rituxan* >$1.6 billion (the number one branded oncology agent in the United States), for non-Hodgkin's lymphoma, *Xolair* monoclonal antibody for asthma treatment.

Near approval: *Avastin* breast cancer, *Lucentis* for macular degeneration, *Raptiva* additional indications, *Tarceva* cancer.

GENZYME CORPORATION
500 Kendall Street
Cambridge, MA 02139
617.252.7500
genzyme.com

Summary: Genzyme specializes in Lysosomal Storage Disorders, Renal, Orthopedic, Burn Treatment, Immune Mediated Diseases, Adhesion Prevention, Immune Mediated Diseases, Cardiovascular, Cancer, Chronic Debilitating Diseases, and Diagnostic Product Services.

History: In 1981, Genzyme founded by Henry Blair and Sherry Snyder. In 1985, *Ceredase* is designated an orphan drug by FDA. In 1986, Genzyme becomes a public company with an initial public offering. In 1994, FDA grants marketing approval of *Cerezyme*. In 1996, approval to market *Seprafilm* is obtained. 1997 brings a biologics license application approval for *Carticel* to repair cartilage in the knee - the first for a cell therapy product. The late nineties bring FDA approval for *Renagel*, *Thyrogen, Synvisc* and *Thymoglobulin*. In 2000, *Sepramesh* and *Renagel 800 mg* and *Renagel 400 mg* tablets are launched. *Fabrazyme*, with orphan drug status receives approval in 2003 and partner BioMarin receives approval of *Aldurazyme*.

CEO: Henri A.Termeer

Sales force: 275

Major Brands: *Fabrazyme* fabry disease, *Synvisc* (with Wyeth) arthritis, *Aldurazyme* for MPS I, *Carticel* cartilage for the knee, *Ceredase*, *Cerezyme* Gauchers disease *Epicel* severe burns, *Renagel* for renal disease, *Seprafilm* for adhesions barrier, *Sepramesh* biosurgical composite, *Thyrogen* treatment for thyroid cancer, *WellChol* lipid lowering agent (marketed by Sanko Pharma).

Near Approval: *Synvisc* for hip, *Sangtat* for Crohn's disease and ulcerative colitis, *Thyrogen* for ablation of thyroid cancer, *Myozyme* for Pompe disease.

GLAXOSMITHKLINE
FIVE MOORE DRIVE
RESEARCH TRIANGLE PARK, NC 27709
919.483.2100
GSK
gsk.com

Summary: As the largest based European pharmaceutical concern Glaxo SmithKline (GSK) therapeutic categorics include, anesthesiology, bacterial and viral, anti-infectives, cardiology, central nervous system disorders, dermatology, gastrointestinal disorders, oncology and respiratory ailments. In 2000, Glaxo Wellcome and SmithKline Beecham completed a merger that would create one of the world's leading research-based pharmaceutical companies now known as GlaxoSmithKline (GSK) based in Greenford, United Kingdom. Currently GSK has eight medications among the world's top 50 pharmaceutical agents and is widely recognized as the second leading pharmaceutical concern behind Pfizer.

History: In 1873, Englishman Joseph Nathen started Glaxo in New Zealand. Nathan obtained the rights to produce powdered milk. The company went public in 1947 and Glaxo diversified in the fifties with acquisitions of veterinary, instrument and drug distribution firms. Only in the late seventies, did Glaxo establish its first United States operations. In the eighties Glaxo focused on its pharmaceutical segment, divesting other non-pharmaceutical operations. Glaxo launched *Zanta* in 1981. SmithKline started in 1830 as a small Philadelphia pharmacy. *Tagamet* introduced in 1976 became the worlds leading selling pharmaceutical product at the time. Beecham merged with SmithKline Beckman in 1989. Thomas Beecham established an apothecary in England in 1847 and opened the world's first drug making factory in 1859. In 1995 Glaxo, purchased U.K. based Burroughs Wellcome for $14.9 billion. Founded by Silas Burroughs and Henry Wellcome (Americans) in 1880, Burroughs Wellcome reached success with numerous antiviral agents. In 1980 Burroughs Wellcome introduced *Zovirax* and in 1987 *Retrovir*. In 1997, the FDA approved *Zyban*. In 1999, Glaxo Wellcome received approval for *Relenza*. 2000 brought approval for *Trizivir*. 2001 brought approval numerous approvals and launches including *Advair Diskus, Agenerase, Rionavir, Augmentin ES, Flovent Diskus, Dutasteride, Triziver, Twinrix,* and *Ventolin HFA*. In 2002, GSK launched *Paxil CR*. In 2003, GlaxoSmithKline announced that it has entered an exclusive partnership with Chiron for the research, development and commercialization of obesity agents and FDA approval of *Bexxar* and *Pediarix*. *Levitra* was launched in 2003 (with Bayer) and approval of *Lexiva* and *Wellbutrin XL*.

Annual Healthcare Revenue: $31.8 billion

CEO: Jean-Pierre Garnier PhD.

Sales force: 8000

Major Brands: *Advair Diskus, Flovent, Serevent, Seretide, Ventolin*>$4.2 billion for asthma, *Avandia* type 2 diabetes, *Amoxil, Augmentin, Augmentin ES/ER* >$1.8 billion, antibiotics, *Bexxar* for cancer therapy, *Ceftin, Zovirax* anti-infectives, *Coreg* hypertension/heart failure, *Dutasteride* benign prostatic hyperplasia, *Imitrex* >$1.2 billion, migraines, *Agenerase, Combivir, Epivir, Lexiva, Trizivir, Retrovir* and *Ziagen* HIV/ infections, *Paxil, Paxil CR* >$3 billion, depression/anxiety/panic disorder and premenstrual dysphoric disorder, *Pediarix* combination vaccine, *Relenza* influenza, *Twinrix* hepatitis vaccine, *Wellbutrin, Wellbutrin SR* depression, *Zantac* ulcers, *Zovirax, Valtrex* herpes, *Ventolin HFA* bronchospasm, *Zyban* smoking cessation, and numerous *vaccine's*.

Near approval: *Argatroban* thrombosis risk, *Arifo* COPD, *Boostrix* DTP vaccine, *Epivir/Ziagen* for HIV, *Factive* antibiotic, *Hepatyrix* vaccine, hepatitis A, salmonella, *Hycamptin* cancer, *Infanrix* diphtheria, tetanus, pertussis vaccine, *Locilex* diabetic foot ulcers, *Penciclovir* herpes treatment, *Teveten* and *Hydrochlorothiazide* hypertension, *Ventolin Dry Powder Inhaler* pediatric asthma, *Vesicare* for over active bladder.

JOHNSON AND JOHNSON
1 JOHNSON AND JOHNSON PLAZA
NEW BRUNSWICK, NEW JERSEY 08993
732.524.0400
JNJ
jnj.com

Summary: United States based Johnson & Johnson is the largest manufacturer of health products in the world. Pharmaceutical divisions consist of Advanced Care Products, Janssen Pharmaceutica, Johnson and Johnson-Merck (consumer pharmaceuticals), LifeScan (glucose monitoring equipment), McNeil Consumer Products Co., Ortho Biotech, Ortho Dermatological, Ortho-McNeil Pharmaceutical and Centocor. Three main segments consist of pharmaceuticals, consumer products, and professional products. Recent acquisitions include OraPharma Inc., 3-Dimensional Pharmaceuticals, Tibotec-Virco, Link Spine Group Inc., and Scios Inc (for $2.4 billion) in 2003.

History: Brothers James and Edward Johnson founded this medical company in 1885 in New Brunswick, New Jersey. In 1886, another brother, Robert, joined to make and sell the antiseptic surgical dressings he developed. In 1897 Edward left the organization to found the drug company Mead Johnson (currently Bristol-Myers Squibb). Johnson & Johnson bought gauze maker Chicopee Manufacturing in 1916. A product of Robert Johnson's dressing; the **Band-Aid** was introduced in 1921. In 1932, Robert Johnson Jr. became Chairman and served until 1963. In the forties the divisions of Ortho (birth control products) and Ethicon (surgical sutures) were developed. In 1959, the company acquired McNeil Labs, who launched blockbuster **Tylenol** in 1960. Foreign acquisitions included Belgium's Janssen and Switzerland's Cilag-Chemie during the same period. Johnson and Johnson purchased LifeScan, a manufacturer of blood glucose monitoring in eighties and product launches included **Acuvue, Retin-A,** and **Eprex.** In 1996, **Renova** was launched. Company acquisitions included Centocor Inc. Alza in 2000. **Ortho Evra,** was approved in 2001 and 2002 brought **Concerta** and **Remicade**. In 2003, J&J acquired leading biotech concern Scios in 203.

Annual Healthcare Revenue: $36.2 billion

CEO: William C. Weldon

Sales force: 5400

Major Brands: *Aciphex* (Janssen) for ulcers (with Eisai), *Concerta* (Ortho-McNeil) attention deficit disorder, *Ditropan XL* (Ortho Mc Neil) bladder control, *Doxil* oncology agent, *Duragesic* >$1.2 billion transdermal pain patch, *Floxin*, *Levaquin*>$1 billion antibiotics, *Natrecor* (Scios) for congestive heart failure, *Nizoral* antifungal, *Procrit* >$4.2 billion, to reduce need for blood transfusions, *Ortho Novum, Ortho Tri-Cyclin, Ortho Evra* contraceptives, *Retin-A* acne, *ReoPro* (Centocor) cardiac ischemia, *Reminyl/Reminyl Oral Solution* Alzheimer's, *Remicade* <$1.3 billion (Centocor) arthritis and Crohn's disease, *Renova* (Ortho Pharmaceutical) photo damage therapy, *Risperdal* >$2.1 billion, schizophrenia, *Sporanox* (Janssen) antifungal, *Topamax* epilepsy, migraine's, *Ultram, Ultracet* (Ortho-McNeil) pain.

Near approval: *Caelyx* breast cancer, *Dilaudid CR* pain, *Cereport* brain tumors, *Doxil* myeloma, breast cancer, *Intergel* post surgical adhesions, *Oros Hydromorphone* chronic pain, *Ortho Elodose, Ortho Tricept* contraception, *Pennsaid* osteoarthritis, *Risperdal, Resperdal Consta* additional indications, *Topamax* tablets and *Topamax Sprinke* for additional indications, *Zarnestra* pancreatic cancer.

KING PHARMACEUTICALS
501 Fifth Street
Bristol, Tennessee 37620
800.776.3637
KG
kingpharm.com

Summary: King is headquartered in Bristol, Tennessee, which manufactures, markets, and sells primarily branded prescription pharmaceutical products. Therapeutic categories include cardiovascular, respiratory, anti-infectives, endocrinology, women's health, and critical care areas. The firm contracts its excess manufacturing capabilities to outside pharmaceutical companies. Subsidiary Monarch Pharmaceuticals sells King's products to physicians and health care facilities.

History: In1994 the Gregory family purchased the Bristol facility (Beecham laboratories) and assumed contracts to manufacture pharmaceutical products for such companies as GlaxoSmithKline, and Novartis. The company adopted its strategy of selectively acquiring branded prescription pharmaceutical products. In 1998, King acquired 15 branded pharmaceutical products from Warner-Lambert and three branded prescription pharmaceutical products from Aventis, which included *Altace*. In 1999, King purchased *Lorabid* from Eli Lilly. King's merger in with Medco Research in 2000 brought such products as *Adenocard* and *Adenoscan*. King acquired from Weyth Laboratories *Nordette*, *Bicillin*, *Wycillin* and *Altace*. Jones Pharma Incorporated of St. Louis was acquired in 2000 adding *Levoxyl, Cytomel, Triostat, Thrombin-JMI* and *Brevital Sodium*.   In 2001, King entered agreements to co-market *Estrasorb* and *Androsorb*. In addition, King acquired Bristol-Myers Squibb's *Corzide, Delestrogen* and *Florinef* in 2001. In 2003 King purchased Ireland-based Élan Pharmaceutical Company's United States primary care field sales force and products, *Sonata* and *Skelaxin* In 2003, *Estrasorb* and *Intal HFA* gained approval.

Annual Healthcare Revenue: $872 million

CEO: Jefferson J. Gregory

Salesforce: 1235

Major Brands: *Altace*, an ACE inhibitor, *Estrasorb* a transdermal estrogen
Levoxyl for thyroid disease, **Intal, Intal HFA** inhaler, *EpiPen* for anaphylactic shock**, *AtroPen* nerve gas antidote, *Sonata* for insomnia, *Skelaxin* muscle relaxant**.

Near Approval: *Sonata* additional formulations, *Estrasorb* hormone replacement.

Mellisa Popa 276-0950 Team der

ELI LILLY AND COMPANY
LILLY CORPORATE CENTER
INDIANAPOLIS, IN 46285
317.277.2162
LLY
Lilly.com

Summary: This Indianapolis based pharmaceutical concern produces antibiotics, insulin, growth hormones, antiulcer, and cancer agents, cardiovascular products, sedatives, vitamins, and feed additives. In 2001, Eli Lilly announced that it would significantly expand its sales force around the globe in late 2003.

History: In 1876, pharmacist, Colonel Eli Lilly, started Eli Lilly and Company. Eli Lilly died in 1898, and his son and grandsons ran the organization until the mid fifties. Lilly introduced insulin in 1923, and blockbusters including, **Merthiolate, Seconal.** Lilly's **Darvon,** at one time, was the leading prescription analgesic in the United States. In 1979, Lilly introduced **Ceclor.** The eighties brought the first biotechnology product **Humulin,** and first in class blockbuster, **Prozac** and **Axid.** Lilly introduced **ReoPro,** in 1995. Recent introductions include **Humalog, Gemzar** and **Zyprexa.** 2001 was a remarkable year with the introduction of **Evista, Prozac Weekly, Zyprexa,** and **Xigris.** In 2002, Eli Lilly received approval for **Forteo** and **Strattera.** Lilly obtained approval for **Symbyax** and **Cialis** (with Icos) in 2003.

Annual Healthcare Revenue: $11 billion

CEO: Sidney T

Sales force: 53

Major Brand ... agents, **Cialis** erectile dysfunction (with Icos), **D** ... is, **Gemzar** cancer, **Humatrope** growth failure ... osteomyelitis, **Prozac, Prozac Weekly** and **S** ... hroric treatment, **ReoPro** cardiovascula ... rder (the first new type of medication for attention ... depression, **Zyprexa, Zyprexa Zydis** >$3.6

Near appro ... er, **Cymbalta** depression, **Duloxetine** ... **emcitabine** breast, ovarian cancer, **Humalog** ... **PL** diabetes, **Olanzapine** psychosis, bipolar dep ... **Resiquimod** genital herpes, **Somatrop** ... on, **Zyprexa IntraMuscular** schizophr

708
647
9335
ISAAC Greeno

Isaac Green
708-647-9335
708 259-6341

Susan Deford-Bolanos
317-276-9460
800-575-1296

400-612-0372

MERCK AND COMPANY INC.
1 MERCK DRIVE
WHITEHOUSE STATION
NEW JERSEY 08889-0100
908.423.1000
MRK
merck.com

Summary: This New Jersey based manufacturer is ranked as one of the largest pharmaceutical concerns in the world.. Merck markets a broad range of human and animal health care products and services. Merck-Medco Managed Care Inc., subsidiary broker's drug purchases for managed care and employee health plans. Therapeutic areas include cardiovascular and gastrointestinal diseases, infections, ophthalmic disorders, prostate disease, and osteoporosis.

History: Theodore Weicker came to the United States from Germany in 1887 to set up an American branch of E. Merck of Germany. George Merck came in 1891 and established the firm, which imported and sold drugs and chemicals from Germany. In 1903, it opened a plant in Rahway, New Jersey. Wicker sold out to George Merck in 1904 and bought a controlling interest in competitor Squibb (now BMS). During WWI Merck gave the United States government the 80% company owned stock owned by the family in Germany. After the war, Merck stock was sold to the public. Merck research did pioneering work on vitamin B12 and developed cortisone (the first steroid). Five Nobel prizes were awarded to Merck scientist in the forties and fifties. In 1952, Merck merged with pharmaceutical producer Sharp & Dome of Philadelphia. Merck introduced *Diuril* in 1958, *Indocin* and *Aldomet* in the early sixties. In the late seventies increased research and development brought forth such products as *Clinoril, Flexeril* and *Timoptic.* In the eighties such products as *Mevacor* and *Vasotec* were introduced, leading their therapeutic classes in sales. Merck purchased pharmaceutical benefit manager (PBM) Medco containment Services in the early nineties for $6.6 billion. Sales for Medco exceeded $23 billion in 2000. Product approvals in 2001 include *Cancidas,* and *Fosamax Once Weekly.* In 2003, Merck agreed to purchase the remaining 49% stake in Banyu Pharmaceutical Co. Ltd. Of Japan for $1.3 billion, establishing Merck's largest wholly owned subsidiary, outside of the United States. 2003 brought FDA approval for *Emend.* In late 2003 Merck completed the spin off of Medco Health (pharmaceutical benefit manager), creating a totally separate organization which issued stock. Merck plans to file 11 new drugs and vaccines for approval by 2006.

Annual Healthcare Revenue: $51.7 billion

CEO: Raymond V. Gilmartin

Sales force: 6,500

Major Brands: *Aggrastat* angina, *Cancidas* fungal infections, *Cozaar, Hyzaar, Vasotec* >$2.1 billion, and *Prinivil* >$1 billion, hypertension agents, *Crixivan, Stocrin* HIV/AIDS, *Fosamax Fosamax Once Weekly* >$2.2 billion, for osteoporosis, *Emend* for nausea and vomiting during chemotherapy, *Maxalt* migraines, *Mevacor, Zocor* >$6 billion cholesterol lowering agents, *Pepcid* and *Prilosec* for ulcers, *Propecia* hair loss, *Proscar* prostate enlargement, *Singulair* >$1.5 billion, the number one asthma treatment in United States, *Vioxx* >$2.5 billion, for arthritis, *Zocor* >$6.6 billion cholesterol agent, currently the top selling drug in the world, *Cosopt* and *Trusopt* elevated intraocular pressure, and numerous *Vaccines.*

Near approval: *Arcoxia* for arthritis, *Cancidas* esophageal candidiasis, *Human Papillomavirus Vaccine* human papillomavirus infections, *Invanz* injectable antibiotic, *Pepcid* pediatric usage, *Singulair & Claritin* (with Schering Plough) allergic rhinitis/asthma, *Vioxx* additional indications, *Zetia/Zocor* for cholesterol, *Zoster Vaccine* prevention of herpes zoster.

NESTLE
ALCON LABORATORIES INC.
P.O. BOX 6600
FORT WORTH, TEXAS 76115
817.293.0450
GALDERMA LABORATORIES INC.
3000 ALTA MESA BLVD., SUITE 300
FORT WORTH, TEXAS 76163
817.263.2600
NSRGY
alconlabs.com
ACL
galderma.com

Summary: Nestle is the worlds #1 food company sells more than 8,500 products in over 100 countries around the world. Nestlé's five segments are 1) beverages, 2) milk products, nutrition and ice cream, 3) chocolate and confectionery, 4) prepared dishes, cooking aids and miscellaneous 5) pharmaceuticals. Pharmaceuticals divisions include 75% ownership of Alcon Laboratories Inc., and Galderma Laboratories Inc. (a joint venture of Nestle and L'Oreal).

History: Henri Nestle purchased a Vevey, Switzerland factory that made products ranging from nut oils to rum. In 1863 Nestle was established in Switzerland. In 1867 Henri Nestle developed a powder made from cow's milk and wheat flour as a substitute for mother's milk. In 1904 Nestle began selling chocolate, and in 1929 Nestle acquired Cailler (the first company to mass-produce chocolate bars) and Swiss General (the inventor of milk chocolate). In 1938 the company introduced Nescafe, the first instant coffee. Other product introductions included Nestlé's Crunch bar in 1938, Quik drink mix 1948, and Taster's Choice coffee in 1966. Most of Nestlé's expansion took place with acquisitions in the 1970's and 1980's including Beringer Brothers wines, Stouffer, Libby, Carnation, Hills Brothers coffee, Buitoni pastas, and Butterfinger and Baby Ruth candies. Nestle first moved beyond foods in 1974 when it acquired a stake in French cosmetics company L'Oreal. Pharmaceutical company Alcon was acquired in 1977. Galderma is a joint venture formed by Nestle and L'Oreal group in 1989. In May 1998, Alcon entered a research alliance with ChiroScience Group PLC. *Loceryl* was acquired in early 1999 from Hoffmann-La Roche. *Differin* was launched in 2000. *Travatan* obtained FDA approval in 2001. In July 2002 the FDA approved *Tri-Luma.* In 2003, *Clobex* was approved.

Annual Healthcare Revenue: $3 billion

CEO Alcon: Timothy Sear

Sales force: 270

Major Brands: Galderma dermatological products: *Capex* dermatitis, *Clobex* topical steroid *Differin* topical anti-acne medication, *Clindagel, Benzac AC, BenzaClin,* benoyl peroxide, *DesOwen* topical steroid, *Loceryl* nail fungus, *Metro-gel/Rozex* rosacea therapy, *Mistamine* antihistamine for urticaria. *Tri-Luma* pigment disorder.

Alcon ophthalmological products: *AcrySof* cataract surgery, *Azopt Timolol GFS* glaucoma, *Betopic, Betopic S,* intraocular pressure, *Ciloxan* ophthalmic infections, *Eye-Stream* irrigating solution, *Patanol* allergic conjunctivitis, *TobraDex* sterile ophthalmic suspension, *Travatan* elevated intraocular pressure.

Near approval: *Anecortave Acetate* age-related macular degeneration, *Metvix PDT* actinic keratosis, basal cell carcinoma

NOVARTIS
556 MORRIS AVENUE
SUMMIT, NJ 07901
908.277.5293
NVS
novartis.com

Summary: Novartis is the result of the $27 billion merger of Ciba-Geigy and Sandoz in 1996. This Basel, Switzerland-based company holds top global positions in all its core businesses: Pharmaceuticals, and Nutritionals. The company is also the #1 maker of chemicals for agriculture protection and the world's largest producer of jarred baby food (Gerber), and business segments in Vision, Animal health, Medical nutrition. The pharmaceutical division accounts for over 40% of total sales, includes products for areas as asthma, immunology, inflammatory diseases, central nervous system disorders, cardiovascular problems, endocrine and metabolic diseases, cancer and dermatology. The nutrition division is one of the world's largest providers of medical nutrition products to patients in hospitals, clinics, and nursing homes residences. Novartis has nearly doubled its United States sales force over the past three years.

History: In 1758 Johann Geigy began promotion of spices and dyes in Switzerland. Following generations of Geigy's continued for a century and synthetic dyes were invented in 1859. At the same time another Swiss company entered the market. Alexander Clavel joined the synthetic dye trade, forming the Gesellschaft fur Chemische Industrie (CIBA). In the early 1900's Ciba was Switzerland's #1 chemical business. Alfred Kern and Edouard Sandoz established Kern and Sandoz in 1886 in Basel also to produce dyes. Ciba, Geigy, and Sandoz were forced to compete with the Germans and the Swiss formed their own cartel Basel AG in 1918. The cartel was dissolved in 1951. All companies continued to branch out through the 1950's. Ciba and Geigy merged in 1970 and began a series of acquisitions in the United States. Ciba-Geigy entered a joint venture with biotech concern Chiron in 1986 and purchased 49% of the company in 1994. In 1996, 45 years after the breakup of Basel AG, Ciba-Geigy and Sandoz recognizing a strategic fit, reunited forming Novartis. 2000 brought the introduction of *Trileptal* and *Exelon*. In 2001 Novartis AG acquired a 21.3% stake in Roche Holding AG, valued at $2.79 billion and obtained approval of *Gleevec, Foradil, Starlix, Zometa.* In 2002, product approvals included *Zelnorm, Ritalin LA* and *Elidel Cream*. Novartis increased its shareholder stake in Roche Holding AG to 32.7% and combined its 14 generic companies under one name, "Sandoz". In addition, Novartis acquired Idenix Pharmaceuticals and their significant pipeline in hepatitis treatments, and the approval of *Stalevo* and *Enablex*.

Annual Healthcare Revenue: $20.9 billion

CEO: Daniel L. Vasella M.D.

Sales force: 6000

Major Brands: *Aredia* tumor induced hypercalceia, *Exelon* Alzheimer's disease, *Gleevec, Femara, Sandostatin* oncology agents, *Enablex* incontinence, *Foradil* asthma, *Diovan, Co-Diovan* >$1.6 billion, heart failure and cardiovascular agent, *Elidel Cream* atopic dermatitis, *Lotrel, Lotensin,* cardiovascular agents, *Lescol XL* lipid lowering agent, *Lamisil* nail fungal infections, *Miacalcin* postmenopausal osteoporosis, *Neoral* immunosuppressant, *Rescula* glaucoma, *Focalin, Ritalin, Ritalin LA* attention deficit disorder, *Stalevo* Parkinson's disease, *Starlix* type 2 diabetes, *Trileptal* epilepsy, *Visudyne* macular degeneration, *Vivelle* postmenopausal osteoporosis, *Zelnorm* irritable bowel syndrome, *Zometa* hypercalcemia of malignancy.

Near approval: *Apligraf* wounds, *Cataflam* migraines, *Certican* for organ rejection, *Prexige* arthritis, *Femara* breast cancer, *Gimatecan* for cancer, *Foradil Certihaler* for asthma, *Letrozole* breast cancer, *Myfortic* rejection in renal transplant, *Prexige* arthritis, pain, *Provigil* excessive daytime sleepiness, *Xolair* allergic rhinitis/asthma, *Zelnorm* constipation, *Zometa* bone metastases.

NOVO NORDISK A/S
405 LEXINGTON AVENUE
STE. 6400
NEW YORK, NY 10017
212.867.0123
NVO
novonordisk.com

Summary: This Copenhagen, Denmark-based company is the worlds leading producer of insulin. Novo's health care products account for a total of 75% of sales. In addition to insulin, it produces injection and monitoring systems for diabetes care. Other therapeutic segments include women's hormone replacement products, human growth hormones, and agents for depression, epilepsy and hemophilia. The company is also a world leader in the industrial enzyme market, investing heavily in the natural protein catalyst, which are often derived from microorganisms. Enzymes are developed for many uses including removing the fat out of foods to even managing toxic spills. The Novo Nordisk Foundation owns 25% of the company. In 2000, Novo Nordisk announced that it would separate into two independent companies, the enzymes business Novozymes A/S and health care business Novo Nordisk A/S.

History: The 1989 merger of Danish insulin producer's Novo and Nordisk formed Novo Nordisk. Engineer Harald Pedersen and brother Thorvald (a pharmacist) established Novo Industri in 1925 to manufacturer insulin and designed a syringe so that patients could administer their own injections. Within a decade Novo was in 40 countries selling insulin. During W.W.II the company produced its first enzyme, *Trypsin,* used to soften leather. In 1947, it introduced penicillin, its first product manufactured by fermentation. In the fifties products such as *Heparin* (for blood clots). In 1982 Novo was the first to produce human insulin. By 1989 it was the worlds #2 maker of insulin (behind Eli Lilly) and the world's largest producer of industrial enzymes. August Krogh (winner of the Nobel Prize in physiology) founded Nordisk in 1923. In 1936 the company introduced the first slow acting insulin. In 1946 the company created a new product called *NPH insulin* (protamine insulin with rapid-acting insulin), which became the leading longer-acting insulin. 1980 has brought the *Nordisk Infuser, NovoPen.* and *Insuject pen.* After the merger Novo Nordisk introduced the *NovoLet.* The company introduced agents for depression, epilepsy and hemophilia in the 1990's. In 1998, Novo Nordisk and Aradigm Corporation signed an agreement to jointly develop pulmonary delivery system for administering insulin by inhalation. In 1999, *NovoSeven* was introduced. 2000 brought *NovoLog,* and *Velsulin BR.* ZymoGenetics is a biopharmaceutical company spin-off of Novo Nordisk's which focus is the discovery, development and commercialization of protein therapeutics for human diseases. In 2002, *NovoPen Junior* was approved.

Annual Healthcare Revenue: $3.1 billion

CEO: Lars Rebien Sorensen

Sales force: 1000

Major Brands: *NovoLog, NovoRapid* insulin product, *Norditropin Simple Xx* growth hormones, *NovaFine NovaLet, InnoLet, FlexPen, and NovoPen 3, NovoPenMate* insulin injection systems, *NovoSeven* hemophilia, *Prandin* type 2 diabetes, *Velsulin BR* DNA origin buffered regular insulin.

Near approval: *Novolin 85/15 Penfill* for diabetes mellitus, *AERx Diabetes Management System* and *Insulin Detemir* for type 1 diabetes, *Seroxat CR* premenstrual dysphonic disorder.

PFIZER INCORPORATED
235 EAST 42ND STREET
NEW YORK, NY 10017
212.573.2323
PFE

pfizer.com

Summary: Based in New York City Pfizer is not only the oldest American based pharmaceutical concern, but also the largest. The combined organization is established in pharmaceuticals, consumer health care, confectionery products, and animal medications. Acquiring Warner-Lambert in 2000 and Pharmacia in 2003 propelled Pfizer the world's largest pharmaceutical concern.

History: Charles Pfizer started his operation in Brooklyn 1849. The company incorporated in 1900 as Chas. Pfizer & Co. Pfizer was pulled into the modern drug business when the company mass-produced penicillin during the war effort in 1941. Pfizer purchased the drug maker Roerig in 1953. Sales reached a total of $2 billion in the late seventies. The eighties brought such blockbusters as *Feldene* and *Glucotrol* . In the nineties Pfizer released *Zoloft, Zithromax* and *Norvasc.* In 1998 Pfizer introduced *Viagra.* February of 2000 Pfizer acquired Warner Lambert. William Warner opened a drugstore in Philadelphia area 1856. In the late 1800's he began the manufacturing of drugs by opening William R. Warner & Co. In fifties Warner purchased Chilcott Labs forming Warner-Chilcott and Lambert Pharmaca of St. Louis (Listerine). Parke-Davis of Detroit was acquired in 1970 (*Dilantin, Benadryl*). Pharmacia begun in Sweden in early nineteen hundreds.. By the mid 1980's Pharmacia was involved in biotechnology, health care, ophthalmology and diagnostics. A pharmacist, Gideon Daniel Searle, formed his pharmaceutical concern in the mid 1800's in Indiana. In late eighteen hundreds the company was relocated to Chicago. Dr. William Upjohn formed the Upjohn Pill and Granuyle Company in Kalamazoo, Michigan in 1886. The blockbuster *Motrin* was introduced in 1974. *Xanax* and *Halcion* were introduced in the eighties. Pharmacia acquired Upjohn in 1995 in a $6 billion deal. 1999 brought *Celebrex*. In 2000, Searle and Pharmacia and merged. In 2001, Pharmacia gained approval to market numerous agents such as: *Axert, Azulfidine EN-Tabs, Detrol LA, Genotropin, Lunelle,* and *Trelstar LA.* 2002 brought the FDA approvals of *Bextra, Relpax, Rebif, Geodon I.M.* and *Vfend.* 2003 brought the completion of the acquisition of Pharmacia by Pfizer for $60 billion.

Annual Healthcare Revenue: $32.3 billion

CEO: Henry A. McKinnell Jr.

Sales force: 12,000

Major Brands: *Accupril* antihypertensive, *Aricept* Alzheimer's disease, *Camptosar* cancer *Diflucan, Vfend* >$1 billion antifungals, *Bextra, Celebrex* >$2 billion, analgesic, anti-arthritic, *Lipitor* >$7.9 billion, cholesterol agent, *Neurontin* >$2.27 billion, epilepsy, neuropathic pain, *Norvasc* >$3.85 billion, cardiovascular agent, *Rebif* multiple sclerosis, *Relpax* migraine, *Viagra* >$1.7 billion, erectile dysfunction, *Zithromax* >$1.52 billion antibiotic, *Zyrtec, Zyrtec-D* >$1 billion antihistamine/decongestant, *Zoloft* >$2.74 billion, anti-depressant, *Activella* osteoporosis, *Genotropin* growth hormone deficiency, *Fragmin* thrombosis, *Lunelle* pregnancy prevention, *Mirapex* Parkinson disease, *Trelstar LA* prostate cancer, *Xalatan* glaucoma.

Near Approval: *Benilas* rheumatoid arthritis, *Deramciciane* anxiety, *Epierenone* hypertension, *Indiplon* insomnia, *Roflumilast* asthma, *Somavert* acromegaly, *Thrombopoietin* thrombocytopenia, *Tifacogin* sepsis, *Vestra* depression, *Xalacom* glaucoma. *Asenapine* for schizophrenia, *Avasimibe* vascular dementia, *Capravirine* HIV infection, *Cardura XL* hypertension, benign prostatic hyperplasia, *Pregabalin* epilepsy, neuropathic pain, *Exubera* inhaled insulin, *Torcetrapib* cholesterol, *Varenicline* smoking cessation, *Caduet (Lipitor/Norvasc) dual therapy*, *Spiriva* pulmonary disease, COPD (with Boehringer Ingelheim).

PROCTER & GAMBLE
1 PROCTER & GAMBLE PLAZA
CINCINNATI, OH 45202
513.983.1100
PG
pg.com

Summary: Procter & Gamble has five main business segments. These are Laundry and Cleaning, Paper Products, Beauty Care, Food and Beverages, and Healthcare. Products include *Tide, Cascade, Bounty, Pampers,* and *Oil of Olay, Cover Girl, Folgers, Jif, Crest,* and *Scope.* Health care is the smallest of the five business segments.

History: William Procter and soap maker James Gamble merged their businesses in 1837 to form Procter and Gamble. By the mid 1800's Procter and Gamble had sales over 1 million dollars. Family descendants operated the company until 1930 when William Deupree became president. *Tide* detergent was introduced in 1947, and *Crest* in the mid fifties. In 1985 Procter and Gamble pushed into the healthcare arena with the purchase of Richardson-Vicks and *Metamucil,* a fiber laxative from Searle. Procter and Gamble's over the counter segment includes *Pepto-Bismol, Vicks* cough and cold line, and *Aleve* pain reliever. Procter and Gamble pipeline includes collaborations with Alexion Pharmaceutical, Regeneron Pharmaceutical, TheraTech Inc., and AstraZeneca. In 1998, brought osteoporosis agent, *Actonel.* In 2001, Proctor & Gamble announced that its health care unit was its strongest businesses unit with sales up 14% over the previous year. In 2002, a once a week dosage form of *Actonel* was launched.

Annual Healthcare Revenue: $5.7 billion

CEO: Alan G. Lafley

Sales force: 850

Major Brands: *Actonel* (with Aventis) post-menopausal osteoporosis, *Asacol* ulcerative colitis, *Didronel* osteoporosis, *Macrobid* urinary tract infections.

Near approval: *Actonel* osteoarthritis, *Estradiol* vasomotor symptoms in postmenopausal women, *Intrinsa* sexual dysfunction, *Pexelizumab* inflammation from bypass surgery, angioplasty, thrombolysis, and myocardial infarction, *Stedicor* arrhythmias.

PURDUE PHARMA L.P.
1 Stamford Forum
201 Tresser Boulevard
Stamford, CT 06901-3431
203.588.8000
purduepharma.com

Summary: Purdue is part of an international group of associated independent companies engaged in the research, development, production, sales, and licensing of both prescription and OTC medications and hospital products. The company is a private company and no stock is traded on pubic exchanges. The company seeks to continually develop and sell new, high quality, innovative pharmaceutical agents. Therapeutic areas include new pain treatments, along with the therapeutic areas of chronic asthma, COPD, relief of constipation and prevention of infection.

History: In 1892, Dr. John Purdue Gray and George Grederick Bingham start the company in New York City. In 1952 present owners, Dr. Raymond and Mortimer Sackler purchase The Purdue Frederick Company, with annual sales slightly above $20,000. In the fifties, *Senokot* and *Cerumenex* the first prescription eardrops are introduced. In 1966, Purdue acquires *Betadine* the broad-spectrum microbicide. They eighties brought *MS Contin Tablets* and *Uniphyl* with patented *Contin* system. 1991 Purdue Pharma In 1995, *OxyContin* is launched in the United States. In 2000, long-lasting local anesthetic *Chirocaine* is launched. Purdue Pharma L.P. and The Purdue Frederick Company relocate to One Stamford Forum, the state of the art office tower in Stamford, CT. In 2000, Purdue's U.S. sales top $1 billion. In 2001, Purdue constructs new headquarters building for discovery research in Cranbury, NJ. 2002 - Purdue Pharma L.P. announced today that an associated company has purchased the over-the-counter product portfolio of Shire Pharmaceuticals Group plc. The acquisition brings with it some well-known, established brands of laxatives and dietary supplements, including *Colace* Stool Softeners, *Peri-Colace Capsules*, and *Slow-Mag Tablets*. In 2003, *Spectracef* was launched.

Annual Healthcare Revenue: $2.5 billion

CEO: Michael Friedman

Salesforce: 1000

Major Products: *MS Contin, OxyContin, OxyFast, OxyIR* for moderate, severe and chronic pain, *Spectratracef* anti-infective, *T-Phyl, Trilisate, Uniphyl, Betadine* topical antibiotics, *Colace, PeriColace, Gentlax, Senokot, Senokot S* laxatives, *Slow-Mag* mineral supplement, *X-Prep bowel* evacuant liquid.

Near Approval: *OxyContin* line extensions, Purdue's top priority is to continue to discover and develop new pain treatments.

ROCHE (HOFFMANN-LA ROCHE INC.)
340 KINGSLAND ST.,
NUTLEY, NEW JERSEY 07110
973.235.5000
ROHHY
rocheusa.com

Summary: This Switzerland based pharmaceutical concern is one of the worlds largest with over 2/3 of its sales attributed to prescription medications. The Roche family has retained a controlling interest in the company since its founding over 100 years ago. Therapeutic areas include central nervous system, infectious diseases, oncology, virology, cardiovascular diseases, inflammatory and autoimmune diseases, dermatology, metabolic disorders, and respiratory diseases. In 2002 Roche divested of both the vitamin and chemical business, focusing solely on the prescription drug and diagnostic markets.

History: Fritz Hoffmann-La Roche founded F. Hoffman-La Roche & Co. in 1896. Hoffmann sold *Thiocal* (cough medicine), *Digalen* (digitalis) and other products under the Roche name. Roche expanded and became the world's leading vitamin manufacturer. Roche continued to develop successful drugs such as *Librium* (1960) and *Valium* (1963). *Valium* was the world's best selling drug. Though now a current practice, Roche became one of the first to co market another company's products when it agreed to co promote Glaxo's *Zantac* ulcer treatment in the United States in the early eighties. The company acquired the majority stake in leading genetic engineering firm, Genentech in 1990. In 1994, Roche purchased Syntex, for $5.3 billion, solidifying its position in the North American marketplace. 1999 brought FDA approval of *Xenical* and *Tamiflu*. In 2000, Roche divested its fragrance and flavor division. Novartis AG acquired a 22.3% ownership of Roche Holding AG valued at 2.79 billion in 2001. In May of 2002 Roche agreed to collaborate with Vernalis Plc. to develop antidepression/anxiety agents. In 2002, approval for the merging of Chugaui Pharmaceutical Co. with Roche of Japan was obtained. In early 2003, Novartis paid an additional $2.1 billion to raise its stake in Roche to 32.7%. Product launches in 2003 include *Fuzeon*, and *Xolair*. Currently Roche holds 59% of biotech concern Genentech's outstanding stock.

Annual Healthcare Revenue: $19 billion

CEO: Dr. Franz B. Humer

Sales force: 1750

Major Brands: *Accutane* acne, *CellCept, Zenapax* organ rejection prevention, *Cytovene, Valycyte* viral infections associated with organ transplantation, *Fuzeon* for HIV, *Kytril* for nausea and vomiting during chemotherapy, *Lexotan* anxiety/tension, *Madopar* Parkinson disease, *Pegasys* for hepatitis C, *Rocephin* >$1 billion, anti-infective, *Roferon-A* hepatitis B and C, cancer, *Rocaltrol* osteoporosis, *Tamiflu* influenza, *Ticlid* thrombosis, *Versed* anesthesia, *Fortovase, Invirase, Valcyte, Viracept* HIV agents, *Xeloda, Furtulon, Herceptin MabThera/Rituxan, NeoRecormon,* and *Xeloda* oncology agents, *Xenical* obesity, *Xolair* for asthma.

Near approval: *Fuzeon* for HIV, *Pegasys* additional indications, *Valcyte* for cytomegalovirus disease in organ transplantation, *Avastin, Bondronat, Tarceva,* and *Taxotere* cancer agents.

SANKYO PHARMA
TWO HILTON COURT
PARSIPPANY, NJ 07054
973.359.2600
sankyopharma.com

Summary: Sankyo is Japan's second-largest pharmaceutical company (behind Takeda). Clinical, regulatory and commercial operations are based in New York, New Jersey and California. The company's research and development efforts are concentrated on allergies, antibiotics, arthritis, cancer, cardiovascular disease, diabetes, neurological agents, and obesity. Sankyo develops its drugs through an extensive independent network of laboratories in Europe, South America, and the United States. In addition to prescription pharmaceuticals, the company makes OTC medications, veterinary drugs, food ingredients, and agricultural chemicals.

History: Sankyo was established in 1899 in Japan. In 1910 a Sankyo scientist, discovers vitamin B12 1971 Sankyo discovered the origination of this statin class. Other discoveries included lovastatin and pravastatin. Sankyo independently markets pravastatin around the world. Pravastatin is marketed as *Pravachol* (Bristol Myers Squibb) in the United States. Sankyo is also the originator of *cefpodoxime proxetil,* a cephalosporin antibiotic sold in over 50 countries around the world. After several decades of continued growth Sankyo built the Sankyo Research Institute in San Diego and established Sankyo USA just in 1985. Sanko-Parke-Davis incorporated in 1996 and marketed *Rezulin* until its withdrawn form the market in 2000. Sankyo launched *WellChol* in the United States in 2000. In 2001, Sankyo purchased the Parke Davis share (from Warner Lambert, now Pfizer) of Sankyo-Parke-Davis. Sankyo now operates as a fully independent integrated pharmaceutical concern in the United States. In 2001, Sankyo and Cygnus signed a joint promotion of the *GlucoWatch Biographer,* a device that provides glucose readings automatically and noninvasively up to three times and hour. In 2002, brought approval of *Benicar* and 2003 *Benicar HCT*.

Annual Healthcare Revenue: $3.6 billion

CEO: Tetsuo Takato

Sales force: 560

Major Brands: *Benicar, Benicar HCT* hypertension (with Forest), *WellChol* lipid lowering agent (developed by Genzyme), *GlucoWatch G2 Biographer* novel glucose monitoring device (comarketed with Cygnus Incorporated).

Near approval: *Calblock* hypertension, *Oxytrol* urinary incontinence, *Pitavastatin* for cholesterol.

SANOFI-SYNTHELABO PHARMACEUTICALS
90 PARK AVENUE
NEW YORK, NY 10016
212.551.4314
SNY
sanofi-synthelabo.com

Summary: Sanofi-Synthelabo participates in four primary disease segments, cardiovascular, central nervous system, oncology, and internal medicine. The combination of Sanofi and Synthelabo established in 1999 formed the second largest pharmaceutical concern in France, after Aventis. Sanofi-Synthelabo believe their $10 billion merger will move them into one of the top ten pharmaceutical companies in the United States market. Currently 88% of sales are based in Europe, Japan, and the rest of the world. Sanofi-Synthelabo has 50 new drugs in its pipeline with more than half of those already in clinical trials. In 2002, Sanofi agreed to buy Bristol Myers Squibb Companies Hungarian subsidiary Pharmavit.

History: This company developed by of an acquisition of United States based pharmaceutical concern Sterling-Winthrop in 1994 by France based Sanofi. Sanofi continued its acquisitions with acquiring Bock Pharmacal of St Louis, its products and salesforce infrastructure.. In 1999, shareholders approved a merger of Sanofi with Synthelabo of France. Both companies primarily participate in the same clinical areas. Of the over 20 pharmaceutical concerns in France in the early seventies, approximately 15 of them are inside the current Sanofi-Synthelabo organization today. *Arixtra* launched in 2002 with co marketing partner Organon. Sanofi-Synthelabo acquired full marketing and promotional responsibility for *Ambien* from Pharmacia in May of 2002. An oncology agents, *Eligard* and *Eloxatine* was introduced in the United States in 2002. In 2003, Sanofi-Synthelabo launched **Uroxatral.**

Healthcare Revenue: $7 billion

CEO: Tim Rothwell (North America)

Sales force: 2300

Major Brands: *Ambien* sleep disorders, *Arixtra* thrombosis after orthopedic surgery *Avapro* (with BMS) hypertension, *Eligard, Eloxatine* cancer agents, *Fraxiparine* thrombosis, *Primacor* acute congestive heart failure, *Plavix* >$1.8 billion (with BMS), *Uroxatral* for benign prostatic hyperplasia.

Near approval: *Dalcipran* depression, *Oxaliplatin* cancer, *Pleconaril* viral infections, *Plenaxis* prostate cancer, *Rimonabant* obesity, *Tiraprazamine* cancer.

SCHERING-PLOUGH CORPORATION
2000 Galloping Hill Road
Kenilworth, NJ 07033
908.298.4000
SGP
sgp.com

Summary: Schering-Plough is a global leader in the areas of allergies, respiratory disorders, oncology, infectious disease, and cardiovascular disorders. The pharmaceutical division accounts for approximately 90% of the companies' sales. The company also operates in the veterinary medicine segment. Schering-Plough also includes such consumer goods as *Dr. Scholl's, Coppertone, Afrin, Drixoral* and *Gyne-Lotrimin*. In 2003, Schering-Plough Corporation was named as one of the 100 Best Companies for Working Mothers by Working Mother magazine. This is the seventh time that Schering-Plough is among the 100 best.

History: Ernst Schering, a German chemist formed this company in the mid 1800's to provide products to pharmacists. In the mid 1900's Schering introduced *Chlor-Trimeton* (one of the first antihistamines), and the cold medicine *Coricidin* to market. In the 1960's the company introduced such novel agents as *Garamycin, Tinactin,* and *Afrin.* In the seventies Schering merged with Plough, Incorporated of Memphis, Tennessee, forming Schering-Plough. Product introductions in the seventies included *Lotrimin,* and *Vaceril.* In the eighties, *Netromycin, Proventil* and *Drixoral* was introduced. Also in the eighties , one of the firsts to enter the biotechnology field Schering -Plough acquired DNAX Research Institute of Palo Alto, California as was traditional Pharma companies Key Pharmaceuticals and Cooper Companies. In 1993, blockbuster product *Claritin* was introduced followed by *Claritin-D.* Other approvals in the nineties included *Cedax, Uni-Dur,* and *Intron-A* and *Temodar.* In 2000, *Tequin* and *Nasonex* nasal spray were launched. In 2001, Schering Plough, Cor Therapeutics, and Genentech entered a collaborative agreement to promote *Integrilin* and Genentech's *TNKase* and *Activase.* In 2002, *Clarinex* and *Clarinex Reditabs* was approved. In 2003, *Clarinex* over the counter sale was approved and *Zetia* (comarketed with Merck) was launched.

Yearly Sales: $10.1 billion

CEO: Fred Hassan

Sales force: 3,500

Major Brands: *Intron A, Peg-Intron* and *Rebetron* >$2.74 billion, cancer, hepatitis C agents, *Integrilin* coronary syndrome, *Imdur, K-Dur,* and *NitroDur* cardiovascular agents, *Integrilin* platelet aggregation inhibitor, *Elocon, Lotrisone* dermatologicals, *Clarinex, Clarinex Reditabs* >$2.3 billion, allergies, *Nasonex, Asmanex Twisthaler,* and *Vancenase* respiratory products, *Rebetol* chronic hepatitis C infections, *Tequin* antibiotic, *Temodar* brain tumors, *Zetia* hypercholesterolemia.

Near approval: *Caelyx, Sarasar* cancer, *Loratadine* allergic rhinitis, *Temodar* cancer, *Zetia/Zocor* combination for cholesterol-management.

SERONO INCORPORATED
100 LONGWATER CIRCLE
NORWELL, MA 02061
781.982.9000
SRA
serono.com

Summary: Swiss based Serono is the Europe's largest biotechnology concern and ranks as the worlds largest. Serono's focus is in the three therapeutic areas of Reproductive Health, Multiple Sclerosis, and Growth Metabolism. Serono is the world leader in the infertility market. Serono has a presence in over 45 countries, with distribution of products in over 100 countries. Serono's genetic engineering facilities are located in the United States, Israel and Spain. The Serono Pharmaceutical Research Institute is headquartered in Switzerland.

History: Serono originally established in 1906 in Rome, Italy under the name of Istituto Farmacologico Serono. During the war years, the company extracted insulin from beef pancreases. In the early 1960's, the first child to be conceived using infertility agent *Pergonal* was born. Expansion of the company outside Italy started in the early seventies with the United States operation Serono Laboratories, Inc. established to service the needs of the infertility marketplace. The mid seventies brought expansion into Germany, Great Britain and Argentina and the transfer of Serono's headquarters to Switzerland. In the late 1980's Serono continued expansion into numerous international markets and 1989 the approval of *Saizen* for growth hormone deficiency, the first recombinant drug. The nineties brought the launch of *Serostim, and Gonal-F.* In 1998, Geneva Medical Research Institute was acquired from Glaxo-Wellcome. *Ovidrel* and *Cetrotide* were launched in 2001. *Rebif* for multiple sclerosis launched in 2002 with co promotion partner Pfizer. In 2002, Serono acquired Genset to further develop drug discovery. *SeroJet* was introduced in 2002. Currently Serono has six recombinant products on the market in 2003. December 2003, brought FDA approval of *Zorbtive* .

Yearly Sales: $1.5 billion

CEO: Ernesto Bertarelli

Sales force: 400

Major Brands: *Cetrotide, Metrodin HP, Pergonal, Profasi, Luveris,* and *Ovidrel* infertility treatments, *Crinone* progesterone gel, *Gonal-F, Gonal F Multi-Dose* ovulation disorders, *Rebif* multiple sclerosis, *Saizen* growth hormones, *Serostim* AID's wasting, *Serophene* ovulatory failure, *Zorbtive* for short bowel syndrome, *SeroJet* needle free drug delivery systems.

Near Approval: *Lutropin Alfa* female infertility, *r-FSH Improved Formulation* fertility agent.

SHIRE PHARMACEUTICALS
One Riverfront Place
Newport, KY 41071
859.669.8000
Shpgy
shire.com

Summary: U.K. based Shire is a global specialty pharmaceutical company. Shire currently focuses on three therapeutic areas, Central Nervous System disorders, Gastrointestinal and Renal. Shire has a risk-balanced R&D portfolio with clear focus on future product needs. Shire's global research and development expertise is supported by in licensing of various agents and has currently provided a substantial pipeline. In addition another division is Shire Laboratories Incorporated is an advanced drug delivery company, which offers a full range of technologies and development capabilities.

History: Founded in 1986, Shire Pharmaceuticals Group PLC has a significant emphasis on the treatment of CNS disorders. Products include *Adderall*, *Adderall XR*, *Reminyl*, and *Carbatrol* for epilepsy. Together these products contributed over 50% of the company's recent revenues. In 1997, Shire acquired drug delivery company, Pharmavene Inc. and the specialty sales organization, Richwood Pharmaceutical Company, Inc. This followed in 1999 by the acquisition of the German, French and Italian sales and marketing subsidiaries of Fuisz Technologies Ltd. Also in 1999, Shire acquired Roberts Pharmaceutical Corporation of New Jersey. The growth rates for revenues were 22% for 2002 over the prior year. October 2003, brought an approvable letter from the FDA for the indication of usage of *Adderall XR* once daily formation in adult population for ADHD..

Yearly Sales: $1.5 billion

CEO: William Nuerge

Sales force: 560

Major Brands: *Adderall XR, Addrerall* for attention deficit hyperactivity disorder (ADHD), *Reminyl* for Alzheimer's disease (with Johnson and Johnson).

Near Approval: *Methypatch* for attention deficit hyperactivity disorder, *Fosrenol* for hyperphosphataemia, *Troxatly* pancreatic cancer, leukemia, *Xagrid* essential thrombocythaemia

SHIRE PHARMACEUTICALS
One Riverfront Place
Newport, KY 41071
859.669.8000
Shpgy
shire.com

Summary: U.K. based Shire is a global specialty pharmaceutical company. Shire currently focuses on three therapeutic areas, Central Nervous System disorders, Gastrointestinal and Renal. Shire has a risk-balanced R&D portfolio with clear focus on future product needs. Shire's global research and development expertise is supported by in licensing of various agents and has currently provided a substantial pipeline. In addition another division is Shire Laboratories Incorporated is an advanced drug delivery company, which offers a full range of technologies and development capabilities.

History: Founded in 1986, Shire Pharmaceuticals Group PLC has a significant emphasis on the treatment of CNS disorders. Products include *Adderall*, *Adderall XR*, *Reminyl*, and *Carbatrol* for epilepsy. Together these products contributed over 50% of the company's recent revenues. In 1997, Shire acquired drug delivery company, Pharmavene Inc. and the specialty sales organization, Richwood Pharmaceutical Company, Inc. This followed in 1999 by the acquisition of the German, French and Italian sales and marketing subsidiaries of Fuisz Technologies Ltd. Also in 1999, Shire acquired Roberts Pharmaceutical Corporation of New Jersey. The growth rates for revenues were 22% for 2002 over the prior year. October 2003, brought an approvable letter from the FDA for the indication of usage of *Adderall XR* once daily formation in adult population for ADHD..

Yearly Sales: $1.5 billion

CEO: William Nuerge

Sales force: 560

Major Brands: *Adderall XR, Addrerall* for attention deficit hyperactivity disorder (ADHD), *Reminyl* for Alzheimer's disease (with Johnson and Johnson).

Near Approval: *Methypatch* for attention deficit hyperactivity disorder, *Fosrenol* for hyperphosphataemia, *Troxatly* pancreatic cancer, leukemia, *Xagrid* essential thrombocythaemia

SOLVAY AMERICA INC.
901 SAWYER ROAD
MARIETTA, GA 30062
770.578.9000
SVYSY
solvay.com

Summary: Solvay is based in Brussels, Belgium. Solvay produces numerous plastic compounds for construction and auto industries. Solvay' customers are manufacturers and commercial businesses operating in areas of construction, consumer and capital goods and services sectors. Plastics account for more than half of the corporation's revenue. The pharmaceutical division accounts for 25% of Solvay's total revenue. In the United States, the company operates through Solvay Pharmaceuticals, Inc.

History: Ernest Solvay discovered Solvay in 1863. Solvay had developed a unique process for producing sodium carbonate (soda ash). In the late, 1800's Solvay had soda ash plants in most of Europe and became the world's leading producer. In the fifties Solvay started selling polyvinyl chloride (PVC) and in the seventies a range of polypropylene products including automobile parts, pipes and interior decoration goods. In 1980, Solvay with its experience in organic chemistry set up a separate health sector. Solvay acquired various pharmaceutical concerns including KaliChemie (Germany), Latema, and Sarbach (France) Duphar (Netherlands) and Reid-Rowell (USA) in 1986 (presently Solvay Pharmaceuticals Inc., USA). In 1999, Solvay Pharmaceuticals Inc. agreed to acquire Unimed Pharmaceuticals Inc. of Chicago in a deal valued at over $123 million. Solvay acquired hypertension product *Aceon* from Servier SA of France. Solvay markets *Estratest* and *Prometrium* with Duramed in the United States. 2000 brought *AndroGel* and the acquisition of Sintofarma Pharmaceuticals of Brazil. In 2001, Solvay acquired *Marinol* (from Roxane Laboratories). Solvay agreed to sell U.S. marketing rights for *Teveten* and *Teveten HCT* in 2002 to Biovail Corporation. Late 2003 brought Solvay's acquisition of *Cetrorelix* from Zentaris, a German biopharma company.

Healthcare Revenue: $1.7 billion

CEO: Alois Michielsen

Sales force: 1000

Major Brands: *Aceon* hypertension, stroke risk, *AndroGel* (with TAP) testosterone deficiency, *Cenestin* menopause, *Cetrorelix* endometriosis, uterine fibroids, benign prostatic hypertrophy, *Creon* pancreatic deficiencies, *Estratest, Estratab* estrogen replacement therapy, *Lithobid* manic-depressive illness. *Marinol* appetite stimulant, *Prometrium* oral progesterone, *Physiotens* hypertension.

Near approval: *Anoheal* anal fissures, *Incostop* incontinence, *Cilansetron* irritable bowel syndrome, *Estratest* expanded indications, *Estrogel* estrogen replacement therapy, *Fluvoxamine* obsessive compulsive disorder, *Tedisamil* arrhythmia's, *Omacor* secondary prevention of myocardial infarction.

TAKEDA PHARMACEUTICALS NORTH AMERICA, INC.
MILLBROOK BUSINESS CENTER
475 HALF DAY ROAD
LINCOLNSHIRE, ILLINOIS 60069
847.383.3000
TDCHF
tpna.com

Summary: Japan's top drug maker, Takeda Chemical Industries Ltd., makes and markets pharmaceuticals, vitamins, food additives, bulk vitamins and chemical products. Areas of research and development include treatments for ulcers, prostate cancer, hypertension, and diabetes. Development partners include Novo Nordisk, and Celera Genomics. German firm BASF and Takeda have combined their bulk vitamin operations in the United States. In 2003 the international division of the largest pharmaceutical company in Japan has been reorganized into three separate units that will operate independently.

History: Over two centuries ago in 1781, 32-year-old Chobei Takeda started a business selling traditional Japanese and Chinese medicines. In 1895, the Company established its own factory and became a pharmaceutical manufacturer. During the late forties Takeda produced antibiotics, cardiac agents, and vitamins. In the fifties Takeda steadily expanded its pharmaceutical business and even began exports to the United States, Russia and China. The sixties brought expansion into Asia, and the seventies brought expansion into Europe. In 1985, Takeda first enters the United States market by forming TAP Pharmaceuticals Inc. (now TAP Pharmaceutical Products Inc.) in the U.S. in a 50:50 joint venture with Abbott Laboratories. TAP began marketing *Lupron* in the same year, followed by *Lupron Depot* in 1989, and *Prevacid* in 1995. Established in 1998, Takeda Pharmaceuticals North America was created to take advantage of Takeda Chemical Industries' growing, international pharmaceutical presence. *Actos* was launched as Takeda Pharmaceutical North America's first product. In 2002, *Prevacid* reached the number one prescribed proton pump inhibitor in the United States. In 2003, Takeda Pharmaceuticals announced an addition of a specialty salesforce for targeting leading U.S. Hospital based teaching institutions and the co-promotion with Kos Pharmaceuticals with their products *Niaspan* and *Advicor.*

Annual Healthcare Revenue: $8.1 billion

President North America: Mark Booth

Sales force: 1200

Major Brands: *Actos* <$1 billion (with Eli Lilly) type 2 diabetes, *Atacand* (marketed by AstraZeneca) hypertension, *Lupron, Lupron Depot* >$1 billion (marketed by TAP) prostate cancer, *Prevacid* (marketed by TAP) >$3 billion, ulcer treatment, *Niaspan* (extended-release niacin) and *Advicor* (extended-release niacin/lovastatin), two products developed by Kos for the treatment of cholesterol.

Near approval: *Biopress* heart failure, *Prevacid* additional indications, *Risedronate Sodium* osteoporosis, *Apomorphine* erectile dysfunction

WYETH PHARMACEUTICALS
5 GIRALDA FARMS
MADISON, N.J. 07940
973.660.5000
WYE
wyeth.com

Summary: This diversified chemical maker's products include pharmaceuticals, consumer health products, veterinary products, and human vaccines. Subsidiaries include Wyeth Pharmaceuticals. , Wyeth Consumer Healthcare (over the counter pharmaceuticals, *Advil, Cultrate, Centrum, Chap Stick, Dimetapp* and *Robitussin*), and Fort Dodge Animal Health (veterinary products). Pharmaceutical division Wyeth Pharmaceuticals focuses on woman's health, infant nutritionals, cardiovascular, neuroscience therapies, gastroenterology, anti-infectives, vaccines, oncology and musculoskeletal therapies.

History: Established in 1926, American Home Products acquired over 30 food and drug companies through the depression (including John Wyeth and Brother) increasing its size dramatically. *Preparation H,* was a sunburn treatment acquired in the thirties as was *Anacin* aspirin product. Canadian company Ayerst Laboratories including blockbuster *Premarin* was acquired in forties. Ayerst developed *Inderal* in sixties. Acquisitions continued with the acquisition of A.H. Robins in the late eighties. In 1994, American Home Products purchased American Cyanamid (Lederle) for a reported price of $9.6 billion. In the forties, Lederle discovered the antibiotic chlortetracycline *(Aureomycin.)* American Home Products introduced various new products in the United States including in 1996, the antidepressant *Effexor.* 1997 brought *Lodine XL* and *Prempro.* 1999 brought *Enbrel, Meningitect* and *Rapamune.* In 2000, products launches included, *Mylotarg, ReFacto, Prevnar,Protonix* and the sale of Cyanamid agricultural division to BASF. In 2001, AHP obtained approval of *Effexor XL.* In addition, AHP formed *Wyeth Women's Healthcare* as global business unit within Wyeth-Ayerst Pharmaceuticals. In 2002 American Home Products changed the name of their organization to Wyeth, paying tribute to one of the company's oldest prescription medicine business and founder John Wyeth. 2003 brought approval of *Enbrel* in a once weekly dose, and the launch of *FluMist.* Late 2003, brought the divestiture sale of products *Ativan* and *Isordil* to Biovail Corp.

Annual Healthcare Revenue: $14.5 billion

CEO: Robert A. Essner

Sales force: 4,900

Major Brands: *Altace* (with King Pharmaceuticals) hypertension, *Cordarone I.V.* arrhythmias, *LoOvral, Min-Ovral, Nordette* and *Triphasil* oral contraceptives, *Effexor, Effexor XR* >$2.0 billion, antidepressant/anxiety, *Enbrel, Enbrel Once Weekly* (with Amgen) arthritis (international sales only), *Flu Mist* nasal influenza vaccine *FluShield* influenza virus vaccine, *Rapamune* prevention of organ rejection, *Mylotarg, Neumega* oncology agents, *Novatrone* multiple sclerosis, *Premarin, Prempro, Premphase* >$1.8 billion, hormonal replacement, *Prevnar* >$1 billion, pneumococcal disease vaccine, *Protonix, Protonix I.V.*>$1billion for ulcers/heartburn, *Rapamune* organ rejection, *ReFacto* hemophilia, *Zosyn* anti-infective and numerous *Vaccines.*

Near approval: *Alesse* acne, *Effexor XL* additional indications, , *InFuse Bone Graft* acute long bone fractures, *ReFacto AF* hemophilia, *Premarin Low Dose* hormonal replacement, *Tigecycline* antibiotic.

CONTRACT SALES ORGANIZATIONS (CSO'S)

Contract sales organizations (CSO's) are well established in the pharmaceutical sales channel. The utilization of CSO's is widely recognized as a solid business strategy, one that plugs in trained professionals that can be integrated or act alone offering maximum agility and effectiveness. Contracts can range from temporary fill-ins while a representative is out of a territory to contracts of two to three years in duration. Often contracts will provide an option clause by which the traditional pharmaceutical concern has the opportunity to adopt the CSO representatives into their own company's sales force. CSO's are a cost effective, efficient marketing strategy. CSO's possess a strong stable of experienced pharmaceutical reserves that are waiting to be called into action. CSO's may have up to 300 representatives ready to meet any manufactures needs quickly and efficiently. Some needs that CSO's meet in the marketplace:

- Traditional pharmaceutical companies need to increase their sales force for a successful product launch
  Rx prescription drugs are shifting to over-the-counter status that requires a separate sales force
- An emerging, foreign, or start up pharmaceutical/biotech company who does not possess the infrastructure and competencies by which to manage a sales force in the United States
- Regional business strategies to meet specific segments in the industry, such as: managed care pull-though strategies, long term care, retail pharmacies, distribution
  A mature product that has not received appropriate promotional attention
- Staffing for convention exhibits, trade shows, medical conferences to keep from pulling staff from their territories
- Providing mirror territories to the traditional pharmaceutical company increasing reach, frequency, and voice in the marketplace

As with any sales position, CSO's like any of us, are held to reaching their numbers. Contracts include measurement tools by which to assess the contribution made by the CSO.

Candidates find that CSO's provide for an excellent entry to the pharmaceutical industry, or a graceful exit. Candidates are interviewed in the same manner as traditional pharmaceutical companies, with the same requirements and competency expectations. CSO's may be more relaxed in the necessity of a four-year degree with those candidates that are registered nurses (with A.A. degree's or diploma programs). CSO's also offer increased flexibility to many individuals with both full and part time employment. Career paths for sales management and sales training are similar to those of traditional pharmaceutical concerns. Marketing careers are limited by the nature of the CSO business (no ownership of specific products).

Imagine the impact and knowledge delivered by a 30-year pharmaceutical sales veteran who now has decided to cut back to 20 hours a week in semi-retirement; the rapport he has established with his a clientele may even open new doors for the CSO. The flexibility of a part-time job for the working mother as she sets her own hours during the workweek to continue her professional career is also a benefit. This helps fill the large void in the United States.

CSOs do not want to be the "minor league" of the pharmaceutical industry. Representatives are compensated by a base salary and commission, or may be paid by the number of sales calls. Total compensation packages have been traditionally less than full time positions, but this gap has closed in recent years.

Their training is similar to full time sales professionals. Sound business decisions and excellent customer needs are paramount, perhaps requiring adjusting their territories to fit their timeframe. The physicians' needs for continuing education must be met; the days of leaving brochures and samples are gone. These Representatives must be able to sell, and close the sale. Some CSO's have their own training departments, while others use the contracting company's training programs. As with traditional companies, training consists of home study, significant classroom time, product knowledge, and selling skills.

Physicians, pharmacists, and managed care institutions are unaware that they are interfacing with a CSO Representative. All sales material, literature, samples, and business cards are provided by the traditional pharmaceutical company under contract. At other times, a small designation of the CSO is listed on the Representative s business card. Unlike the *Insight* strategy for networking with traditional Pharma companies, *Insight* recommends making direct contact with these organizations through their websites. Listed below is a sampling of some of the major contract sales organizations.

D E NDRITE I NTERNATIONAL, I NC.
1200 MT. KEMBLE AVENUE
MORRISTOWN, NJ 07960 973.425.1200
973.425.2100
DENDRITE.COM

V ENTIV H EALTH U.S. SALES 200
COTTONTAIL LANE SOMERSET
NJ 08873 800.390.5003
800.228.4343
212.768.8000
VENTIV.COM

I NNOVEX I NC.
WATERVIEW CORPORATE CENTRE
10 WATERVIEW BLVD
PARSIPPANY, NJ 07054
800.605.3230 973.257.4500
INTERVIEW WITH THE INTERACTIVE VOICE RESPONSE (IVR) SYSTEM, USE REFERENCE NUMBER
1234
INNOVEXGLOBAL.COM

MCKESSON PHARMACEUTICAL PARTNERS 101
COLLEGE ROAD EAST PRINCETON, NJ 08540
609.919.3900
609.919.3931
MCKHBOC-PPG.COM

NELSON PROFESSIONAL SALES 2000
LENOX DRIVE, SUITE 100
LAWRENCEVILLE, NJ 08648 609.896.4712
800.672.0676
NELSONPROFESSIONALSALES.COM

PROFESSIONAL DETAILING INCORPORATED (PDI) 10
MOUNTAINVIEW ROAD, SUITE C200 UPPER SADDLE RIVER,
NJ 07458 800.242.7494
PDI-INC.COM

ATTACH BUSINESS CARDS HERE
HERE

ATTACH BUSINESS CARDS

DATES AND NOTES FROM TELEPHONE CONTACTS:

CURRENT/FUTURE JOB OPPORTUNITIES:

DISTRICT MANAGER NAME, ADDRESS, PHONE:

PRECEPTORSHIP SCHEDULING:

ADDITIONAL PROFILE AND CONTACT INFORMATION:

Notes:

ATTACH BUSINESS CARDS HERE   ATTACH BUSINESS CARDS
HERE

DATES AND NOTES FROM TELEPHONE CONTACTS:

CURRENT/FUTURE JOB OPPORTUNITIES:

DISTRICT MANAGER NAME, ADDRESS, PHONE:

PRECEPTORSHIP SCHEDULING:

ADDITIONAL PROFILE AND CONTACT INFORMATION:

Notes:

ATTACH BUSINESS CARDS HERE
HERE

ATTACH BUSINESS CARDS

DATES AND NOTES FROM TELEPHONE CONTACTS:

CURRENT/FUTURE JOB OPPORTUNITIES:

DISTRICT MANAGER NAME, ADDRESS, PHONE:

PRECEPTORSHIP SCHEDULING:

ADDITIONAL PROFILE AND CONTACT INFORMATION:

Notes: